Early Praise for *Craft GraphQL APIs in Elixir with Absinthe*

Like GraphQL's meteoric rise, this book is sure to be a breakout hit for readers looking to revolutionize the way they write APIs. Ben and Bruce combine their Absinthe expertise with their production experience to take readers from the basics of GraphQL to exercising its most powerful features with Elixir and Phoenix.

➤ **Chris McCord**
    Author, Phoenix framework

If we're lucky, about once per decade or so we'll come across a technology that has the chance to revolutionize the Web. GraphQL is one such set of technologies. This book is written by two of the industry's experts—co-authors of one of the best and most complete GraphQL implementations. Even if you're not planning to deploy on Elixir, this book will show you GraphQL done right.

➤ **Chad Fowler**
    Microsoft and BlueYard Capital

Absinthe single-handedly made one of the most critical and complex parts of Trailpost's infrastructure the piece I worry about least. This book should be on the radar of anyone developing APIs in Elixir, and probably some who aren't.

➤ **Daniel Pehrson**
    Founder, Trailpost.com

GraphQL is a broad but rewarding topic, and Bruce and Ben have covered it comprehensively. The book introduces the key GraphQL concepts in a very approachable way. It then makes sure you have all the tools and techniques to build robust, well-structured, and incredibly fast GraphQL APIs using Elixir, Absinthe, Ecto, and Phoenix. A killer combination for building amazing applications if ever there was one!

➤ **Josh Price**
    Technical Director, Alembic

GraphQL is a game changer, and now you can use it with Elixir! This book is an invaluable must-read for any Elixir developer. I referred to it often as I helped prepare our web team for the next generation of APIs.

➤ **Daniel Berkompas**
    Senior Software Engineer, Infinite Red; Creator of LearnElixir.tv & LearnPhoenix.tv

Craft GraphQL APIs in Elixir
with Absinthe

Flexible, Robust Services for Queries, Mutations,
and Subscriptions

Bruce Williams

Ben Wilson

The Pragmatic Bookshelf

Raleigh, North Carolina

Many of the designations used by manufacturers and sellers to distinguish their products are claimed as trademarks. Where those designations appear in this book, and The Pragmatic Programmers, LLC was aware of a trademark claim, the designations have been printed in initial capital letters or in all capitals. The Pragmatic Starter Kit, The Pragmatic Programmer, Pragmatic Programming, Pragmatic Bookshelf, PragProg and the linking *g* device are trademarks of The Pragmatic Programmers, LLC.

Every precaution was taken in the preparation of this book. However, the publisher assumes no responsibility for errors or omissions, or for damages that may result from the use of information (including program listings) contained herein.

Our Pragmatic books, screencasts, and audio books can help you and your team create better software and have more fun. Visit us at *https://pragprog.com*.

The team that produced this book includes:

Publisher: Andy Hunt
VP of Operations: Janet Furlow
Managing Editor: Brian MacDonald
Supervising Editor: Jacquelyn Carter
Series Editor: Bruce A. Tate
Copy Editor: Nicole Abramowitz
Indexing: Potomac Indexing, LLC
Layout: Gilson Graphics

For sales, volume licensing, and support, please contact *support@pragprog.com*.

For international rights, please contact *rights@pragprog.com*.

ISBN-13: 978-1-68050-255-8
Book version: P2.0—April 2020

Contents

Part II — Publish Your API

Part III — Use Your API

Acknowledgements

We'd like to thank our editor, Jackie Carter, and the rest of the staff at The Pragmatic Bookshelf for their guidance and assistance turning this book into a reality. While it's a cliché, writing a book is hard work...and it would have been immeasurably more difficult without your help. Likewise, a small army of technical reviewers—Andrea Leopardi, Brian O'Grady, Chad Wooley, Chengyin Liu, Gabor Hajba, Jack Marchant, James Fish, Jesse Cooke, Kim Shieir, Lou Xun, Mark Goody, Nate Vick, Paulo A. Pereira, Rodrigo Franco, and Sebastian Kosch—helped us improve the content and code in this book. Any remaining issues fall squarely and solely on our shoulders.

Bruce would like to thank his wife, Melissa, and their three sons—Braedyn, Jamis, and Cole—without whose love, support, and deep, abiding well of patience, no book would be worth writing (or would get done in the first place). He'd also like to thank Maria Gutierrez, a dear friend who he'll eventually forgive for the gentle nudge that convinced him to invest the time to write another book.

Ben is grateful to his colleagues, friends, and family for their seemingly endless willingness to listen, offer advice, and humor the most insane ideas throughout this process. In particular, Ben wants to thank his wife, Becca, whose constant care and dedication to those around her serves as both an inspiration and a daily joy.

Finally, we'd like to show our appreciation for those who have contributed to Absinthe, the project this book covers.

We deeply appreciate the time and encouragement given to us by José Valim and Chris McCord as the Absinthe project has grown. Their answers to hard questions and warnings about pitfalls, their open minds and imaginations, have made all the difference between the project becoming a fun yet subtly broken toy, and a robust, useful tool for the Elixir/Phoenix community they lead.

In the same vein, we'd like to thank the dozens of contributors to Absinthe's many packages. Absinthe is an ambitious project. Like many ambitious projects, it started out as a crazy dream—and as it turns out, it found plenty of crazy-smart, friendly people to share it...and make it so much better. Thank you!

Introduction

GraphQL is an exciting newcomer to the world of web service protocols. It arrived on the scene at exactly the right time for us, struggling as we were with a complicated, inflexible REST API that was wearing a little of the shine off our fancy new Elixir application in production.

We decided to give GraphQL a try.

Little did we know that along the way, we'd discover an approach to building APIs and collaborating across the backend/front-end divide that was more flexible, maintainable, and fun for our team.

We wrote Absinthe, the GraphQL toolkit for Elixir, because we thought GraphQL might be a good fit for our problem, our development process, and our platform. Since that time, a community has grown up around the project. We wrote this book because we think that it might just be a good fit for yours, too.

It's certainly a great fit for Elixir!

About This Book

This book is organized into three parts.

Part I introduces you to the core concepts behind GraphQL, then guides you through building a GraphQL API in Elixir. You'll learn about queries, mutations, and subscriptions, and end up with a functional example by the time you're through.

Part II addresses the most common security, maintainability, and performance questions that people have about GraphQL in production, focusing on building real-world solutions that turn naive implementations into rock-solid, scalable APIs that are easy to maintain.

Part III is all about using your GraphQL API. You'll learn how to support client-side GraphQL frameworks that access it over HTTP or directly from within your Elixir applications.

The book wraps up by providing a useful appendix to use as a quick reference when building your GraphQL schema and interacting with your API.

What This Book Isn't

This book isn't an introductory book on Elixir or Phoenix. While the book's code should be straightforward reading for most developers, we will cover some more advanced topics that would benefit from a firm grounding in the Elixir language and the Phoenix web framework. We recommend the following supplementary books to readers who might be coming at this book from a different background:

- *Programming Elixir 1.6 [Tho18]*
- *Programming Phoenix 1.4 [TV19]*

This book isn't a lengthy diatribe about REST or JSON APIs. While we'll take time to compare GraphQL with other technologies—building on your experience—this isn't going to be a point-by-point takedown of other choices; GraphQL is a compelling choice, and while we'll often touch on why, we'll move on to actually building things with it rather quickly.

Who This Book Is For

If you're a developer who writes modern web APIs, this book is for you. You know the rewards and challenges of building a RESTful API using JSON, working with databases, and aggregating data from remote services. This book is for you because you're in a good position to experience the "aha moment" of GraphQL full-force. You already know the problem space.

If you write Elixir (or Erlang) code, this book is for you. You use the Erlang/OTP platform for a reason—it's robust, fault-tolerant, and battle-tested. This book is for you because GraphQL is the web API and (data retrieval/mutation) technology that Elixir/Erlang deserves, and you're using a platform that can take GraphQL to the next level.

If you write Node.js code, and especially if you're already supporting GraphQL APIs for JavaScript-based web frameworks, this book is for you. Maybe you're looking for an alternative backend technology, and you've heard a lot about Elixir and Phoenix. You already know a fair bit about GraphQL, but you want to take it *further.* This book is for you because it will help you take the jump to Elixir with the confidence and knowledge to make your APIs even better.

How to Read This Book

If you're brand new to GraphQL and want the full background story, or if you've played a bit with it before but would like a solid refresher, start at the beginning. In Chapter 1, Meet GraphQL, on page 3, you'll learn about its origins and walk through the core concepts that you'll need as you read the rest of the book.

If you've used GraphQL before in another language and want to jump straight into building your first Elixir GraphQL API, then Chapter 2, Building a Schema, on page 15 is the chapter for you. It's where you'll be introduced to Absinthe, the GraphQL toolkit for Elixir, and start building the GraphQL schema for our example application.

Readers who have already had some experience building GraphQL APIs using Elixir and are looking for specific answers might want to start at Part II, Publish Your API, on page 121; its chapters are focused on common challenges GraphQL developers face taking their dreams to reality. If you're ready to use your Absinthe-based GraphQL API, take a look at Part III, Use Your API, on page 193, where you'll learn about supporting fancy JavaScript GraphQL-fluent, client-side frameworks over HTTP and even building some custom processing logic to use GraphQL directly from elsewhere in your Elixir applications.

Regardless of where you start reading the book, check out the "Moving On" section at the end of each chapter. You're sure to find ideas and challenges there that will help you take your understanding of GraphQL and its use in Elixir to the next level.

About the Code

The sample code and examples included in this book are written using the Elixir programming language, and will focus on how to use Absinthe,[1] the GraphQL toolkit for Elixir. As the authors of Absinthe, we can't wait to show you the ropes.

Absinthe is distributed as a number of separate, focused packages, and we'll be using several; absinthe provides the core GraphQL functionality, absinthe_plug supports handling requests over HTTP/S, and absinthe_phoenix adds support for GraphQL subscriptions over Phoenix channels. You learn about each of these, and more related packages, as we build out the examples.

---

1. http://absinthe-graphql.org

System Dependencies

The Elixir example code for the book assumes that you've installed the following system dependencies. This can be done by using your favorite package manager or downloading and installing them as pre-built binaries from the associated websites.

- Erlang[2] (v20.0+)
- Elixir[3] (v1.5.0+)
- PostgreSQL[4] (v9.4+)

The final chapter of the book covers integration with JavaScript client-side frameworks, and we recommend Node.js[5] v8.9.0+.

Online Resources

You can find all the example code for this book on its Pragmatic Bookshelf website,[6] alongside a handy community forum if you'd like to reach out for help along the way.

While we've worked hard to make our code examples and explanations bug-free and clear in every way for our readers, we've written enough software to know that we're fallible. Thanks in advance for reporting any issues that you find in the book code or text via the errata form, also conveniently found on the book website.

Welcome to the world of GraphQL—using Elixir. We can't wait to see what you build!

Bruce Williams & Benjamin Wilson
March 2018

---

2. https://www.erlang.org
3. https://elixir-lang.org
4. https://www.postgresql.org
5. https://nodejs.org
6. https://pragprog.com/book/wwgraphql/craft-graphql-apis-in-elixir-with-absinthe

Part I

Build a GraphQL API

In this first part, you'll learn GraphQL's core concepts (or enjoy a refresher) and build a basic functional API in Elixir from start to finish. You'll discover how to use queries to get information, mutations to make modifications to data, and live subscriptions over Phoenix channels to keep your API users up to date with changes.

## CHAPTER 1

Meet GraphQL

There was a time when the primary job of a web server was supplying HTML content to a web browser for display, but these days—to support mobile and rich client-side applications—a lot of the work that we need to do on the backend involves building APIs.

Building an API that can support a wide range of possible clients can quickly become a challenge. The needs of applications that use the API can quickly diverge and force us to make tough decisions; what starts as a simple *REST* API can quickly become more complex as we work to make its endpoints more flexible to support clients.

Let's explore a different way to build APIs—one that addresses this modern problem head on and comes packed with other benefits: *GraphQL*.

GraphQL is a query language that gives the users of an API the ability to describe the data that they want, and lets creators of the API focus on data relationships and business rules instead of worrying about the various data payloads the API needs to return.

In this chapter, we're going to look at some of the key concepts behind GraphQL, including how these query documents are structured and how a GraphQL server interprets them. Along the way, we'll draw some comparisons with the most common technology driving web services today: REST.

On the Client

To illustrate conventional GraphQL communication practices, let's imagine how a web or mobile application might request data from a server over HTTP. At a high level, this conversation looks something like the figure on page 4.

The application sends a GraphQL document to the server, and the server responds with a JSON document, having consulted a *schema* that describes

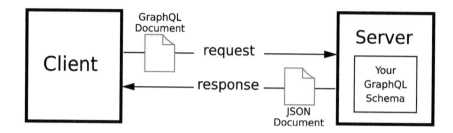

data it has available to query and to modify. Because of the schema, the server is empowered to flexibly fulfill the requests sent by clients on a case-by-case basis.

Let's see how this compares to REST, looking at a specific example: retrieving information about a specific user record. In a REST API, we'd do an HTTP request that would look something like this (assuming a user ID of 123):

```
GET /users/123
```

As a client of this REST API, you have very limited control over what is returned. Perhaps the server will give you the user's ID and a name, or maybe it will return the entirety of the user's profile and every other record associated with the user. The contract between the client and the server is fairly one-sided: the client gets what the server wants to give it.

REST API authors attempting to address this problem use a number of different techniques and conventions:

- Writing detailed, custom documentation about API responses, so clients at least know what to expect

- Supporting query parameters (like include and fields) that act as flags to select information, adding some limited flexibility

- Including references (either IDs or URLs) to related data, rather than embedding it, effectively splitting the query across multiple requests

- Using different resources to model different levels of data inclusion (for example, /users/123 as a full set of data and /profiles/123 as a sparse set of data), duplicating or reusing large chunks of code

- Splitting the API completely, perhaps by platform (for instance, exposing /desktop/users/123 and /mobile/users/123), to support the needs of different types of clients

- Some combination of all of these

REST's simplicity falls away pretty suddenly as the needs of clients become more varied and the surface area of the API expands.

The GraphQL approach to this problem is more standardized (being based on a specification) and cohesive: GraphQL is an expressive query language focused on flexibly meeting API client needs. If a GraphQL client wanted to retrieve user 123's name and email address, for instance, they'd explicitly specify those *fields*:

```
{
  user(id: 123) {
    name
    email
  }
}
```

We don't need to get hung up on the details now, but what you're looking at here are three fields: user, name, and email, with name and email being children of user. This makes sense, structurally, as a user has a name and an email address. We're passing an id argument here, too, specifying which user we'd like to use.

The request is made to a single GraphQL endpoint (URL) via an HTTP GET or a POST request, and the structure of the GraphQL document determines exactly what the server's response will look like. There are no hidden, default values forced upon the client; the response is tailored based on the request. Here's an example response based on our previous GraphQL document:

```
{
  "data": {
    "user": {
      "name": "Joe Bob",
      "email": "joe.bob@example.com"
    }
  }
}
```

The GraphQL server has the schema and knows what a User is, how to retrieve one by ID, and what information it can contain. It can respond to the client with the information about the user that the client specifically requested.

It knows how to find data related to the user, too.

Including Relationships

Often the most valuable pieces of data end up being the relationships between entities rather than the entities themselves. That is certainly true in social networking applications, where the interconnectedness of people—their social graph—serves as the functional core of the product. Social networks could hardly be considered social without friendships.

It shouldn't be much of a surprise then that GraphQL, originating at Facebook, excels at helping clients query across relationships—across the graph of related entities. It's even in the name!

But let's take a step back and think about how we might handle getting related information from a REST API first. Joe—our user 123—has friends, and we'd like to know their names, too.

When using a REST API, here are some questions we should probably ask ourselves:

- Can we get a user's friends via /users/:id, or do we need to use a different resource URL?

- Are friends (or their names) included by default, or do we need to specify that we want them? How do we do that?

- When information about friends is returned, where will it be in the result?

- Is each friend's data embedded, or just referenced, forcing us to do more requests to retrieve it? Will we need to paginate the friends list? How will this affect our performance on mobile devices, where bandwidth may be limited and additional requests have a negative effect on performance and battery life?

This is a lot of unnecessary mental overhead, requiring researching documentation (if it exists and is complete) and doing exploratory testing just to determine how to access the data we need from the API.

GraphQL Simplifies Things

GraphQL can shorten your development time because you don't need to ask these questions.

If you know that a GraphQL server supports users having friends (you'll learn about introspection in Running Our Query with GraphiQL, on page 24), you also know that you can query across that relationship, getting exactly the information that you want to receive in a single request, all the while using a standardized query language.

We simply ask for the data using GraphQL:

```
{
  user(id: 123) {
    name
    email
    friends {
      name
    }
  }
}
```

The result is much as it was with our earlier user example, but with the additional data about friends a level deeper:

```
{
  "data": {
    "user": {
      "name": "Joe Bob",
      "email": "joe.bob@example.com",
      "friends": [
        {"name": "Fred Jones"},
        {"name": "Jane Smith"},
        {"name": "Rebekah Jones"}
      ]
    }
  }
}
```

Looking at the client-side code, you know exactly what you can expect to be there because you have a GraphQL query at hand that tells you the shape of the response you'll get back from the server, taking the guesswork (and documentation spelunking) out of the picture. This lets you focus on more product-specific concerns.

From a backend perspective, because queries are coming in as a declarative query language detailing what clients need, you gain an incredibly detailed picture of what information your clients actually need. Gone are the days of sending as much data across the wire that any client, someday, might use, or building in custom inclusion and exclusion logic that you have to maintain.

This isn't necessarily a new concept either. If you've ever used a database system that supports SQL, you're already familiar with query languages that allow you to retrieve exactly what you want. GraphQL is a lot simpler than SQL for users, however, and the backend data retrieval logic (that gets the data the user wants) is a lot easier to customize.

Let's take a closer look at that backend logic next and talk about what needs to be done on the GraphQL server for it to give us this level of flexibility.

On the Server

GraphQL is incredibly powerful, but it isn't magic. GraphQL query documents can be flexible because the server holds a complete schema describing the shape of data that the API models and the input that it can expect from clients. This means that you, as the API developer, are responsible for accurately building a representation of your data. If this sounds like a lot of work, take heart in that it means the GraphQL server can free you up from more mundane details being mixed into your business logic.

We'll get into the nitty gritty of how GraphQL schemas are built in the next chapter, but let's take a look at one of the more important benefits that providing one gives us automatically: user input validation. We'll start with a little vignette showing how this usually works in a REST API.

User Input Validation in REST

Suppose, in your REST API, you have an endpoint that will return a list of upcoming events. You want to support filtering these events by the date and location where they are going to take place. This would give you something like:

```
GET /events?date=2016-11-22&location_id=4
```

You can't trust API users to give you correct input values. The location_id could be "hello world" instead of a number, for example. The date could be given in an invalid or unsupported date format. Users might even pass in superfluous parameters that they think should work, but do not.

REST, as a standard, doesn't really have much to say about data validation, so enforcing rules about incoming data is left up to the code that handles the request—code that we have to write ourselves.

This validation code can add a lot of complexity to backend controllers, which are often responsible for a long list of other tasks: retrieving the information the client wants, formatting the result as the client expects, and sending the response back across the HTTP connection. This can quickly become a mess. Here's an example of our events endpoint using a Phoenix controller action. Remember, its only job is to return a list of filtered events, and yet...

```
Line 1  @valid_filters ~w(date location_id name)a
  -     def index(conn, params) do
  -       filters =
  -         @valid_filters
  5         |> Enum.reduce(%{}, fn key, filters ->
  -           case Map.fetch(params, Atom.to_string(key)) do
  -             {:ok, value} ->
```

```
          add_filter(filters, key, value)
          _ ->
10          filters
      end
    end)

    render("index.json", events: Event.list(filters))
15 end

  defp add_filter(filters, :date, date) do
    case Date.from_iso8601(date) do
      {:ok, date} ->
20        Map.put(filters, :date, date)
      {:error, _} ->
        filters
    end
  end
25 defp add_filter(filters, key, value) do
    Map.put(filters, key, value)
  end
```

This is a lot of code! Did you catch where the controller action actually retrieved the requested data—its main purpose? There it is on line 14, tucked away in the wash of boilerplate. This is without even trying to return nice errors to the client in the event they do something wrong, or letting them know they've sent something extra.

The controller is trying to do three distinct tasks:

1. Validate the input from the user.
2. Get the data the user wants.
3. Respond to the user in the correct format.

Even when you leverage packages and other utilities to try to make data validation simpler, the central problem is still the same: you're doing too much work here that's outside your core goal, which is getting the events.

Using GraphQL, this is a completely different story.

GraphQL Inputs

GraphQL simplifies this dramatically by inverting the problem. With GraphQL you have a predefined schema with declared types and rules about the input that you can receive from users to retrieve data. When someone sends you data, it is checked by these rules before your code is executed.

This keeps your code focused on its primary objective: doing what the user wants.

To use our previous example, you would declare that location_id has to be an integer, and that date has to be formatted as a date. Then, to support a comparable GraphQL query like the following:

```
{
  events(location_id: 4, date: "2016-11-22") {
    name
    location {
      name
    }
  }
}
```

You could write code that just focuses on using the filters (that will be validated and parsed for us) to get the events you want:

```
def events(filters, _) do
  {:ok, Event.list(filters)}
end
```

Validation Errors Skip Execution

A GraphQL server doesn't just verify that a request is well formed. It also validates that it meets the requirements defined by the schema.

Requests that fail to pass validation never get the chance to execute your business logic, resulting in faster error responses and less bugs for you to track down later.

If the client sends something extra, they'll be given a detailed error message in the response to that effect. If API users fail to send something that's required, or if they send something that is invalid, they'll be notified as well. As developers, we don't have to worry about any of those scenarios! Once we have a schema in place, the input data given to our code is guaranteed to have met the rules we've declared about it, and we can get right down to business.

Your GraphQL server's knowledge of your schema also helps it determine what data is available to be output.

Queries and Schemas

Remember our user example from earlier, and how our GraphQL server knew that the client could receive the name, email, and friends of a user? The reason that worked is rooted in the correspondence between the structure of GraphQL queries and the structure of the graph of types maintained in the schema. In the next couple of chapters, we'll be covering how we actually write Elixir code that builds this schema graph, but let's look at a few diagrams that demonstrate this correspondence.

Let's talk about another query—returning the data for a user profile. A basic diagram of the GraphQL schema might look like this:

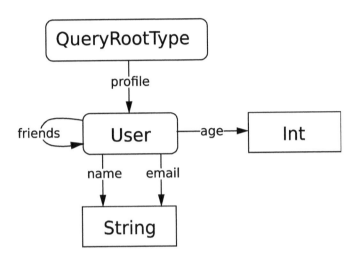

This is a graph showing User (a custom type in our schema) and String and Int (built-in types) as nodes, with the fields name, email, age, and friends as edges, representing the relationships between the types. (We'll talk about QueryRootType in a moment.)

Nodes and Edges

GraphQL developers and the GraphQL community commonly borrow terms from graph theory, which is the study of mathematical structures that model the relationships between objects.

In graph theory terminology, the relationships between objects are commonly referred to as "edges" (drawn as lines), and the objects themselves are called "nodes" (drawn as shapes connected by those lines).

A User type is related to a String type both by its name and its email fields.

Because the User type has fields and represents a complex value, GraphQL refers to it as an *object type*, whereas Int and String are simple values that it refers to as *scalar types*; they have no fields of their own. GraphQL's type system models a number of different types and defines a number of ready-to-use, built-in types. You will learn more about others in the next few chapters.

Object types can have fields that point to themselves, which is what we see with the User type's friends edge. This means that all objects in our graph that are of the User type can have friends, and that each of those friends will also be of type User.

Incoming queries are matched up against the schema. Sometimes it's useful to represent the relationships visually. For instance, if we graph the following query document:

```
{
  profile {
    name
    email
    friends {
      name
    }
  }
}
```

It will look something like this:

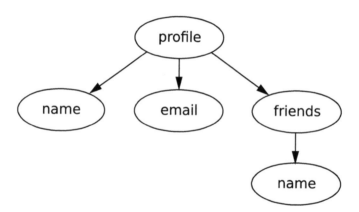

We can see a lot of similarities with our schema graph. Each node in our query tree lines up exactly with the name of an edge we have in our schema graph. When we query a GraphQL schema, we're really just walking these edges and getting the data associated with them. All queries start at a root object we have on our schema graph (we're calling it RootQueryType). Our query then has us follow the profile edge, which gets us to a User. From there, we also want to follow the name and email edges, which get us to string values. Finally, our friends edge just gets us back to a User, letting us know that we can get a name, age, or email of the friend if we want...and their friends, too!

Building a schema presents two major categories of work: describing the types and the edges between types (both by defining them and adding built-in documentation, which you'll see later), and writing the business logic that edges use to find their data.

If a query needs to walk from a user to its friends, how does that actually happen? Are we going to hit the database? If we do, will trying to get the friends of friends result in terrible database access patterns?

These are the kinds of questions that we're going to take on as we work through this book. To do this, we are going to be building an application piece by piece that will put these problems front and center in a concrete way.

Absinthe and the Tech Stack

For the rest of the book, we'll be focusing on improving an application that we've provided called PlateSlate. PlateSlate models the menu, ordering, and order fulfillment needs of a quick-service restaurant chain. We'll incrementally build out the domain model and add features to its API that will expose you to deeper, trickier aspects of GraphQL (and Elixir) as we go. If you haven't already downloaded the application, please go to Online Resources, on page xiv, and follow the instructions there.

This application makes use of a few Elixir packages, the most important of which is *Absinthe*. Absinthe lets you build GraphQL schemas and execute documents against them using Elixir. It provides a host of features that we'll be covering throughout this book to make your GraphQL APIs straightforward to build, idiomatic, and perform well.

We're also going to leverage a couple of packages for exposing our GraphQL API via the web, specifically *Plug* and *Phoenix*. In many ways, Absinthe replaces a lot of the things you'd normally find in a Phoenix-based API like controllers and views. Little to no knowledge of either of these technologies is assumed; we'll cover the bits you need to know along the way.

Finally, we're going to have some packages we use to get underlying data. One of the core value propositions of GraphQL is its ability to provide a common interface to different types of data stores, and we'll try to illustrate that as we build our application. This means we'll eventually use a basic HTTP client to make HTTP requests to other APIs and use Ecto to access an SQL database. Strong proficiency with these packages is not required, but a basic grasp of how to interact with a relational database will help.

At a high level, this is how a GraphQL request is handled, using these packages:

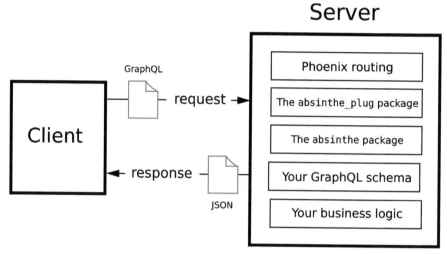

Most of our time will be spent focusing on how to define our GraphQL schema and tie it to our application business logic, and that's what we will move on to next.

Moving On

In this chapter, we've introduced a lot of key GraphQL concepts and talked about how GraphQL compares to REST. We've talked about how clients communicate with servers using GraphQL documents, and how servers use a schema to validate and retrieve the data requested. You've learned how this approach makes client requests more flexible, and how the schema simplifies the concerns that your server business logic needs to handle manually.

Here are a couple of challenges for you before we move on:

1. Think of a domain familiar to you and write down the types that belong to that domain. Draw in relationships between those types. Remember, these relationships are often what we think of as properties on an entity.
2. Add a root object, and think about how you might want to connect it with your graph. From there, write down some GraphQL queries that would be possible to handle from that point. What kinds of responses might come back for these?

Once you've thought through these problems, get ready to jump into defining your first GraphQL schema with Elixir using Absinthe.

## CHAPTER 2

Building a Schema

GraphQL APIs are shaped by their schemas. In fact, it's fair to say that because GraphQL schemas are more than just structural metadata and actually define behavior, they're the API implementation itself.

The schema is used by GraphQL servers as the canonical source of information when deciding how to respond to a request. They're the reason that GraphQL documents can be as flexible as they are, while still giving backend developers the mechanisms that they need to ensure the API is safe and reliable.

In Elixir, you can use the Absinthe package to build GraphQL APIs. In this chapter, we'll help you get acquainted with how Absinthe's schemas are defined by building the foundation of our example application, PlateSlate. The knowledge you'll pick up in this chapter will serve as the foundation for the rest of the book.

First, let's kick the tires on our example application, making sure it's up and running and ready for a GraphQL API.

Preparing the Application

Let's start by making sure that you've set up your development environment. Your system will need to have the prerequisites listed in the System Dependencies, on page xiv, installed and ready to go, and you'll need to download the example application source code via one of the methods explained in Online Resources, on page xiv.

Once that's done, make sure that you're looking at the directory for this chapter. We're going to be running a few commands using the mix build tool.

Make sure that you're running the correct versions of Elixir, just to make sure that you don't download and compile packages using the wrong version:

```
$ elixir --version
Erlang/OTP 20 «Build details»

Elixir 1.5.0
```

Great, with Elixir 1.5 (and Erlang/OTP 20), you're ready to go.

Let's retrieve the Elixir package dependencies of the PlateSlate application using the deps.get task:

```
$ mix deps.get
Running dependency resolution...
«Dependency installation output»
```

Now that we have our dependencies, let's get the PostgreSQL database for the application configured correctly, the Ecto migrations run, and our seed data loaded. Handily, we've included a single alias in our mix.exs, ecto.setup. Just run it, and you should see the following:

```
$ mix ecto.setup
The database for PlateSlate.Repo has been created
«Database setup output»
```

If something goes wrong here, it's usually a missing PostgreSQL role.[1] (If you encounter this problem, you can find the configuration we're trying to use for PostgreSQL in config/dev.exs.)

Seed data for the project will be used both in development and in testing, so it's been extracted to a module PlateSlate.Seeds in /dev/support/seeds.ex. The ecto.setup process will have already loaded these values, but you may want to give them a look so that you're familiar with the data you'll have on hand.

Once our mix ecto.setup has run successfully, we're ready to move on to defining our first GraphQL object type. It's time to start building our schema.

Our Schema Module

To build a GraphQL API, you'll need to construct a GraphQL schema, which defines its domain model and how data is retrieved. That can seem pretty overwhelming at first, so we'll help you start by showing you where to put the schema and ease you into your first query.

We want this schema to support clients of our API accessing a list of menu items. An example query from a client might look something like this:

---

1.   https://www.postgresql.org/docs/current/static/app-createuser.html

```
{
  menuItems {
    name
  }
}
```

If the user was talking to us, this would translate to "Give me the names of all of the menu items that you have." Here's a sample of the type of JSON they'd expect in response:

```
{
  "data": {
    "menuItems": [
      {"name": "Reuben"},
      {"name": "Croque Monsieur"},
      {"name": "Muffuletta"}
    ]
  }
}
```

To make this happen, we need to define a GraphQL object type for our menu items.

Defining an Object Type

All data in GraphQL has an associated type. Our menu item type is what GraphQL refers to as an *object*, since it contains a number of *fields* (like name). Let's define our menu item object type so that clients can retrieve information about the structure of menu items. We do this using the object macro that using Absinthe.Schema gives us.

Your Schema in an Abstraction Layer

Keep in mind that your API and the underlying data representations do not need to be identical, or even have the same structure. One of the main values in modeling GraphQL types is that they can serve as an abstraction over whatever backing data store (or service) contains the associated data, transforming it before it's transmitted to API users.

Here are the beginnings of the schema module, with the boilerplate for our new menu item type. You can see we're also stubbing out the query definition for now (more on that soon):

```
02-chp.schema/1-start/lib/plate_slate_web/schema.ex
defmodule PlateSlateWeb.Schema do
  use Absinthe.Schema

  query do
    # <<Ignore this for now>>
  end

  object :menu_item do
    # <<We'll add fields soon>>
  end
end
```

Before we add any fields, let's fire up Interactive Elixir from the root directory of our application:

```
$ iex -S mix
iex(1)>
```

Don't Forget -S mix

 It's important that you run iex with the -S mix option. Without it, your application code won't be automatically compiled, started, and available to you from your session.

Once the prompt shows up, let's take a look at how the menu item object type is modeled in our schema module. We'll use the handy Absinthe.Schema.lookup_type function:

```
iex(1)> Absinthe.Schema.lookup_type(PlateSlateWeb.Schema, "MenuItem")
```

The result looks something like this (we're omitting some of the private internals that are just around for record keeping, and ordering the contents roughly by importance):

```
%Absinthe.Type.Object{
  identifier: :menu_item,
  name: "MenuItem",
  description: nil,
  fields: %{},
  interfaces: [],
  is_type_of: nil
}
```

Absinthe models the types we define as Elixir structs. We haven't added much to our menu_item type yet, so you can see the definition is rather sparse, but it's still worth pointing out some of the main features. First, some internals:

identifier

> The internal identifier Absinthe uses to refer to this type. As we define the schema, we'll be using it a lot, too.

The rest of the Absinthe.Type.Object struct defines values that we can customize as needed:

description

> Documentation we can provide for an object type that will automatically be available to API users using GraphQL's built-in *introspection* features. We'll be talking about this more in Running Our Query with GraphiQL, on page 24.

name

> The canonical GraphQL type name. While required, this will be generated for you automatically if you don't provide it yourself, based on the Absinthe identifier. While we could customize this for our :menu_item object, the default of "MenuItem" works just fine.

fields

> The real meat and potatoes of our object types. We'll add some next.

is_type_of and interfaces

> Support GraphQL's Union and Interface abstract types, which we'll talk more about in Understanding Abstract Types, on page 63.

This is how Absinthe represents the types that you'll be building. Now let's move on to filling in your first type.

Adding Fields

Adding a field to an object type is as simple as using the field macro. The macro takes an identifier atom, a type reference, an optional keyword list of attributes, and a further optional block for more in-depth configuration. We'll start with the basics and add :id, :name, and :description fields to our :menu_item object:

```
02-chp.schema/2-object/lib/plate_slate_web/schema.ex
object :menu_item do
  field :id, :id
  field :name, :string
  field :description, :string
end
```

The identifiers that we've chosen for the fields will give the fields canonical GraphQL names of "id", "name", and "description". (Like object types, the canonical GraphQL names of fields are generated for us automatically.)

The second argument to the field macro here defines the field type. These fields are simple scalar values, and the GraphQL specification defines a number of

built-in scalar types you can use. We've including a handy, detailed reference
in Appendix 1, GraphQL Types, on page 261, but here are the basics:

GraphQL	Absinthe	Description
Int	:integer	Signed 32-bit numeric non-fractional values
Float	:float	Signed double-precision fractional values as specified by IEEE 754[2]
String	:string	Textual data, represented as UTF-8 character sequences
Boolean	:boolean	true or false
Null	:null	Null values, represented as the keyword null
ID	:id	A unique identifier, often used to re-fetch an object or as the key for a cache; not intended to be human-readable

The built-in ID (:id) and String (:string) types are great fits for our :id and :name fields.

Custom Scalar Types

We can add our own scalar types too (we'll learn more about that
in Creating Your Own Scalar Types, on page 50).

Let's review our object by starting iex -S mix and then using Absinthe.Schema.lookup_
type/2 to see the fields we've added:

```
iex(1)> Absinthe.Schema.lookup_type(PlateSlateWeb.Schema, "MenuItem")
```

This gives us something like this (again, shortened a bit for clarity):

```
%Absinthe.Type.Object{
  identifier: :menu_item,
  name: "MenuItem",
  description: nil,
  fields: %{
    id: %Absinthe.Type.Field{
      identifier: :id,
      name: "id",
      type: :id,
      args: %{},
      default_value: nil,
      deprecation: nil,
      description: nil,
      resolve: nil
    },
```

---

2.   http://en.wikipedia.org/wiki/IEEE_floating_point

➤
```
  name: %Absinthe.Type.Field{
    identifier: :name,
    name: "name",
    type: :string,
    args: %{},
    default_value: nil,
    deprecation: nil,
    description: nil,
    resolve: nil
  }
},
interfaces: [],
is_type_of: nil
}
```

There are additional options we can pass to the field macro to build out our Absinthe.Type.Field structs, but we'll get into those soon enough. First let's see about building a basic query.

Making a Query

A GraphQL query is the way that API users can ask for specific pieces of information. We've defined the shape of our GraphQL MenuItem type, but to support users getting menu items, we need to provide two things:

- A way for users to request objects of the type
- A way for the system to retrieve (or resolve) the associated data

The key to the first objective is defining a special object type to serve as the entry point for queries on a GraphQL schema. We already defined it when we used the query macro earlier.

The query macro is just like object, but it handles some extra defaults for us that Absinthe expects. Since we've already defined a blank query object, let's take a look at what it looks like in IEx, too:

```
iex(1)> Absinthe.Schema.lookup_type(PlateSlateWeb.Schema, "RootQueryType")
```

The result looks something like this:

```
%Absinthe.Type.Object{
  identifier: :query,
  name: "RootQueryType",
  description: nil,
  fields: %{},
  interfaces: [],
  is_type_of: nil
}
```

As you can see, there's nothing special about the root query object type structurally. Absinthe will use it as the starting point of queries, determining what top-level fields are available.

Let's add the field we need, :menu_items, for our menu item listing query. We'll use the same field macro we used when we were building our :menu_item object:

```
query do
  field :menu_items, list_of(:menu_item)
end
```

list_of is a handy Absinthe macro that we can use to indicate that a field returns a list of a specific type. Technically, here it's shorthand for %Absinthe.Type.List{of_type: :menu_item}. That's a little long to type every time you need to return a list. We'll use menu_items, since it should return information about more than one menu item.

Supporting Language Conventions

GraphQL is often used by front-end languages like JavaScript that have slightly different conventions than Elixir. In Elixir, it's more conventional to use :menu_items, but in JavaScript, we'd expect menuItems (which is the GraphQL convention, as well).

Lucky for us, Absinthe handles translating between these two conventions automatically so that both the client and the server can work using the formats most familiar to them. The functionality is extensible, too; if you want to use a different naming convention in your GraphQL documents, you can.

Our :menu_items field doesn't actually build the list of menu items yet. To do that, we have to retrieve the data for the field. GraphQL refers to this as *resolution*, and it's done by defining a *resolver* for our field.

A field's resolver is the function that runs to retrieve the data needed for a particular field. Let's build our first one for the :menu_items field. Our menu item data is modeled using Ecto:[3]

```
02-chp.schema/2-object/lib/plate_slate/menu/item.ex
defmodule PlateSlate.Menu.Item do
  use Ecto.Schema
  import Ecto.Changeset
  alias PlateSlate.Menu.Item

  schema "items" do
    field :added_on, :date
    field :description, :string
```

---

3.   https://hex.pm/packages/ecto

```
    field :name, :string
    field :price, :decimal

    belongs_to :category, PlateSlate.Menu.Category

    many_to_many :tags, PlateSlate.Menu.ItemTag,
      join_through: "items_taggings"

    timestamps()
  end

  @doc false
  def changeset(%Item{} = item, attrs) do
    item
    |> cast(attrs, [:name, :description, :price, :added_on])
    |> validate_required([:name, :price])
    |> foreign_key_constraint(:category)
  end
end
```

To retrieve all the menu items, do the following:

```
PlateSlate.Repo.all(PlateSlate.Menu.Item)
```

Since this is exactly what our :menu_items field needs to do, let's wire that in as the result of its resolver, using Elixir's alias to shorten the module names for readability:

```
02-chp.schema/2-object/lib/plate_slate_web/schema.ex
alias PlateSlate.{Menu, Repo}

query do

  field :menu_items, list_of(:menu_item) do
    resolve fn _, _, _ ->
      {:ok, Repo.all(Menu.Item)}
    end
  end

end
```

We've passed a function to the resolve macro to set the field's resolver. Because the field doesn't need any parameters, we can ignore the function arguments and just return an :ok tuple with the list of menu items. That lets Absinthe know that we were able to resolve the field successfully.

You don't need to define a resolver function for every field. For example, this query will attempt to resolve a menu item's :name field:

```
{
  menuItems {
    name
  }
}
```

If a resolver is not defined for a field, Absinthe will attempt to use the equivalent of Map.get/2 to retrieve a value from the parent value in scope, using the identifier for the field. You'll learn more about how that works in Setting Defaults, on page 132.

Resolution starts at the root of a document and works its way deeper, with each field resolver's return value acting as the parent value for its child fields. Because the resolver for menuItems (that is, the resolver we defined in our schema for the :menu_items field) returns a list of menu item values—and resolution is done for each item in a list—the parent value for the name field is a menu item value. Our query, in fact, boils down to something very close to this:

```
for menu_item <- PlateSlate.Repo.all(PlateSlate.Menu.Item) do
  Map.get(menu_item, :name)
end
```

Of course, our GraphQL request gets this information bundled up, nicely labeled in a JSON response from Absinthe.

Let's take a break from editing the schema to play with GraphiQL, a handy user interface we can use to query our fledgling GraphQL API.

Running Our Query with GraphiQL

GraphiQL is "an in-browser IDE for exploring GraphQL," and to make things easy for the user, Absinthe integrates with three versions of GraphiQL: the official interface,[4] an advanced version,[5] and GraphQL Playground.[6] All three are built in to the absinthe_plug[7] package and ready to go with just a little configuration.

The absinthe_plug dependency is already in our mix.exs file from the initial setup, but we need to now configure the Phoenix router to use it. Replace the existing "/" scope with the following block:

```
02-chp.schema/2-object/lib/plate_slate_web/router.ex
scope "/" do
  pipe_through :api

  forward "/api", Absinthe.Plug,
    schema: PlateSlateWeb.Schema
```

---

4. https://github.com/graphql/graphiql
5. https://github.com/OlegIlyenko/graphiql-workspace
6. https://github.com/graphcool/graphql-playground
7. https://github.com/absinthe-graphql/absinthe_plug

```
  forward "/graphiql", Absinthe.Plug.GraphiQL,
    schema: PlateSlateWeb.Schema,
    interface: :simple
end
```

Really, we're setting up two routes: "/api" with the regular Absinthe.Plug, and "/graphiql" with the GraphiQL plug. The former is what API clients would use and what we'll use in our tests, and then the latter provides the "in-browser" IDE we'll use now. Specifically, we're going to use the simplified, official GraphiQL interface, set with the interface: :simple option.

Let's start our application by running the following:

```
$ mix phx.server
```

Since the server will start on port 4000, visit http://localhost:4000/graphiql (adding the path where you have mounted GraphiQL) and see the GraphiQL user interface.

There's a lot to see here, but let's give our query a shot before we dig into it much further. Start by typing your query into the text area to the top left.

Did you notice that while you were typing, GraphiQL helpfully suggested some autocompletions? That's because when you loaded the page, it automatically sent an introspection query to your GraphQL API, retrieving the metadata it needs about PlateSlateWeb.Schema to support autocompletion and display documentation.

When you press the play button above the query, you can see the JSON result in the right-hand text area as shown in the top figure on page 26.

Success! Now, let's try this one, adding the :id field:

```
{
  menuItems {
    id
    name
  }
}
```

Here's the result:

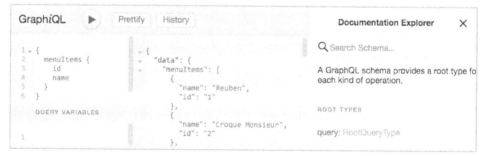

It's handy being able to specify additional fields in our query without having to modify the schema any further! We already defined the :id field on our :menu_item type, so it works out of the box. We just weren't asking for it before.

What else can we query? Let's look at the API documentation that GraphiQL has collected for us. To the right of the GraphiQL interface, there's a "Docs" link that, when clicked, will open up a new sidebar full of API documentation:

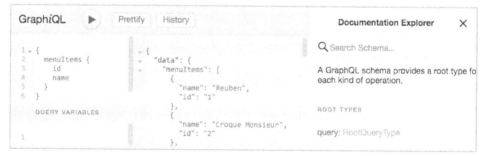

If you click on RootQueryType, you can see the menuItems field with its type, [MenuItem], displayed, but it's missing a more detailed description. You can add one by editing your schema.

Let's do that now. Back in web/schema.ex, you can add a :description value as part of the third argument to the field macro:

```
field :menu_items, list_of(:menu_item),
    description: "The list of available items on the menu" do
  «Menu item field definition»
end
```

If you look back at GraphiQL (refresh the page), your description will now be displayed.

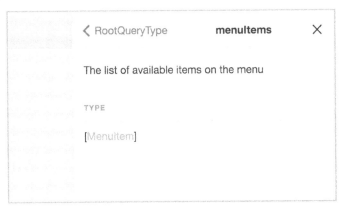

There's another technique you can use to add descriptions, using a module attribute, @desc, just as you would with Elixir's @doc:

```
@desc "The list of available items on the menu"
field :menu_items, list_of(:menu_item) do
  «Menu item field definition»
end
```

Because the latter approach supports multiline documentation more cleanly and sets itself off from the working details of our field definitions, it's the approach we'll use in our application.

Testing Our Query

GraphiQL is a great tool to explore our API and when we'd like to manually run a query, but it's not a replacement for a test suite. We'll use *ExUnit* to add tests for our Absinthe schema to make sure our queries work now and later on to prevent regressions. Our future selves will appreciate the forethought.

ExUnit is bundled with Elixir, so no dependencies are required. Since our PlateSlate application is using Phoenix, ExUnit has already been set up with a preconfigured test harness that we can use.

Because we know our users are going to use the API by hitting /api, we can treat our API just as we would a Phoenix controller, using the PlateSlate.ConnCase helper module that Phoenix generously generated for us:

02-chp.schema/2-object/test/plate_slate_web/schema/query/menu_items_test.exs

```
Line 1  defmodule PlateSlateWeb.Schema.Query.MenuItemsTest do
   -      use PlateSlateWeb.ConnCase, async: true
   -
   -      setup do
   5          PlateSlate.Seeds.run()
   -      end
   -
   -      @query """
   -      {
  10        menuItems {
   -          name
   -        }
   -      }
   -      """
  15      test "menuItems field returns menu items" do
   -        conn = build_conn()
   -        conn = get conn, "/api", query: @query
   -        assert json_response(conn, 200) == %{
   -          "data" => %{
  20            "menuItems" => [
   -              %{"name" => "Reuben"},
   -              %{"name" => "Croque Monsieur"},
   -              %{"name" => "Muffuletta"},
   -              # «Rest of items»
  25            ]
   -          }
   -        }
   -      end
   -
  30  end
```

The setup block loads our seed data as a convenience. The test itself starts by building a connection. Then it passes the @query module attribute we defined previously (making use of Elixir's handy multiline """ string literal) as the :query option, which is what Absinthe.Plug expects. The response is then checked to make sure that it has an HTTP 200 status code and includes the JSON data that we expect to see.

Running the test gives us exactly what we were hoping for:

```
$ mix test test/plate_slate_web/schema/query/menu_items_test.exs
.

Finished in 0.2 seconds
1 test, 0 failures
```

After a little compilation, a passing test!

We'll continue to build tests out this way as our API grows. These tests exercise a lot of our system, from HTTP requests through JSON serialization, helping to reduce our stress by keeping us confident that changes elsewhere in the application aren't affecting our GraphQL users.

Moving On

In this chapter, we learned how to build the foundation of a GraphQL schema in an Elixir application, defining an object type that we exposed via a query field, and we tested our fledgling API using a popular tool, GraphiQL.

Here are a couple challenges for you before we move on:

1. We've defined :id and :name fields for our MenuItem object type. The backing Ecto schema, PlateSlate.Menu.Item, has a number of other fields we could also expose in our GraphQL schema. Define another one using one of the built-in scalar types we mentioned earlier.
2. Add descriptions for the fields inside the MenuItem object type, using the @desc form. Don't stop there: you can use it to add a description for the object type itself, too. Verify that GraphiQL is displaying the descriptions.

Once you're done, we're going to look at supporting user input in the next chapter, which will open up a whole range of new and interesting API possibilities.

## CHAPTER 3

Taking User Input

Web APIs need to define and validate input from users, whether it's used to query information or to modify it. In most web frameworks, this input definition is ad hoc and often mixed in with the business logic of the application. GraphQL takes a more declarative approach, however, by defining input as part of your API schema and supporting type validations as a core feature.

In this chapter, you'll see that by articulating the rules about our data in the schema, we can have the Absinthe package enforce them for us, allowing our Elixir application code to focus on more core application concerns. This will make our code more readable and easier to maintain.

We'll dig into the nuts and bolts of user input in GraphQL, covering the different ways users can provide it and the constraints we can set. You'll learn about new input types and how to apply them to make your GraphQL schemas more descriptive, accurate representations of your API.

Let's start by looking at GraphQL's most fundamental user input concept, the field argument.

Defining Field Arguments

GraphQL documents are made up of fields. The user lists the fields they would like, and the schema uses its definition of those fields to resolve the pieces of data that match. The system would be pretty inflexible if it did not also allow users to provide additional parameters that would clarify exactly what information each field needed to find. A user requesting information about menuItems, for instance, may want to see certain menu items or a certain number of them.

It's for this reason that GraphQL has the concept of field *arguments*: a way for users to provide input to fields that can be used to parameterize their queries. Let's take a look at our example application and see how we can extend our Absinthe schema by defining the arguments that our API will accept for a field, and then see how we can use those arguments to tailor the result for users.

We've already built a field in our API that we could make more flexible by accepting user input: the list of menu items. Our schema's menuItems field, if you remember, looks something like this:

03-chp.userinput/1-start/lib/plate_slate_web/schema.ex
```
Line 1  alias PlateSlate.{Menu, Repo}
   -
   -    query do
   -
   5      field :menu_items, list_of(:menu_item) do
   -        resolve fn _, _, _ ->
   -          {:ok, Repo.all(Menu.Item)}
   -        end
   -      end
   10
   -    end
```

On line 7, the field's resolver just returns all the menu items, without any support for filtering, ordering, or other modifications to the scope or layout of the result. The field isn't declaring any arguments, so the resolver doesn't receive anything with which we could modify the list of menu items retrieved.

Let's add an argument to our schema to support filtering menu items by name. We'll call it matching, then configure our field resolver to use it when provided:

03-chp.userinput/2-matchinginline/lib/plate_slate_web/schema.ex
```
Line 1  alias PlateSlate.{Menu, Repo}
   -    import Ecto.Query
   -
   -    query do
   5
   -      field :menu_items, list_of(:menu_item) do
   -        arg :matching, :string
   -        resolve fn
   -          _, %{matching: name}, _ when is_binary(name) ->
   10            query = from t in Menu.Item, where: ilike(t.name, ^"%#{name}%")
   -            {:ok, Repo.all(query)}
   -          _, _, _ ->
   -            {:ok, Repo.all(Menu.Item)}
   -        end
   15      end
   -
   -    end
```

On line 7, we defined matching as a :string type. If you remember from the previous chapter, :string is a built-in type. We can use it as an input type, too.

We're not making the matching argument mandatory here, so we need to support resolving our menuItems field in the event it's provided, and in the event it isn't. You can see Elixir's pattern matching capability used in the two separate function heads of our resolver to handle those two cases.

The second function head, on line 12, serves as the fall-through match and is identical to our original resolver.

It's the first function head, on line 9, that adds our new behavior. On line 10, we make use of the matched argument as name (in the from macro that Ecto.Query[1] provides) to build our Ecto query. We pulled the Ecto.Query macros in on line 2. By declaring our inputs up front, Absinthe has a bounded set of inputs to work with and can thus give us an atom-keyed map to work with as arguments, unlike Phoenix controller action params.

Resolvers and Field Arguments

 Absinthe only passes arguments to resolvers if they have been provided by the user. Making a map key match of the arguments resolver function parameter is a handy way to check for a field argument that's been specified in the request.

Writing complicated resolvers as anonymous functions can have a negative side effect on a schema's readability, so to keep the declarative look and feel of the schema alive and well, let's do a little refactoring and extract the resolver into a new module. Because filtering menu items is an important feature of our application—and could be used generally, not just from the GraphQL API—we'll also pull the core filtering logic into the PlateSlate.Menu module, which is where our business logic relating to the menu belongs.

Here's our new resolver module:

03-chp.userinput/3-matching/lib/plate_slate_web/resolvers/menu.ex
```
defmodule PlateSlateWeb.Resolvers.Menu do
  alias PlateSlate.Menu

  def menu_items(_, args, _) do
    {:ok, Menu.list_items(args)}
  end
end
```

You can see that the resolver is calling PlateSlate.Menu.list_items/1, passing the arguments. The logic inside PlateSlate.Menu looks like this:

---

1. https://hexdocs.pm/ecto/Ecto.Query.API.html

```
03-chp.userinput/3-matching/lib/plate_slate/menu/menu.ex
def list_items(%{matching: name}) when is_binary(name) do
  Item
  |> where([m], ilike(m.name, ^"%#{name}%"))
  |> Repo.all
end
def list_items(_) do
  Repo.all(Item)
end
```

This code should look pretty familiar; it's been extracted out of our anonymous resolver function and restructured into a named function. Doing this makes both the resolver and the overall schema more readable.

The Point of "Pointless" Modules

While it might seem like adding resolver modules just to have them call functions from other modules is superfluous, it's important to set up a solid separation of concerns early on in our project.

In general, a resolver's job is to mediate between the input that a user sends to our GraphQL API and the business logic that needs to be called to service their request. As your schema gets more complex, you'll be glad you made space in the overall architecture of your application to keep your resolver and domain business logic separate.

We'll cover structural decisions like these in more detail in Chapter 4, Adding Flexibility, on page 59.

Now let's wire our resolver back into our :menu_items field in the schema:

```
03-chp.userinput/3-matching/lib/plate_slate_web/schema.ex
alias PlateSlateWeb.Resolvers

query do

  field :menu_items, list_of(:menu_item) do
    arg :matching, :string
    resolve &Resolvers.Menu.menu_items/3
  end

end
```

Using Elixir's & function capture special form[2] here lets us tie in the function from our new module as the resolver for the field and keeps the schema declaration tight and focused.

Let's explore using this new field argument that we've defined with some GraphQL queries that cover a range of scenarios.

---

2.   https://hexdocs.pm/elixir/Kernel.SpecialForms.html#&/1

Providing Field Argument Values

There are two ways that a GraphQL user can provide argument values for an argument: as document literals, and as variables.

Using Literals

Using document literals, values are embedded directly inside the GraphQL document. It's a straightforward approach that works well for static documents. Here's a query that uses a document literal for the matching argument that we've added to retrieve menu items whose names match "reu":

```
{
  menuItems(matching: "reu") {
    name
  }
}
```

Argument values are given after the argument name and a colon (:), and the literal for a :string argument is enclosed in double quotes ("). Let's use this query in a new test, just as we did in Testing Our Query, on page 27:

```
03-chp.userinput/3-matching/test/plate_slate_web/schema/query/menu_items_test.exs
@query """
{
  menuItems(matching: "reu") {
    name
  }
}
"""
test "menuItems field returns menu items filtered by name" do
  response = get(build_conn(), "/api", query: @query)
  assert json_response(response, 200) == %{
    "data" => %{
      "menuItems" => [
        %{"name" => "Reuben"},
      ]
    }
  }
end
```

Running the test, we can verify that our literal argument value is being passed through, and the query successfully filtering the menu items returned:

```
$ mix test test/plate_slate_web/schema/query/menu_items_test.exs
..

Finished in 0.4 seconds
2 tests, 0 failures
```

It works! Now let's see what happens when a user provides a bad value:

03-chp.userinput/3-matching/test/plate_slate_web/schema/query/menu_items_test.exs
```
@query """
{
  menuItems(matching: 123) {
    name
  }
}
"""

test "menuItems field returns errors when using a bad value" do
  response = get(build_conn(), "/api", query: @query)
➤  assert %{"errors" => [
➤    %{"message" => message}
➤  ]} = json_response(response, 400)
➤  assert message == "Argument \"matching\" has invalid value 123."
end
```

The first thing to notice here is that we're getting an HTTP 400 response code from Absinthe. This indicates that one or more errors occurred that prevented query execution. Helpfully, the error given in the response tells the user of the API what they're doing wrong.

This is great! Our API can respond appropriately to user-provided values, without any intervention by any custom type-checking code. By consulting our schema, Absinthe handles it for us.

Let's run it to make sure the error is returned:

```
$ mix test test/plate_slate_web/schema/query/menu_items_test.exs
...

Finished in 0.4 seconds
3 tests, 0 failures
```

Now that we have both valid and invalid tests working correctly, let's talk about how users might use this query in the real world. In the examples we're using for our tests, we're using literal argument values directly in the GraphQL document. This isn't very reusable.

Imagine a user interface that took a search term from end users and then called out to our API. If the front-end application only used document literals, it would need to interpolate the search terms directly into the GraphQL document. For each user request, a completely new document would have to be generated, likely using string interpolation. To do this while ensuring that the GraphQL document wouldn't be malformed, it would need to sanitize the input—making sure, for instance, that no double quotes were provided that would prematurely end the string value and cause a parse error from the GraphQL server.

This is a great use case for GraphQL *variables*—a way to insert dynamic argument values provided alongside (rather than inside) the static GraphQL document.

Using Variables

GraphQL variables act as typed placeholders for values that will be sent along with the request, a concept that may be familiar to you if you've used parameterized SQL queries for insertion and sanitization of values. GraphQL variables are declared with their types—before they're used—alongside the *operation* type. We haven't had to think about operation types before, so let's talk a little bit about what operations are and how they fit inside the GraphQL document.

Understanding Operations

A GraphQL document consists of one or more operations, which model something that we want the GraphQL server to do. Up to this point, we've been asking the server to provide information—an operation that GraphQL calls a query. GraphQL has other operation types too, notably mutation for persisting a change to data, and subscription to request a live feed of data. We'll get into those later.

We've been using a simplified way of typing up a *query operation*, which just uses an outer set of curly braces ({}) to demarcate where it starts and ends:

```
{
  menuItems { name }
}
```

GraphQL assumes that if you're providing a single operation like this, its operation type is query. The previous example is equivalent to this, where we explicitly mark the operation as a query:

```
query {
  menuItems { name }
}
```

In simple cases, we omit the operation type, but when we're using variables, we need to use the more formal, verbose syntax and fully declare the operation. This gives us a place to list and describe the variables that we'll be using in the operation. Let's declare a variable for use in our menu item search query.

Naming Operations

You can also provide a name for operations, which can be useful for identifying them in server logs. The name is provided after the operation type—for instance, query MenuItemList { ... }. You'll see named operations later in the book.

Declaring Variables

Here's our menu items query operation with a definition for a variable we'll be using, $term, and then its use for the matching argument:

```
query ($term: String) {
  menuItems(matching: $term) {
    name
  }
}
```

Variable declarations are provided directly before the curly braces that start the body of an operation, and are placed inside a set of parentheses. Variable names start with a dollar sign ($), and their GraphQL types follow after a colon (:) and a space character. If we were declaring multiple variables, we'd list them separated by commas.

The variable's GraphQL type isn't the snake_cased form as declared in our schema. As you discovered in the previous chapter, Absinthe uses snake_cased atom identifiers for GraphQL types (like :string) so that our Elixir code feels idiomatic. In GraphQL documents, however, we need to use the canonical GraphQL type names (like String), which are CamelCased. (If you're ever unsure of the canonical name for a built-in GraphQL type and how they map to Absinthe types, take a peek at Appendix 1, GraphQL Types, on page 261, where we've laid them all out for you.)

We used the String type for our $term variable, since that's exactly the type of argument value that we defined for the matching argument in our schema.

Variable Types Aren't Extraneous

While it might seem like having to declare an argument type and a variable type (that will be used for that argument) is overkill, it allows the GraphQL server to give clearer error messages about the expected vs. provided variable value and lets the GraphQL document writer make values mandatory to support client-side validation.

Of course, if you've taken the time and effort to declare a variable and sprinkle its values throughout a document, you probably want to know how to provide values for it.

Providing Values for Variables

Variable values are provided alongside GraphQL documents. Let's modify the test that we used previously to illustrate how:

```
03-chp.userinput/3-matching/test/plate_slate_web/schema/query/menu_items_test.exs
@query """
query ($term: String) {
  menuItems(matching: $term) {
    name
  }
}
"""
@variables %{"term" => "reu"}
test "menuItems field filters by name when using a variable" do
  response = get(build_conn(), "/api", query: @query, variables: @variables)
  assert json_response(response, 200) == %{
    "data" => %{
      "menuItems" => [
        %{"name" => "Reuben"},
      ]
    }
  }
end
```

You notice that we're passing the value of term (without the $ prefix) along in variables. We're still using a GET request here, but a POST would also work. In either case, the value of variables should be JSON-encoded (a detail that—since we're inside a test—we can ignore).

We can run the test with mix to verify that our variable value is being passed correctly:

```
$ mix test test/plate_slate_web/schema/query/menu_items_test.exs
....

Finished in 0.4 seconds
4 tests, 0 failures
```

We can also play with the query in the GraphiQL interface that we learned about in the previous chapter, provided for us as part of the absinthe_plug project dependency. To do that, we start our application to access the GraphiQL interface:

```
$ mix phx.server
[info] Running PlateSlateWeb.Endpoint with Cowboy using http://localhost:4000
```

Open up a browser and point it at http://localhost:4000/graphiql.

First, enter this query in the pane on the left:

```
query ($term: String) {
  menuItems(matching: $term) {
    name
  }
}
```

Then, make sure the "Query Variables" section is open and define the value for the term variable in a JSON object. It should all look something like this:

When we run the query, GraphiQL sends a POST with a body that looks something like this:

```
{
  "query": "query ($term: String) { menuItems(matching: $term) { name } }",
  "variables": "{\"term\": \"reu\"}"
}
```

The response, sent back from Absinthe, is formatted nicely for readability and is exactly what we expect to see:

GraphQL makes it easy to plug in dynamic values from outside the document. This capability makes for flexible, reusable GraphQL documents that we can use over and over with different use values. Let's look at another example, tackling a common user interface need (list ordering) while introducing a new, useful GraphQL type: enumerations.

Using Enumeration Types

A GraphQL enumeration (or *enum*, as it's generally called) is a special type of scalar that has a defined, finite set of possible values. Here are some examples of values that are well represented by enums:

- Available shirt sizes: S, M, L, and XL
- Color components: RED, GREEN, and BLUE
- Ordering: ASC and DESC

Enums are a good choice if the possible values are well defined and unlikely to change, if those values are short (one or maybe two words long), and if they're not a pair of values that are more clearly represented by a boolean flag.

Let's use the ASC and DESC ordering example for a list of menu items that we'll allow users to retrieve in ascending or descending order.

We'll start by adding our enum type, :sort_order, using the enum and value macros. The enum macro works just like object, but it defines an enumeration instead of an object. The value macro defines a possible value of the enum. For our use case, :asc and :desc will do:

```
03-chp.userinput/4-ordering/lib/plate_slate_web/schema.ex
enum :sort_order do
  value :asc
  value :desc
end
```

To allow users to dictate a :sort_order for our :menu_items field, we need to declare a new argument. We'll call it :order, too:

```
field :menu_items, list_of(:menu_item) do
  arg :matching, :string
  arg :order, :sort_order
  resolve &Resolvers.Menu.menu_items/3
end
```

There are a few things to notice about the argument declaration. First, as with the :matching argument for the :menu_item type, the standard form for an argument declaration is arg NAME, TYPE. If this seems a bit confusing, we can make the type more explicit by providing it as a :type option. Let's do that, and provide the argument a default value for good measure:

```
arg :order, type: :sort_order, default_value: :asc
```

The second argument to the arg macro can be a keyword list to support additional options. Here we dictate that the :order argument should have a default value of :asc if one is not provided; that way, our users don't have to declare an order if they don't care about it, but our resolver can always expect to find a value for it. Let's modify the PlateSlate.Menu.list_items/1 to handle those two cases:

- When the order is given (or it defaults) as :asc
- When the order is given as :desc

```
03-chp.userinput/4-ordering/lib/plate_slate/menu/menu.ex
def list_items(filters) do
  filters
  |> Enum.reduce(Item, fn
    {_, nil}, query ->
      query
    {:order, order}, query ->
      from q in query, order_by: {^order, :name}
    {:matching, name}, query ->
      from q in query, where: ilike(q.name, ^"%#{name}%")
  end)
  |> Repo.all
end
```

Here we use Ecto's order_by to take the value of our :order argument directly—since it just happens to use :desc and :asc for ordering. We execute the query to retrieve the menu items, which are then returned. If we run the tests at this point, you'll notice our default order is causing a failure:

```
$ mix test test/plate_slate_web/schema/query/menu_items_test.exs
.
1) test menuItems field returns menu items
   (PlateSlateWeb.Schema.Query.MenuItemsTest)
     test/plate_slate_web/schema/query/menu_items_test.exs:16
     Assertion with == failed
     «Lots of details»
...

Finished in 0.3 seconds
4 tests, 1 failure
```

This happens because the test doesn't provide a desired order, so the order falls back to the default value. This causes the menu items to be returned in an order the test doesn't expect. If we change the order of the menu items in the test to match the default value, the test will pass:

```
03-chp.userinput/4-ordering/test/plate_slate_web/schema/query/menu_items_test.exs
test "menuItems field returns menu items" do
  conn = build_conn()
  conn = get conn, "/api", query: @query
  assert json_response(conn, 200) == %{"data" => %{"menuItems" => [
    %{"name" => "Bánh mì"},
    %{"name" => "Chocolate Milkshake"},
    %{"name" => "Croque Monsieur"},
```

```
      %{"name" => "French Fries"},
      %{"name" => "Lemonade"},
      %{"name" => "Masala Chai"},
      %{"name" => "Muffuletta"},
      %{"name" => "Papadum"},
      %{"name" => "Pasta Salad"},
      %{"name" => "Reuben"},
      %{"name" => "Soft Drink"},
      %{"name" => "Vada Pav"},
      %{"name" => "Vanilla Milkshake"},
      %{"name" => "Water"}
  ]}}
end
```

We also want to make sure specifying a sort order works. Let's write another test that will attempt to get the list of menu items, ordered descending, and check the name of the first menu item returned:

03-chp.userinput/4-ordering/test/plate_slate_web/schema/query/menu_items_test.exs
```
@query """
{
  menuItems(order: DESC) {
    name
  }
}
"""
test "menuItems field returns items descending using literals" do
  response = get(build_conn(), "/api", query: @query)
  assert %{
    "data" => %{"menuItems" => [%{"name" => "Water"} | _]}
  } = json_response(response, 200)
end
```

We're providing the order as DESC, and without quotes. By convention, enum values are passed in all uppercase letters; the value macro that we used to declare the enum values sets up a mapping for us, accepting enum values as literals and variables in all uppercase and converting them to atoms automatically.

Unconventional Enum Values

While the value macro does support customizing the external representation used for enum values, the GraphQL specification explicitly recommends the uppercase convention that Absinthe sets up for you automatically.

Unless you have a very good reason, you should stick with the recommendation given by the specification so that your API provides as comfortable an experience as possible to users that are already familiar with GraphQL.

You provide variable values for enum types just as you do for String. Let's revisit the test we just ran, but using variables to insert the argument value:

```
03-chp.userinput/4-ordering/test/plate_slate_web/schema/query/menu_items_test.exs
@query """
query ($order: SortOrder!) {
  menuItems(order: $order) {
    name
  }
}
"""
@variables %{"order" => "DESC"}
test "menuItems field returns items descending using variables" do
  response = get(build_conn(), "/api", query: @query, variables: @variables)
  assert %{
    "data" => %{"menuItems" => [%{"name" => "Water"} | _]}
  } = json_response(response, 200)
end
```

Because the "Water" menu item is the first item in descending order, we're checking that it's the first item returned.

Notice the type name that we're using for our :sort_order enum variable, $order. It starts with SortOrder, as you'd expect given the way Absinthe type identifiers are automatically converted to title case for their canonical GraphQL names—but it ends in an exclamation mark (!). This denotes that, as the person writing the GraphQL query document, you're making the variable mandatory. This is a handy tool on the client side, giving front-end developers the ability to enforce additional input constraints. A document that doesn't meet its variable requirements won't be executed if it's received by Absinthe, and some client-side frameworks even enforce variable checks to prevent inadequately filled GraphQL documents from being sent at all.

We can make arguments mandatory at the schema level as well, adding non-null constraints to our argument types. We'll cover that shortly, but first let's take a look at how we can organize field arguments into groups using a mechanism that GraphQL calls *input object* types.

Modeling Input Objects

Up to this point, we've been adding arguments directly onto our fields, but this can get messy. Imagine, for instance, if we wanted to add various filtering options to our :menu_items field. We could just add them à la carte:

```
@desc "Matching a category name"
arg :category, :string
```

```
@desc "Matching a tag"
arg :tag, :string

@desc "Priced above a value"
arg :priced_above, :float

@desc "Priced below a value"
arg :priced_below, :float
```

Mixed in with other arguments that we add to the field, this can quickly become a hodgepodge of various flags and options that would be better organized into related groupings. GraphQL gives us a tool to do this: input object types.

We can collect multiple arguments and model them as a special object type used just for argument values. Let's take the :category, :tag, :priced_above, and :priced_below arguments and group them together into a new input object type, :menu_item_filter:

```
03-chp.userinput/5-inputobjects/lib/plate_slate_web/schema.ex
@desc "Filtering options for the menu item list"
input_object :menu_item_filter do

  @desc "Matching a name"
  field :name, :string

  @desc "Matching a category name"
  field :category, :string

  @desc "Matching a tag"
  field :tag, :string

  @desc "Priced above a value"
  field :priced_above, :float

  @desc "Priced below a value"
  field :priced_below, :float

end
```

We've taken the filters and placed them inside an input_object macro block that demarcates the limits of our new :menu_item_filter type. You'll also notice that we're not using arg anymore; just like normal object types, input objects model their members as fields, not arguments. Fields for input objects, however, don't have any arguments (or a resolver) of their own; they're merely there to model structure.

Let's plug this new type in as an argument for the :menu_items field:

```
03-chp.userinput/5-inputobjects/lib/plate_slate_web/schema.ex
field :menu_items, list_of(:menu_item) do
  arg :filter, :menu_item_filter
  arg :order, type: :sort_order, default_value: :asc
  resolve &Resolvers.Menu.menu_items/3
end
```

To support the filter, we modify PlateSlate.Menu.list_items/1, reworking it to build a query using either or both of the :order and :filter arguments:

```
03-chp.userinput/5-inputobjects/lib/plate_slate/menu/menu.ex
def list_items(args) do
  args
  |> Enum.reduce(Item, fn
    {:order, order}, query ->
      query |> order_by({^order, :name})
    {:filter, filter}, query ->
      query |> filter_with(filter)
  end)
  |> Repo.all
end

defp filter_with(query, filter) do
  Enum.reduce(filter, query, fn
    {:name, name}, query ->
      from q in query, where: ilike(q.name, ^"%#{name}%")
    {:priced_above, price}, query ->
      from q in query, where: q.price >= ^price
    {:priced_below, price}, query ->
      from q in query, where: q.price <= ^price
    {:category, category_name}, query ->
      from q in query,
        join: c in assoc(q, :category),
        where: ilike(c.name, ^"%#{category_name}%")
    {:tag, tag_name}, query ->
      from q in query,
        join: t in assoc(q, :tags),
        where: ilike(t.name, ^"%#{tag_name}%")
  end)
end
```

We use the order_by and where macros from Ecto.Query as we iterate over the key/value pairs of the filter and build up the query with Enum.reduce/3.[3] To understand how the filter can be sent to Absinthe, let's build and run a couple of tests. In the first test, we'll provide the filter as a literal:

```
03-chp.userinput/5-inputobjects/test/plate_slate_web/schema/query/menu_items_test.exs
@query """
{
  menuItems(filter: {category: "Sandwiches", tag: "Vegetarian"}) {
    name
  }
}
"""
```

---

3. https://hexdocs.pm/elixir/Enum.html#reduce/3

```
test "menuItems field returns menuItems, filtering with a literal" do
  response = get(build_conn(), "/api", query: @query)
  assert %{
    "data" => %{"menuItems" => [%{"name" => "Vada Pav"}]}
  } == json_response(response, 200)
end
```

Here we're providing the filter argument value formatted just as you might expect from a JavaScript object, using curly braces and bare, unquoted identifiers for the field names. Once the filter argument passes schema checks, it is restructured to match the schema naming, handling camelCase to snake_case conversion, if appropriate. Not much needs to be done to the filter input object value; the arguments map passed to our menu items resolver looks exactly like the GraphQL document, using atom keys:

```
%{category: "Sandwiches", tag: "Vegetarian"}
```

We've seen how input objects can be provided as literals, but usually complex arguments will be sent as variables, so let's look at how this same request might look using a $filter variable:

```
03-chp.userinput/5-inputobjects/test/plate_slate_web/schema/query/menu_items_test.exs
@query """
query ($filter: MenuItemFilter!) {
  menuItems(filter: $filter) {
    name
  }
}
"""
@variables %{filter: %{"tag" => "Vegetarian", "category" => "Sandwiches"}}
test "menuItems field returns menuItems, filtering with a variable" do
  response = get(build_conn(), "/api", query: @query, variables: @variables)
  assert %{
    "data" => %{"menuItems" => [%{"name" => "Vada Pav"}]}
  } == json_response(response, 200)
end
```

It looks very similar; as in previous examples, the variable value is sent alongside the query. Here, for the test case, the value of the filter variable is defined using an Elixir map type, which is how Absinthe will receive the value after the JSON object sent as part of the request is parsed by Plug.Parsers and the absinthe_plug package.

Having replaced the matching arg with the filter arg, you'll also want to take a moment to go through the existing tests that are now failing and turn any matching: "..." inputs into filter: {name: "..."}. Pay attention to the error message you get back in the failing tests. Once again, we can see Absinthe at work validating input without any code necessary in our resolvers.

Rules for Input Objects

Here are some things to keep in mind when building input objects:

- Input objects can be nested. You can define an input object field as having an input object type. This nesting can be arbitrarily deep.

- Input object types, unlike normal object types, do not support circular references. You can't have two input types that refer to each other, either directly or through an intermediary.

- Input object type fields can be of any type that a field argument might use. It's best to just think of them as structured arguments.

We've just scratched the surface of input objects. We'll dig in deeper in Chapter 5, Making a Change with Mutations, on page 77, where we'll learn about how we can use input objects to model data for changesets.

In the meantime, let's address non-null constraints, the mechanism that GraphQL schemas use to enforce that a given argument is provided in documents before they are executed.

Marking Arguments as Non-Null

In the last section, you saw variable declarations that featured use of exclamation marks to ensure variable values were provided. It looked something like this:

```
query ($filter: MenuItemFilter!) {
  menuItems(filter: $filter) {
    name
  }
}
```

The document here declares that the $filter variable is a MenuItemFilter, while the addition of an exclamation mark denotes that a value is mandatory. This is a constraint that the document designer (usually a front-end developer) builds into the query, but the schema designer can enforce non-null constraints on the backend as well.

Let's say, for instance, that we wanted to ensure that a filter was always provided to the :menu_items field, regardless of what the document says should be mandatory. We can do this by using the Absinthe non_null macro, wrapping the argument type:

```
field :menu_items, list_of(:menu_item) do
  arg :filter, non_null(:menu_item_filter)
  arg :order, type: :sort_order, default_value: :asc
  resolve &Resolvers.Menu.menu_items/3
end
```

Like the list_of macro, non_null is a handy shortcut for building a struct—in this case, %Absinthe.Type.NonNull{of_type: :menu_item_filter}.

Our use of non_null here ensures that the :filter argument is always provided. If it isn't, execution of the document won't occur, the field resolver function won't even be invoked, and the user will get back a blunt message that looks something like this (omitting some line number information):

```
{
  "errors": [
    {
      "message":
      "In argument \"filter\": Expected type \"MenuItemFilter!\", found null."
    }
  ]
}
```

Granted, sending an empty filter object is enough to count as meeting this constraint; to force values in the filter, we'd have the flexibility to handle those directly. For instance, in the event we wanted to force the menu items list to always be filtered by category, we could also mark that field as non-nullable:

```
input_object :menu_item_filter do
  field :category, non_null(:string)
  field :tag, :string
  field :priced_above, :float
  field :priced_below, :float
end
```

Non-Nullability

 When the field for an input object is non-nullable—just as with arguments—validation will fail when a non-null value isn't provided for that field. It's different for normal (output) object fields. Declaring an output object field as non-nullable means that the schema will guarantee the field resolver's result will always be non-null.

Non-nullability for input object fields means the client needs to provide a non-null value as part of the request. Non-nullability for output object fields means the server needs to provide a non-null value as part of the response.

> ## Dealing with Dependent Arguments
>
> You may encounter situations where you've defined many arguments for a field only to discover that certain arguments should be non-nullable—but only in the event another argument isn't present...or is. Here are two differing solutions that you can evaluate:
>
> - Make the field arguments more complex: try grouping arguments that go together into input objects, like we did with menu item filtering. This lets you leave the input object nullable but individual input object fields as non-nullable. Sometimes it's more important to keep a field cohesive.
>
> - Make the field simpler: split it into multiple, simpler fields that handle narrower use cases and have their own documentation (via @desc). Don't be afraid to create more, case-specific fields, each with a narrow focus. You can always share resolution logic and output types.

With this constraint in place, any filter that's provided that omits a value for :category would get a similarly helpful error message after failing validation.

Defining arguments (and input object fields) as non-nullable is an important part of building an effective GraphQL schema that accurately models the data constraints that your API needs to operate.

There are certain situations that are fairly cut and dry. For instance, if the purpose of a field is to retrieve a specific piece of data by an :id, it makes sense for that :id to be defined as non-nullable. There may be cases, especially when dealing with mutations (as we'll learn about soon), in which you'll need to carefully assess whether an argument should be nullable and what effect that will have—especially as the nullable status will be clearly denoted in the API documentation that users automatically have available as a feature of GraphQL.

Now that we have a handle on complex argument data structures and some techniques that we can use as we build and configure them, let's focus in a little tighter—on the smallest unit of user input: scalar types.

Creating Your Own Scalar Types

Scalar types form the leaves of your input and output trees. You're already pretty familiar with a number of scalar types that we've used as inputs and outputs. Absinthe's built-in scalar types, from :integer to :string and :id, all have a firm grounding in the GraphQL specification. These types are not special cases, but are built using the same schema tools provided to users of Absinthe.

Building your own scalar types can be handy, too. Let's say, for instance, that we'd like to support a :date scalar type that supports users providing dates in a nice, easy-to-use format, automatically giving us Date structs that are easier for us to use in Elixir.

If we wanted to filter our menu item list by the date prior to which the menu item was added, for instance, it would be nice to support a nicely formatted date as an argument:

```
{
  menuItems(addedBefore: "2017-01-31") {
    name
  }
}
```

We also want to be able to retrieve the date of a menu item in a document like this:

```
{
  menuItem {
    name
    addedOn
  }
}
```

Given what we already know, this could definitely be handled by just making the :added_before argument a :string field. The problem, though, would be that our resolver code would have to go through the effort of parsing that string into an actual %Date{} struct, and handling any errors that might show up if it's in an invalid format. We also lose out on documentation because while the field type will say string, it's really more specific than that.

We would be a lot better off building a :date type, which it turns out is pretty easy to do!

The first thing we'll need is the scalar type itself, which we can build with the scalar macro.

03-chp.userinput/6-customscalar/lib/plate_slate_web/schema.ex
```
scalar :date do
  parse fn input ->
    # «Parsing logic here»
  end

  serialize fn date ->
    # «Serialization logic here»
  end
end
```

Each scalar needs to have two parts defined for it—a parse function and a serialize function:

- parse converts a value coming from the user into an Elixir term (or returns :error).

- serialize converts an Elixir term back into a value that can be returned via JSON.

In this example, the parse function's job is to take the document representation of the scalar (for example, "2016-01-31") and transform it into an Elixir date, validating it along the way. The serialize function's job is just to go the other way, transforming the date back into a string. In our particular case, the actual logic for date parsing and serialization is supplied by Elixir itself, so that part is largely solved for us.

03-chp.userinput/6-customscalar/lib/plate_slate_web/schema.ex
```
scalar :date do
  parse fn input ->
    case Date.from_iso8601(input.value) do
      {:ok, date} -> {:ok, date}
      _ -> :error
    end
  end

  serialize fn date ->
    Date.to_iso8601(date)
  end
end
```

Scalars can be used as both input and output types, as you've already seen with built-in scalars like :string. We track the added-on dates of menu items in the database, and we'd like to support an API that would let users filter menu items by that date.

To do that, let's first add the field to our menu item object:

03-chp.userinput/6-customscalar/lib/plate_slate_web/schema.ex
```
object :menu_item do
  field :id, :id
  field :name, :string
  field :description, :string
  field :added_on, :date
end
```

Now that we have that, let's enhance our menu item filter with :added_before and :added_after fields:

```
03-chp.userinput/6-customscalar/lib/plate_slate_web/schema.ex
@desc "Filtering options for the menu item list"
input_object :menu_item_filter do

  @desc "Matching a name"
  field :name, :string

  @desc "Matching a category name"
  field :category, :string

  @desc "Matching a tag"
  field :tag, :string

  @desc "Priced above a value"
  field :priced_above, :float

  @desc "Priced below a value"
  field :priced_below, :float

➤  @desc "Added to the menu before this date"
➤  field :added_before, :date
➤
➤  @desc "Added to the menu after this date"
➤  field :added_after, :date

end
```

With the filter changes in place, we need to modify list_items/1 to make use of the new filter options:

```
03-chp.userinput/6-customscalar/lib/plate_slate/menu/menu.ex
defp filter_with(query, filter) do
  Enum.reduce(filter, query, fn
    {:name, name}, query ->
      from q in query, where: ilike(q.name, ^"%#{name}%")
    {:priced_above, price}, query ->
      from q in query, where: q.price >= ^price
    {:priced_below, price}, query ->
      from q in query, where: q.price <= ^price
➤    {:added_after, date}, query ->
➤      from q in query, where: q.added_on >= ^date
➤    {:added_before, date}, query ->
➤      from q in query, where: q.added_on <= ^date
    {:category, category_name}, query ->
      from q in query,
        join: c in assoc(q, :category),
        where: ilike(c.name, ^"%#{category_name}%")
    {:tag, tag_name}, query ->
      from q in query,
        join: t in assoc(q, :tags),
        where: ilike(t.name, ^"%#{tag_name}%")
  end)
end
```

What we've done here is pretty similar to what's already in place for prices, checking for an added_on value that falls after :added_after and before :added_before. This works because our custom scalar logic has parsed the input values and converted them into %Date{} structs for us, as we'll show in a moment.

First, let's test this out and see if it works!

```
03-chp.userinput/6-customscalar/test/plate_slate_web/schema/query/menu_items_test.exs
@query """
query ($filter: MenuItemFilter!) {
  menuItems(filter: $filter) {
    name
    addedOn
  }
}
"""

@variables %{filter: %{"addedBefore" => "2017-01-20"}}
test "menuItems filtered by custom scalar" do
  sides = PlateSlate.Repo.get_by!(PlateSlate.Menu.Category, name: "Sides")
  %PlateSlate.Menu.Item{
    name: "Garlic Fries",
    added_on: ~D[2017-01-01],
    price: 2.50,
    category: sides
  } |> PlateSlate.Repo.insert!

  response = get(build_conn(), "/api", query: @query, variables: @variables)
  assert %{
    "data" => %{
      "menuItems" => [%{"name" => "Garlic Fries", "addedOn" => "2017-01-01"}]
    }
  } == json_response(response, 200)
end
```

In addition to our test, let's briefly inspect the arguments that the resolver is passing to the list_items/1 function:

```
03-chp.userinput/6-customscalar/lib/plate_slate/menu/menu.ex
def list_items(args) do
  IO.puts "These are our arguments: #{inspect(args)}"
  args
  |> Enum.reduce(Item, fn
    {:order, order}, query ->
      query |> order_by({^order, :name})
    {:filter, filter}, query ->
      query |> filter_with(filter)
  end)
  |> Repo.all
end
```

Running the test, we not only see that our test passed, but we also see the
output from our IO.puts line:

```
$ mix test test/plate_slate_web/schema/query/menu_items_test.exs
Compiling 7 files (.ex)
«Other tests»
.These are our arguments: %{
  filter: %{added_before: ~D[2017-01-20]},
  order: :asc
}
..

Finished in 0.2 seconds
14 tests, 0 failures
```

As we can see, the date string has been parsed into an actual Elixir date
value! This means we can just pass it directly as part of our filters without
having to do any validation at all in our resolver.

Let's see what happens when a user provides a bad value:

```
03-chp.userinput/6-customscalar/test/plate_slate_web/schema/query/menu_items_test.exs
@query """
query ($filter: MenuItemFilter!) {
  menuItems(filter: $filter) {
    name
  }
}
"""
@variables %{filter: %{"addedBefore" => "not-a-date"}}
test "menuItems filtered by custom scalar with error" do
  response = get(build_conn(), "/api", query: @query, variables: @variables)

  assert %{"errors" => [%{"locations" => [
    %{"column" => 0, "line" => 2}], "message" => message}
  ]} = json_response(response, 400)

  expected = """
  Argument "filter" has invalid value $filter.
  In field "addedBefore": Expected type "Date", found "not-a-date".\
  """
  assert expected == message
end
```

The user will get a helpful error, with no extra effort.

There's actually one more caveat we aren't really going to go into in detail yet,
but it explains why we do input.value in our parse function instead of just input.
The input for our parse function isn't just the string "2017-01-31" but rather a
struct that holds additional information about our input. Right now, for

example, we can make our scalar break by passing in a document that looks like this:

```
{
  menuItems(addedBefore: 123) {
    name
  }
}
```

We can use the extra information provided by the `input` struct to handle these cases nicely, checking the type of the input that was provided:

03-chp.userinput/7-strictcustomscalar/lib/plate_slate_web/schema.ex
```
scalar :date do
  parse fn input ->
    with %Absinthe.Blueprint.Input.String{value: value} <- input,
    {:ok, date} <- Date.from_iso8601(value) do
      {:ok, date}
    else
      _ -> :error
    end
  end

  serialize fn date ->
    Date.to_iso8601(date)
  end
end
```

Instead of accepting any input type, we are pattern matching for string inputs so that we can make sure to give the date-parsing function acceptable input. If we didn't do this, `Date.from_iso8601/1` would raise an exception.

We'll learn more about `Absinthe.Blueprint` structs and how to use them in Chapter 9, Tuning Resolution, on page 167.

Absinthe Custom Types

 Absinthe ships with a number of custom scalar definitions, including several for dates and times. You can find these definitions in `Absinthe.Type.Custom`.

In the next chapter, you'll learn how to import types from other modules.

Adding a custom scalar type gives us the capability to keep our business logic clean and simple by isolating any parsing (and validation) logic inside the scalar type definition itself, while clarifying the date and time input and output formats that we support for our users.

Moving On

In this chapter, you've learned a lot about how to model the input types that users can provide as arguments, and how Absinthe uses the schema to automatically enforce the constraints for you.

Before you move on, here are a couple of challenges for you to look at:

1. We built out a full example using input objects and enums for the :menu_items field. Add a :categories field that supports filtering by name and also supports ordering.

2. Build a custom scalar type that accepts valid email addresses and parses them into {username, domain} tuples, then serializes tuples back out as email addresses. Just use a simple check when parsing the email address; this isn't about crafting the perfect regular expression.

In the next chapter, you'll learn how to better organize your schema and use abstract types to model relationships that will make your GraphQL documents more flexible and reusable.

## CHAPTER 4

Adding Flexibility

Capturing and distilling an entire domain model into a GraphQL schema can be quite the undertaking, and it's important to keep your schema as maintainable and flexible as possible as it grows to describe the needs of your API.

Like any software developer, you likely bridle at the idea of typing countless lines of repetitive boilerplate into an editor, or dealing with restrictions that force you to organize your code in a way that doesn't fit your personal tastes or team conventions. Never fear! We'll start this chapter exploring tools that Absinthe provides that can make your type definitions more reusable, and we'll look at techniques you can employ to more effectively organize your schema.

After you have code organization figured out, we'll dig into some advanced modeling approaches that will help you build a more meaningful, accurate representation of your domain model. You'll discover how using abstract types like interfaces and unions can make your API simpler, and you'll learn how users can leverage GraphQL fragments to keep their documents shorter and easier to understand.

Let's take your schema-writing capabilities to the next level, starting with some brand-new techniques to organize your Absinthe-related code.

Organizing a Schema

Absinthe schemas are compiled, meaning that their types are collected, references are resolved, and the overall structure of the schema is verified against a set of rules during Elixir's module compilation process. Absinthe does this to ensure that GraphQL documents can be processed at runtime using a schema module that's already been checked for common errors and has been optimized for better performance.

That doesn't mean your Absinthe schema needs to be written in a single module. In fact, when a schema grows beyond being a limited sketch of our domain model into something more comprehensive—when it becomes something that we need to maintain—it's a good idea to organize it across multiple modules.

To do this, we need something to wire them all together so that Absinthe can find the portions of the schema we've extracted and organized elsewhere.

Thankfully, Absinthe provides two simple tools to help us: import_types and import_fields. Let's look at how we can use these two handy macros in our schema definitions, using the PlateSlate example application that we've been working on.

Importing Types

During the module compilation process, all the types referenced in an Absinthe schema are bundled together and built into the compiled module. Right now, in our PlateSlate application, all the types are located inside a single module, PlateSlateWeb.Schema, and it just works. Unfortunately, it's getting a bit long and unwieldy.

Let's see about splitting the custom types from the root type definitions (like query). Since all the types we've built so far are menu-related, we'll create a new module, PlateSlateWeb.Schema.MenuTypes, to hold them. Here's what that looks like:

```
04-chp.flexibility/1-start/lib/plate_slate_web/schema/menu_types.ex
defmodule PlateSlateWeb.Schema.MenuTypes do
  use Absinthe.Schema.Notation

  @desc "Filtering options for the menu item list"
  input_object :menu_item_filter do
    # «menu item filter fields»
  end

  object :menu_item do
    # «menu fields»
  end

end
```

Absinthe refers to modules like this one as *type modules*, because their purpose is to contain a set of types for inclusion in a schema. Type modules can be kept for use in your own schema or packaged and published for reuse by others.

It's important to note that unlike a schema module, which makes use of Absinthe.Schema, type modules use Absinthe.Schema.Notation instead. This gives them access to the general type definition macros (like object), without the top-level compilation and verification mechanism that only schemas need.

Use Absinthe.Schema.Notation in Type Modules

Use Absinthe.Schema.Notation in your type modules to import Absinthe's type definition macros. Don't use Absinthe.Schema; it's reserved for schema modules themselves.

Inside of our schema we use the import_types/1 macro and point it at our new module so that the newly extracted types are still usable from within our schema:

```
04-chp.flexibility/1-start/lib/plate_slate_web/schema.ex
defmodule PlateSlateWeb.Schema do
  use Absinthe.Schema

  alias PlateSlateWeb.Resolvers

  import_types __MODULE__.MenuTypes

  query do

    field :menu_items, list_of(:menu_item) do
      arg :filter, :menu_item_filter
      arg :order, type: :sort_order, default_value: :asc
      resolve &Resolvers.Menu.menu_items/3
    end

  end

  # «Common types; :date, :sort_order, etc»
end
```

During compilation, Absinthe will pull in the type definitions from PlateSlate-Web.Schema.MenuTypes, wiring them into our schema module so they work just like they did when they were defined in place.

Notice that we've kept the root query object type around. The query macro is defined in Absinthe.Schema, and can only be used in our schema module. This is to ensure that we don't end up with multiple root query object types when importing different type modules. The same restriction will apply to the other root types that we'll define later: mutation and subscription.

Only Use import_types at the Schema Level

Absinthe's import_types macro should only be used from your schema module. Think of your schema module like a manifest, defining the complete list of type modules needed to resolve type references.

This has really helped clean up our schema, and we can take it even further if we need to later on. Let's talk a bit about Absinthe's other schema structural macro, import_fields.

Importing Fields

Imagine what it might be like down the road for our PlateSlate application when the surface area of the API has expanded to support a wide range of applications. Our user interface will only be the beginning; once we've opened up the API to third-party developers and support integrations with other services, the entry points into our API—the catalog of fields present inside our root query object type—might grow to the point that our schema once again becomes unwieldy, despite our best efforts refactoring other types into type modules.

To support breaking up a large object, Absinthe provides another macro, import_fields, that we can use.

In our hypothetical, successful future for PlateSlate, let's say our root query object type has fields that provide the following:

- Information about menu items
- Specialized search functions for allergens
- Customer and order history queries
- Staff schedule details
- Restaurant location address information for mapping

Instead of having an exhaustive query object in our schema.ex spanning dozens or hundreds of lines, what if it could look like this:

```
query do
  import_fields :menu_queries
  import_fields :allergen_queries
  import_fields :customer_queries
  import_fields :staff_queries
  import_fields :location_queries
  # «Other fields»
end
```

Instead of defining the fields directly in the root query object type, we can pull them out and put them into separate types (which we can place in other type modules). Here's how our :menu_queries type might look, defining the same :menu_items field we've gotten used to seeing in our schema:

```
object :menu_queries do

  field :menu_items, list_of(:menu_item) do
    arg :filter, :menu_item_filter
```

```
    arg :order, type: :sort_order, default_value: :asc
    resolve &Resolvers.Menu.menu_items/3
  end

  # «Other menu-related fields»

end
```

It's just an object type definition—nothing special—and we'd locate it alongside other menu-related objects in our menu_types.ex file. Instead of being used as a type for a field's resolution, however, the :menu_queries object type just serves as a convenient named container to hold the fields we'd like to pull into our root query object type.

Deciding on Structure

The tools that we've covered here—import_types and import_fields—don't establish any structural constraints for the way that you arrange your Absinthe-related modules. It's completely up to you.

We opted for extracting the types along the same lines as our Ecto schemas are organized under the PlateSlate module; the types present in PlateSlate.Menu are represented by GraphQL types located in PlateSlateWeb.Schema.MenuTypes.

Absinthe and Phoenix Contexts

Phoenix v1.3 introduced the concept of bounded context modules. These modules define the business logic for a portion of your overall domain model.

A compelling, more structured choice for laying out your Absinthe-related modules involves grouping your Absinthe types into modules that mirror the names of your Phoenix contexts, then calling functions present in your contexts from your field resolvers.

As you learned in the previous chapter, it's important to keep your business logic inside your context modules—don't pull it into your resolvers or duplicate it there. Think of your resolvers as a way to trigger your business logic, a way to wire it into schema.

Now that you have some ideas about the tools and techniques you can use to arrange your Absinthe schema, let's dig into another important real-world feature set: how to use abstract types to make your schema more flexible and reusable.

Understanding Abstract Types

Up to this point, we've focused on building concrete types that closely model the underlying data, matching up with the Ecto schemas we've built for our PlateSlate application.

To support an easy-to-use, flexible API for your users, you'll need to go beyond this type of modeling and learn how to use abstract types as well.

Let's look at a quick example. A standard feature for a user interface (and the APIs that support them) is a search function. If we were going to implement a search function for our PlateSlate application, allowing users to retrieve both menu items and menu item categories (a grouping of menu items) that match a search term, how would we do it?

With only our concrete types in place, we're stuck with having to build this feature as two separate fields. After all, a GraphQL field can only resolve to a single type. Here's about the best that our users can hope for:

```
query Search($term: String!) {
  searchCategories(matching: $term) {
    # «Select fields from category results»
  }
  searchMenuItems(matching: $term) {
    # «Select fields from menu item results»
  }
}
```

We'll have to define a distinct search field for every type we want to be searchable, looking something like this in our schema:

```
field :search_categories, list_of(:category) do
  arg :matching, non_null(:string)
  resolve fn _, %{matching: term}, _ ->
    # «Search logic»
    {:ok, results}
  end
end

field :search_menu_items, list_of(:menu_item) do
  arg :matching, non_null(:string)
  resolve fn _, %{matching: term}, _ ->
    # «Similar search logic for a similar field»
    {:ok, results}
  end
end
```

This is going to get tedious. Imagine what life will be like in six months after we've fully built out the domain to include allergen information, listings for our various restaurant locations, marketing content we'd like searchable, and so on. A brittle, complicated mess.

What if, instead, we could model all these search results as...search results? It would sure look better if our schema code could read like this:

```
field :search, list_of(:search_result) do
  arg :matching, non_null(:string)
  resolve fn _, %{matching: term}, _ ->
    # «Combined search logic, returning heterogenous data»
    {:ok, results}
  end
end
```

This would make our search feature more adaptable as features are added later. In any case, the code is certainly easier to read, and it would allow user queries to look more like this:

```
query Search($term: String!) {
  search(matching: $term) {
    # «Select fields from a mix of search results»
  }
}
```

Look, no type-specific fields! Just a single field that users can leverage anytime they want to retrieve records by a search term.

Now, to do this, we need to let Absinthe know what a :search_result is and how it relates to the concrete types that we want to be searchable.

We're going to cover a couple of different options that the GraphQL specification gives us: unions and interfaces. After we're done, you should have a solid grounding in both abstract type mechanisms and feel confident about when to use each when modeling your domain model in future applications.

Using Unions

A GraphQL union type is an abstract type that represents a set of specific concrete types. For instance, in our PlateSlate search example, a :search_result could be a union type for both :menu_item and :category.

Let's define that in our schema...but first, we need to add the :category type. It's a straightforward grouping of :menu_item records with a name and description:

```
04-chp.flexibility/2-unions/lib/plate_slate_web/schema/menu_types.ex
alias PlateSlateWeb.Resolvers

object :category do
  field :name, :string
  field :description, :string
  field :items, list_of(:menu_item) do
    resolve &Resolvers.Menu.items_for_category/3
  end
end
```

We've included a resolver to load the menu items for a category when the :items field is selected. At the moment, the implementation is a bit naive:

```
04-chp.flexibility/2-unions/lib/plate_slate_web/resolvers/menu.ex
def items_for_category(category, _, _) do
  query = Ecto.assoc(category, :items)
  {:ok, PlateSlate.Repo.all(query)}
end
```

If the menu items for a list of categories were requested, for example, this would execute a database query per category (an example of the infamous "N+1" problem). This isn't something we'd want in production, and you'll learn how to combat it later in Chapter 9, Tuning Resolution, on page 167.

Notably, though, this is the first resolver we've written where we're using the first argument, which receives the parent value. In our case, this resolver is on the :items field of the :category object, so its parent value is a category. We can then use that category to do a database query for its items.

Now that the object type is out of the way, let's move on and define the :search_result union type:

```
04-chp.flexibility/2-unions/lib/plate_slate_web/schema/menu_types.ex
union :search_result do
  types [:menu_item, :category]
  # «Almost done...»
end
```

This uses a couple of new macros from Absinthe. The union macro is used to create our type, and it works a lot like object. The types macro, used inside the union scope, sets its types.

We need to add one more thing to our type definition. Abstract types like unions (and, as you'll learn about later, interfaces) need a way to determine the concrete type for a value. For our :search_result union type, supporting both :menu_item and :category concrete types, we'll write it like this:

```
04-chp.flexibility/2-unions/lib/plate_slate_web/schema/menu_types.ex
union :search_result do
  types [:menu_item, :category]
  resolve_type fn
    %PlateSlate.Menu.Item{}, _ ->
      :menu_item
    %PlateSlate.Menu.Category{}, _ ->
      :category
    _, _ ->
      nil
  end
end
```

The resolve_type macro takes a 2-arity function. The first parameter of the function will receive the value that we're checking, and the second parameter will receive the resolution information (which we'll just ignore in this case). Recall that a union type means "one of these types." When Absinthe is actually running a document and getting Elixir values, it needs a way to figure out which Elixir value maps to which of the types in the union, and that's what this resolve_type function does for us.

Since the resolved value for the :search_result type will be Ecto schema structs for PlateSlate.Menu.Item or PlateSlate.Menu.Category, determining the associated Absinthe type is straightforward. For completeness, we provide a fall-through match. It returns nil, which denotes that the value doesn't belong to any member type of the union.

Now that we've completed the modeling for the :search_result type, let's build that search field we've been thinking about. We'll add it to our query block in the schema file:

04-chp.flexibility/2-unions/lib/plate_slate_web/schema.ex
```
query do
  # «Other query fields»

  field :search, list_of(:search_result) do
    arg :matching, non_null(:string)
    resolve &Resolvers.Menu.search/3
  end

end
```

To resolve the field, we'll use a search resolver function.

04-chp.flexibility/2-unions/lib/plate_slate_web/resolvers/menu.ex
```
def search(_, %{matching: term}, _) do
  {:ok, Menu.search(term)}
end
```

It just hands off the work to a context function, which runs a search pattern against names and descriptions for each table, and returns the combined results.

04-chp.flexibility/2-unions/lib/plate_slate/menu/menu.ex
```
@search [Item, Category]
def search(term) do
  pattern = "%#{term}%"
  Enum.flat_map(@search, &search_ecto(&1, pattern))
end

defp search_ecto(ecto_schema, pattern) do
  Repo.all from q in ecto_schema,
    where: ilike(q.name, ^pattern) or ilike(q.description, ^pattern)
end
```

While each value returned from this function is a :menu_item or :category, it's also a valid :search_result, owing to the union type definition we added to the schema.

There's one concern that this neat new ability to generalize a field result brings up: if a field can return different results with different shapes, how can users effectively select the data they want in the query?

Let's look at that search query again:

```
query Search($term: String!) {
  search(matching: $term) {
    # «How do we differentiate category and menu item fields?»
  }
}
```

To do this, we make use of an important GraphQL feature, *fragments*. Fragments are a way to write chunks of GraphQL that can target a specific type.

Here's a query that pulls out some information specific to PlateSlate menu items and categories:

```
Line 1  query Search($term: String!) {
          search(matching: $term) {
            ... on MenuItem {
              name
      5     }
            ... on Category {
              name
              items {
                name
     10       }
            }
          }
        }
```

You can see where we're defining and inserting fragments on lines 3 and 6. The ... is referred to as a "fragment spread," and it inserts the inline fragment that follows. This is nomenclature you'll also find in ECMAScript 6 objects,[1] which isn't surprising considering the number of JavaScript developers involved with the creation and maintenance of GraphQL.

The inline fragment targets a type (introduced with on) and defines the set of fields, within the curly braces, that apply for any item that matches the type. You'll learn about named fragments later in this chapter.

---

1. https://developer.mozilla.org/en-US/docs/Web/JavaScript/Reference/Operators/Spread_operator

Let's explore this query a bit with the GraphiQL user interface to see what the results look like.

We've made the search function ridiculously permissive, allowing even single character searches, so let's make use of that. By searching for anything that matches "e", we should be able to get a large volume of results.

First, we start the server:

```
$ mix phx.server
[info] Running PlateSlateWeb.Endpoint with Cowboy using http://0.0.0.0:4000
```

Heading over to http://localhost:4000/graphiql in our browser, we enter the query in the left side panel, define our term variable, and press the "play" button:

In the bottom-right pane, you can see those results: a mix of menu items and categories.

We can make the difference between the results more obvious by using a handy GraphQL tool: introspection.

Introspecting Value Types

The GraphiQL interface uses GraphQL's introspection[2] capabilities extensively to provide nice features like autocompletion and documentation. We can use introspection ourselves, too. Let's decorate our search query with a little introspection:

```
query Search($term: String!) {
  search(matching: $term) {
    ... on MenuItem {
      name
    }
```

---

2. http://graphql.org/learn/introspection

```
      ... on Category {
        name
        items {
          name
        }
      }
      __typename
    }
  }
```

Fields that begin with _ are reserved by GraphQL to support features like introspection. The _typename introspection field that we're using here always returns the concrete GraphQL type name that's in the associated scope.

If we plug it back into our GraphiQL example, we can see it in action:

GraphiQL ▶ Prettify   ‹ Docs

```
                                                   "__typename": "MenuItem"
 1  query Search($term: String!) {                 },
 2    search(matching: $term) {                     {
 3      ... on MenuItem {                             "name": "Lemonade",
 4        name                                        "__typename": "MenuItem"
 5      }                                            },
 6      ... on Category {                             {
 7        name                                        "name": "Vanilla Milkshake",
 8        items {                                     "__typename": "MenuItem"
 9          name                                     },
10        }                                           {
11      }                                             "name": "Chocolate Milkshake",
12      __typename                                    "__typename": "MenuItem"
13    }                                              },
14  }                                                 {
                                                      "name": "Sandwiches",
    QUERY VARIABLES                                   "items": [
                                                        {
                                                          "name": "Vada Pav"
 1  {"term": "e"}                                      },
                                                        {
                                                          "name": "Bánh mì"
                                                        },
                                                        {
                                                          "name": "Muffuletta"
                                                        },
```

Now we can see our results handily annotated with the GraphQL types in the result pane.

Use __typename to See GraphQL Types

 If you're ever curious about the GraphQL type that's being returned, use the built-in _typename introspection field. It will always return the concrete GraphQL type for the surrounding scope, which can be handy for debugging an API or updating client-side caches.

At this point, we have a fully functional search (although one we'll want to tune before we release it to production), and we've played with it in GraphiQL. Let's build a test for it, too. We'll shorten up our query a bit and just make sure that we get a mix of menu items and categories returned:

```
04-chp.flexibility/2-unions/test/plate_slate_web/schema/query/search_test.exs
@query """
query Search($term: String!) {
  search(matching: $term) {
    ... on MenuItem { name }
    ... on Category { name }
    __typename
  }
}
"""
@variables %{term: "e"}
test "search returns a list of menu items and categories" do
  response = get(build_conn(), "/api", query: @query, variables: @variables)
  assert %{"data" => %{"search" => results}} = json_response(response, 200)
  assert length(results) > 0
  assert Enum.find(results, &(&1["__typename"] == "Category"))
  assert Enum.find(results, &(&1["__typename"] == "MenuItem"))
end
```

We'll run mix test to execute our test:

```
$ mix test test/plate_slate_web/schema/query/search_test.exs
.

Finished in 0.2 seconds
1 test, 0 failures
```

It passes; great!

Now let's think a little about how we could make this even better. The simplified search that we've done for our test seems to hint at a sore point: there sure is a lot of duplication involved to get the same field from two different concrete types.

Because unions are about combinations of disparate types that might not have any fields in common, retrieving data from them requires us to use fragments (that target types) to get the data we want. There's another option: interfaces. Let's see if modeling our search results as an interface might make things a bit simpler.

Using Interfaces

GraphQL interfaces are similar to unions, with one key difference: they add a requirement that any member types must define a set of included fields. This might remind you of interfaces in other languages (or perhaps behaviours in Elixir/Erlang).

For search results, we know that we want to easily access the name field. It's fair to say that a search result should always include a name; it's a simple constraint, and one that doesn't require us to add any fields to our :menu_item and :category types. We just need to convert our :search_result to an interface and indicate that our types belong to it.

Let's open up the file with our Absinthe type definitions and make the modifications. First, we'll convert our :search_result type to an interface:

```
04-chp.flexibility/3-interfaces/lib/plate_slate_web/schema/menu_types.ex
interface :search_result do
  field :name, :string
  resolve_type fn
    %PlateSlate.Menu.Item{}, _ ->
      :menu_item
    %PlateSlate.Menu.Category{}, _ ->
      :category
    _, _ ->
      nil
  end
end
```

We use the interface macro instead of the union macro, and because interfaces need to be able to resolve the concrete types of their values just like unions, we get to keep the resolve_type function that we already defined.

We removed the types macro usage, which our union type used to declare which types it included; the object types that implement our new interface declare that themselves, as we'll see in a moment.

The only addition we've made involves the use of the field macro. Here we've indicated any implementing object types must define a :name field that returns a :string value. Easily done, as both :menu_item and :category already do that. All we need to do with them is declare they implement our new interface.

We'll make the addition to :menu_item:

```
04-chp.flexibility/3-interfaces/lib/plate_slate_web/schema/menu_types.ex
object :menu_item do
  interfaces [:search_result]
  field :id, :id
  field :name, :string
  field :description, :string
  field :added_on, :date
end
```

And to :category:

```
04-chp.flexibility/3-interfaces/lib/plate_slate_web/schema/menu_types.ex
alias PlateSlateWeb.Resolvers

object :category do
  interfaces [:search_result]
  field :name, :string
  field :description, :string
  field :items, list_of(:menu_item) do
    resolve &Resolvers.Menu.items_for_category/3
  end
end
```

As you can probably guess from the list value we're passing to interfaces, an object type can implement as many interfaces as you'd like.

Now that we have these changes in place, let's see what difference it can make to our query documents. We'll update the test we just added, but first it's worth pointing out that it should still pass with flying colors:

```
$ mix test test/plate_slate_web/schema/query/search_test.ex
.

Finished in 0.2 seconds
1 test, 0 failures
```

We'll make our change to the search query, removing the now-excessive fragment usage:

```
04-chp.flexibility/3-interfaces/test/plate_slate_web/schema/query/search_test.exs
@query """
query Search($term: String!) {
  search(matching: $term) {
    name
    __typename
  }
}
"""
@variables %{term: "e"}
test "search returns a list of menu items and categories" do
  response = get(build_conn(), "/api", query: @query, variables: @variables)
  assert %{"data" => %{"search" => results}} = json_response(response, 200)
  assert length(results) > 0
  assert Enum.find(results, &(&1["__typename"] == "Category"))
  assert Enum.find(results, &(&1["__typename"] == "MenuItem"))
  assert Enum.all?(results, &(&1["name"]))
end
```

Then, run the tests again:

```
$ mix test test/plate_slate_web/schema/query/search_test.exs
.

Finished in 0.2 seconds
1 test, 0 failures
```

See how the name field is bare, without a wrapping ... on Type { } inline fragment? This works because selecting fields that have been declared on the interface aren't subject to the same type of restrictions as selecting fields on unions (which have no such mechanism).

This doesn't mean, of course, that you can just select any field on an interface and get away with it. If we wanted to retrieve information about menu items that belonged to any categories that were returned from a search, we'd still need to have a wrapping fragment type, like this:

```
query Search($term: String!) {
  search(matching: $term) {
    name
    ... on Category {
      name
      items {
        name
      }
    }
  }
}
```

This is because :items isn't declared on the interface. It's not a field that's shared with other object types (that is, :menu_item) that implement :search_result.

Interfaces are a handy tool, and they're often the right choice when you need an abstract class precisely for the reason that we've illustrated here. If there are fields in common, interfaces allow users to write more simple, readable GraphQL.

Let's talk about another tool along those lines: named fragments. Wouldn't it be nice if we could reuse chunks of GraphQL rather than have the same thing over and over?

Using Named Fragments

In the last section, you were introduced to fragments, using the inline variety to associate parts of GraphQL documents with specific types. Named fragments are just like inline fragments, but they're reusable.

Let's give that search query another look, this time breaking out the fields for menu items and categories:

```
query Search($term: String!) {
  search(matching: $term) {
    ... MenuItemFields
    ... CategoryFields
  }
}
fragment MenuItemFields on MenuItem {
  name
}
fragment CategoryFields on Category {
  name
  items {
    ... MenuItemFields
  }
}
```

Just as before, the ... fragment spread is used to insert an instance of a fragment. This time, however, we're referencing a named fragment that's defined outside the GraphQL operation using the fragment keyword. Notice that the type targeting is still there on the fragment definition. Fragments always target a specific type.

We are ignoring the :search_result interface's ability to return a name field without using fragments in this specific example. That's okay; maintaining a GraphQL document like this has a key benefit: simple extensibility.

For instance, application requirements down the road may mean that searches need to return price information. Handily, for menu items that match directly or for menu items that were returned as part of the category, the user would only have to edit the definition for MenuItemFields:

```
fragment MenuItemFields on MenuItem {
  name
  price
}
```

Since the fields from MenuItemFields are inserted into both the top-level search and used inside the definition for CategoryFields, the new price data would be retrieved at both records.

The benefits to named fragments become even more pronounced if the user is building their application in such a way that they can compose documents from different sources, mixing and matching definitions to serve the data needs of the specific application component they're working on.

Named fragments give users more flexibility to build documents the way they want, with a minimum of fuss. An unavoidable part of an eminently flexible query language like GraphQL is it can be used to build complex documents to service complex needs. Fragments are a nice exit hatch to support programmatic generation of documents to relieve some of the maintenance stress.

Fragments Can't Form Cycles

 Named fragments can include references to other fragments, but can't form cycles (A -> B -> A, A -> A, etc). Absinthe will helpfully detect cycles and self-referential definitions in GraphQL documents and automatically return errors to the user for you.

Moving On

In this chapter, we've looked at a wide range of topics that help make building and using a GraphQL system more flexible and humane.

You've learned how to break up your schema into manageable pieces using Absinthe's import_types and import_fields macros. We've dug deep into GraphQL unions and interfaces, and you've discovered how abstract types can make your API more approachable and usable. Your knowledge of GraphQL document building has expanded as well, now that you've seen fragments and understood how users can define, apply, and reuse fragments, enabling new approaches to GraphQL document authoring.

Before we head on to the next chapter, here are a few thought exercises based on the material in this chapter:

1. Take a look at the schema.ex file. We've kept it simple for the purposes of the book, but think through how you might break up the query definition using import_fields, or where you might relocate the common types at the bottom of the schema (using import_types) if you wanted to keep the file as concise as possible.
2. We settled on using an interface to model search results for PlateSlate. Can you think of any cases you might prefer to use a union?
3. Build a query document that defines a series of named fragments that form a cycle. Why do you think it might be a bad idea to try to execute a query like this? Try to run the document through Absinthe to trigger the error response.

Next up, we tackle a very important topic: mutations! It's been fun building a read-only API, but it's probably time to let our users make changes to our data. We think you'll be pleased with the flexibility you'll have at your fingertips, especially if you have experience building REST APIs.

## CHAPTER 5

Making a Change with Mutations

It's easy to focus on GraphQL's data-fetching capabilities; the flexibility it gives clients when crafting queries is certainly its most striking feature, but it's not a read-only data platform. GraphQL also supports mutations, which allow users of the API to modify server-side data.

If you're familiar with REST APIs, you can think of GraphQL mutations as roughly analogous to POST, PUT, and DELETE operations. Unlike REST, however, the responses from GraphQL mutations can be tailored, just as with GraphQL query operations.

In this chapter, we're going to explore how GraphQL mutations can be used by adding menu-item management features to our PlateSlate application. You'll learn how to add a root mutation type and define fields, get acquainted with modeling new records with input objects, and uncover important strategies that you can use to return error information if something goes wrong.

Let's jump in by building our first mutation, which will let users create menu items using the PlateSlate API.

Defining a Root Mutation Type

To support *mutation operations*, we need to define a root mutation type, just as we did for queries. This will be used as the entry point for GraphQL mutation operations, and it will define—based on the mutation fields that we add—the complete list of capabilities users of our API will have available to modify data.

We define the root mutation type by using the mutation macro in our schema:

05-chp.mutations/1-start/lib/plate_slate_web/schema.ex
```
mutation do
  # «Mutation fields will go here»
end
```

This might strike you as somewhat similar to our use of the query macro when we did the initial build-out of the PlateSlate Absinthe schema, and that's by design. Both macros—query and mutation—are used to define the root object types for their respective GraphQL operations.

A mutation root type won't do us any good unless we define mutation fields. Let's do that next, adding a mutation for menu item creation.

Adding a Mutation Field

Now that we have a place to put our mutations, let's get organized and come up with a plan for menu item creation. Here's the narrative of how we expect this feature to work:

- A user will build out the menu item details in their user interface (website, mobile application, anything that can talk GraphQL).

- The user's client will send the collected data for a menu item to our GraphQL API, indicating the createMenuItem mutation and the data they'd like in response.

- Our API will execute the mutation, create the menu item (if possible), and return the requested data.

Let's build out the mutation field that clients need. Just as we would with query fields and the query root mutation type, we add mutation fields directly inside the mutation block (which defines the root mutation object type). Here, we add a :create_menu_item field:

```
05-chp.mutations/2-create/lib/plate_slate_web/schema.ex
mutation do

  field :create_menu_item, :menu_item do
  end

end
```

Most mutations that create something return it as the result of the field, which is why the mutation here is returning a :menu_item. We'll talk more about why this is handy soon, but first let's get into the nitty gritty of receiving the input to create the menu item.

Modeling with an Input Object

To create menu items, you'll need to accept information from the client. You'll use an input object to model the data that you're expecting. Let's keep it simple for now, just accepting a name, optional description, price, and category ID in a new input object type, :menu_item_input:

05-chp.mutations/2-create/lib/plate_slate_web/schema/menu_types.ex
```
input_object :menu_item_input do
  field :name, non_null(:string)
  field :description, :string
  field :price, non_null(:decimal)
  field :category_id, non_null(:id)
end
```

These fields represent the subset of fields that are needed to support clients creating menu items. We can expand this as the menu management features that we need grow with our application.

Object Types Aren't Input Types

 It's easy to forget that you can't use object types for user input; instead, you need to create *input* object types for use in arguments. While this might seem like unnecessary work at first, you'll come to appreciate the way it forces you to focus on the discrete package of data that you need for specific mutations.

There are also some technical differences between objects and input objects. Input object fields can only be valid input types, which excludes unions, interfaces, and objects. You also can't form cycles with input objects, whereas cycles are permitted with objects.

Our GraphQL schema doesn't know what the :decimal type is yet, so we need to define that as well. Absinthe ships with a :float scalar type—a built-in type to meet the requirements of the GraphQL specification—but a float is a poor choice for monetary math operations. Thankfully, we've already got the decimal package in our mix.exs file, which will let us properly represent our menu item prices.

Let's define the :decimal type using the scalar macro, just as we did in Creating Your Own Scalar Types, on page 50:

05-chp.mutations/2-create/lib/plate_slate_web/schema.ex
```
scalar :decimal do
  parse fn
    %{value: value}, _ ->
      Decimal.parse(value)
    _, _ ->
      :error
  end
  serialize &to_string/1
end
```

Now that we have a decimal type, we can expose a :price field on the :menu_item object type that we defined all the way back in Defining an Object Type, on page 17, too:

```
05-chp.mutations/2-create/lib/plate_slate_web/schema/menu_types.ex
object :menu_item do

  interfaces [:search_result]

  field :id, :id
  field :name, :string
  field :description, :string
➤ field :price, :decimal
  field :added_on, :date
end
```

Let's define an :input argument on our :create_menu_item field, using our :menu_item_input type:

```
05-chp.mutations/2-create/lib/plate_slate_web/schema.ex
mutation do

  field :create_menu_item, :menu_item do
    arg :input, non_null(:menu_item_input)
    resolve &Resolvers.Menu.create_item/3
  end

end
```

We are using the name input here because it's a convention of the Relay client-side framework[1] for mutations, but we could use a different name instead if we were so inclined. (We're not, for now.) We've also wired in the resolver function, located with the other menu-related resolvers in PlateSlateWeb.Schema.Resolvers.Menu.

The actual behavior that will occur when users use createMenuItem in GraphQL documents is the responsibility of the resolver function for our mutation field. We need to make the resolver interpret our client input, attempt to persist the menu item, and respond to users.

Building the Resolver

Let's build the resolver function. It will grab the :input argument for us, and then call a general-purpose PlateSlate.Menu.create_item/1 function that will handle attempting to persist the record:

---

1. https://facebook.github.io/relay/

```
05-chp.mutations/2-create/lib/plate_slate_web/resolvers/menu.ex
Line 1   def create_item(_, %{input: params}, _) do
2          case Menu.create_item(params) do
3            {:error, _} ->
4              {:error, "Could not create menu item"}
5            {:ok, _} = success ->
6              success
7          end
8        end
```

Here's how we've implemented PlateSlate.Menu.create_item/1:

```
05-chp.mutations/2-create/lib/plate_slate/menu/menu.ex
def create_item(attrs \\ %{}) do
  %Item{}
  |> Item.changeset(attrs)
  |> Repo.insert()
end
```

The actual persistence of the menu items is straightforward but requires you to know a little about how Ecto works. The important thing to know here is that an Ecto *changeset* models the data that needs to be inserted or updated—changed—in a database. Here our create_item/1 function takes the menu item attributes, creates an Ecto changeset using PlateSlate.Menu.Item.changeset/1 (helpfully already written for you in the application), and attempts to insert it into the PlateSlate.Repo, aliased for convenience here as Repo.

If you look back at line 2 of the resolver, you'll notice that we use case to handle the result of the create_item function. While the return value of a successful Repo.insert/2 is compatible with a resolution result, the {:error, changeset} that it can return isn't. For the moment, when an error occurs, we just return an error message from the field resolver, but we'll look at some options for error reporting at the end of this chapter.

Let's talk a bit about what happens when the persistence is successful.

Returning Data from Mutations

Remember, when we defined the mutation field, we declared what type of object it would have as a result. We did this by passing :menu_item as the second argument to the field macro:

```
05-chp.mutations/2-create/lib/plate_slate_web/schema.ex
mutation do

  field :create_menu_item, :menu_item do
  end

end
```

What this means is our API clients can query the result object type just like they would in a query operation. They can then extract exactly the information they want from the created object to update the user interface of their application.

Mutations and Client-Side Frameworks

Because mutations change data in the system, and modified data needs to be reflected in user interfaces—forms updated, lists redrawn, and other elements changed —different client-side application frameworks and tools have constraints around how to structure arguments for mutations and how to shape results of mutations.

In this chapter, we're showing how to use GraphQL mutations according to the specification rather than using any specific framework. We'll cover framework-specific configurations later, in Chapter 11, Integrating with the Frontend, on page 221.

Here's an example of a full GraphQL document that uses our new mutation field and requests some information about the resulting menu item:

```
mutation CreateMenuItem($menuItem: MenuItemInput!) {
  createMenuItem(input: $menuItem) {
    id
    name
    description
    price
    category { name }
    tags { name }
  }
}
```

Notice how we can dig into the returned :menu_item object type and pull out any information that we need, like categories and tags. This would be especially useful if, by persisting a new menu item, certain defaults were set on the menu item (or calculated based on information we sent). By supporting a fully tailored query in the same request, our clients can immediately make use of the information without having to make a separate, subsequent request, subject to race condition concerns.

In a perfect world, we'd just *know* that our mutation would work flawlessly the very first time. We know better, so let's give it a test!

Testing Our Request

Testing a mutation doesn't look a whole lot different from testing a query. We'll be passing some variables, shaped just the right way to match our :menu_item_input input object type, and the only real change is that we need to make sure to use post, since that's the HTTP method that GraphQL expects for mutations.

We'll open a new test file and drop in our createMenuItem mutation:

05-chp.mutations/2-create/test/plate_slate_web/schema/mutation/create_menu_item_test.exs

```elixir
defmodule PlateSlateWeb.Schema.Mutation.CreateMenuTest do
  use PlateSlateWeb.ConnCase, async: true

  alias PlateSlate.{Repo, Menu}
  import Ecto.Query

  setup do
    PlateSlate.Seeds.run()

    category_id =
      from(t in Menu.Category, where: t.name == "Sandwiches")
      |> Repo.one!
      |> Map.fetch!(:id)
      |> to_string

    {:ok, category_id: category_id}
  end

  @query """
  mutation ($menuItem: MenuItemInput!) {
    createMenuItem(input: $menuItem) {
      name
      description
      price
    }
  }
  """
  test "createMenuItem field creates an item", %{category_id: category_id} do
    menu_item = %{
      "name" => "French Dip",
      "description" => "Roast beef, caramelized onions, horseradish, ...",
      "price" =>  "5.75",
      "categoryId" => category_id,
    }
    conn = build_conn()
    conn = post conn, "/api",
      query: @query,
      variables: %{"menuItem" => menu_item}

    assert json_response(conn, 200) == %{
      "data" => %{
        "createMenuItem" => %{
          "name" => menu_item["name"],
          "description" => menu_item["description"],
          "price" => menu_item["price"]
        }
      }
    }
  end
end
```

If we run the test from the console, we'll see the test pass. (Flawlessly, the first time! We must have been lucky. This time.)

```
$ mix test test/plate_slate_web/schema/mutation/create_menu_item_test.exs
.

Finished in 0.1 seconds
1 test, 0 failures
```

You might notice something about the response, though. The value that's returned for the menu item is housed inside an object returned under the "createMenuItem" key. The raw JSON response looks something like this:

```
{
  "data": {
    "createMenuItem": {
      "name": "French Dip",
      "description": "Roast beef, caramelized onions, horseradish, ..."
      "price": "5.75"
    }
  }
}
```

While that's not very surprising, given that is the name of the mutation field, it's also not very pretty. It would be a lot nicer to have it called "menuItem". Luckily, we can use a mechanism that GraphQL calls a *field alias* to help.

Using Field Aliases for Nicer (and Unique) Names

Sometimes there's a difference of opinion between what the schema designer decides to call a field and how the user of the API would like results returned. This comes up especially with mutations, since they commonly include verbs as part of their names (in our example, "create").

So, our users probably don't want to have their new menu item returned as "createMenuItem". What can they do?

They can use a field alias, which is done by preceding the field with another name and a colon (:). For example, they can write this to call the result menuItem instead:

```
mutation ($menuItem: MenuItemInput!) {
  menuItem: createMenuItem(input: $menuItem) {
    name
  }
}
```

It almost looks like an assignment, doesn't it? Now our result would look like this:

```
{
  "menuItem": {
    "name": "French Dip"
  }
}
```

This isn't all for vanity's sake, either. Imagine the real possibility that an API client might want to create multiple new menu items at once. A naive attempt might look something like this:

```
mutation CreateTwo($menuItem1: MenuItemInput!, $menuItem2: MenuItemInput!) {
  createMenuItem(input: $menuItem1) { id name }
  createMenuItem(input: $menuItem2) { id name }
}
```

This won't end well! GraphQL doesn't allow duplicate field names in a request, and it wouldn't make much sense in the resulting JSON, either. How would it figure out how to return a single value for "createMenuItem"?

Instead, clients can mark each mutation with separate aliases:

```
mutation CreateTwo($menuItem1: MenuItemInput!, $menuItem2: MenuItemInput!) {
  one: createMenuItem(input: $menuItem1) { id name }
  two: createMenuItem(input: $menuItem2) { id name }
}
```

Now clients would receive two values in the JSON response: one for "one" and one for "two".

This isn't just for mutations either. Structurally, GraphQL queries and mutations are exactly the same, and there are plenty of cases where a user might want to query the same field with different sets of arguments for multiple, separate results. Here's an example of a query we might want to support:

```
query Meal {
  inHand: search(matching: "reu") { name }
  inGlass: search(matching: "lem") { name }
}
```

The aliases here support using a single field multiple times within a GraphQL document; the result would come back with the field data associated with each alias:

```
{
  "data": {
    "inHand": [
      {
        "name": "Reuben"
      }
    ],
    "inGlass": [
      {
        "name": "Lemonade"
      }
    ]
  }
}
```

We've done a little test along the happy path[2] and discussed some complexities when returning data for successful requests, but let's dig a bit deeper and talk about what to do when things go wrong. What if we have business rules that prevent a mutation from being successful? How do we provide useful feedback to our API users?

Handling Mutation Errors

In a perfect world, users would provide the correct data, conditions would always be met, mutations would execute cleanly, and changes would be persisted flawlessly. This isn't a perfect world, however, so we need to deal with errors that might occur when executing our mutations. We'll cover two major strategies that you can use to report errors to users. While you can't always make them happy, you can at least let them know what went wrong.

Before we dig into error handling, we need to set up a good example. Let's add a constraint in our PlateSlate application business logic so that we can easily trigger an error when creating menu items.

Right now in our PlateSlate application, we're very permissive about menu item creation; besides checking that names and prices are provided, we allow any menu item to be created. We even allow menu items with duplicate names; let's add a basic constraint in our database to prevent that.

Since we're using Ecto for our PlateSlate project, we'll use mix to generate a migration:

---

2. https://en.wikipedia.org/wiki/Happy_path

```
$ mix ecto.gen.migration AddIndexForMenuItemNames
* priv/repo/migrations
* priv/repo/migrations/20170826015057_add_index_for_menu_item_names.exs
```

Opening the migration file, we'll add an index with a unique constraint:

05-chp.mutations/3-errors/priv/repo/migrations/20170826015057_add_index_for_menu_item_names.exs
```
defmodule PlateSlate.Repo.Migrations.AddIndexForMenuItemNames do
  use Ecto.Migration

  def change do
    create unique_index(:items, [:name])
  end
end
```

Now, run the migration:

```
$ mix ecto.migrate
«Running migration»
[info] create index menu_items_name_index
[info] == Migrated in 0.0s
```

Now we have the database configured. We'll add the unique constraint to the Ecto changeset for Menu.Item as well:

05-chp.mutations/3-errors/lib/plate_slate/menu/item.ex
```
def changeset(%Item{} = item, attrs) do
  item
  |> cast(attrs, [:name, :description, :price, :added_on])
  |> validate_required([:name, :price])
  |> foreign_key_constraint(:category)
  |> unique_constraint(:name)
end
```

Let's add a test that verifies our expectations for error handling as it stands right now:

05-chp.mutations/3-errors/test/plate_slate_web/schema/mutation/create_menu_item_test.exs
```
test "creating a menu item with an existing name fails",
%{category_id: category_id} do
  menu_item = %{
    "name" => "Reuben",
    "description" => "Roast beef, caramelized onions, horseradish, ...",
    "price" =>  "5.75",
    "categoryId" => category_id,
  }
  conn = build_conn()
  conn = post conn, "/api",
    query: @query,
    variables: %{"menuItem" => menu_item}
```

```
  assert json_response(conn, 200) == %{
    "data" => %{"createMenuItem" => nil},
    "errors" => [
      %{
        "locations" => [%{"column" => 0, "line" => 2}],
        "message" => "Could not create menu item",
        "path" => ["createMenuItem"]
      }
    ]
  }
end
```

Running this confirms that all is well:

```
$ mix test test/plate_slate_web/schema/mutation/create_menu_item_test.exs
..

Finished in 0.2 seconds
2 tests, 0 failures
```

Now you can have some peace of mind that when users create menu items, they will be prevented from using duplicate names. The only question is whether the errors you give your users are informative enough.

We'll cover two approaches that you can use in your Absinthe schema to give users more information when they encounter an error: using simple :error tuples and modeling the errors directly as types.

Using Tuples

Field resolver functions return tuple values to indicate their result. We've already seen this in the resolvers we've built so far in our PlateSlate application. For example, here's the resolver for the :create_menu_item field that we've been working on throughout this chapter:

```
05-chp.mutations/3-errors/lib/plate_slate_web/resolvers/menu.ex
def create_item(_, %{input: params}, _) do
  case Menu.create_item(params) do
    {:error, _} ->
      {:error, "Could not create menu item"}
    {:ok, _} = success ->
      success
  end
end
```

The return value for PlateSlate.Menu.create_item/1 is a tuple, and we use case to do a bit of post-processing on the value to return a nicely formatted value for Absinthe to include in the response. Successful values are returned untouched, but error values (which are Ecto changesets) are replaced with a pretty generic message, "Could not create menu item." We can do better than that!

Here's what a changeset looks like when returned from Ecto after an unsuccessful attempt to create a menu item:

```
#Ecto.Changeset<action: :insert,
  changes: %{name: "Water", price: #Decimal<0>},
  errors: [name: {"has already been taken", []}],
  data: #PlateSlate.Menu.Item<>, valid?: false>
```

Changesets are a pretty complex piece of machinery, and for good reason. We need to extract useful error information from this in a format that Absinthe can consume and return to users. Fortunately, Ecto.Changeset.traverse_errors/2 is a ready-made tool that's perfect for our purposes. Let's plug it into the resolver function, pulling the error information out of the changeset and returning it as part of the tuple:

```
05-chp.mutations/4-errortuples/lib/plate_slate_web/resolvers/menu.ex
def create_item(_, %{input: params}, _) do
  case Menu.create_item(params) do
    {:error, changeset} ->
      {
        :error,
        message: "Could not create menu item",
        details: error_details(changeset),
      }
    success ->
      success
  end
end

def error_details(changeset) do
  changeset
  |> Ecto.Changeset.traverse_errors(fn {msg, _} -> msg end)
end
```

The traverse_errors/2 function takes a changeset and a function to process each error, which is a two-element tuple of the error message. We're transforming the error information into a string with format_error/1.

Errors Need a Message

If you go beyond returning {:error, String.t} and return a map or keyword list, you must include a :message. Anything else is optional, but any error information must be serializable to JSON.

Instead of returning a simple {:error, String.t} value from the resolver, we're now returning an {:error, Keyword.t}, with the error information from the changeset under the :details key. Here's what the return value of the resolver will look like if a user encounters a name collision:

```
{
  :error,
  message: "Could not create menu item",
  details: %{
    "name" => ["has already been taken"]
  }
}
```

It's important to remember that errors are reported separate of data values in a GraphQL response, so the previous error would be serialized to look like this in a response:

```
{
  "data": {
    "createMenuItem": null
  },
  "errors": [
    {
      "message": "Could not create menu item",
      "details": {
        "name": ["has already been taken"]
      },
      "locations": [{"line": 2, "column": 0}],
      "path": [
        "createMenuItem"
      ]
    }
  ]
}
```

Handily, the path to the related field is included, as well as line number information. This makes mapping an error to its originating point in our GraphQL schema (and document) pretty straightforward.

That Pesky Column Number

 Notice that the column value in the error is 0. Due to a current limitation of the lexer that Absinthe uses (leex[3], part of Erlang/OTP), column tracking isn't available...yet. For the moment, to be compatible with client tools, Absinthe always reports the column value as 0.

---

3. http://erlang.org/doc/man/leex.html

Let's verify we get this error by modifying our test along the same lines:

```
05-chp.mutations/4-errortuples/test/plate_slate_web/schema/mutation/create_menu_item_test.exs
test "creating a menu item with an existing name fails",
%{category_id: category_id} do
  menu_item = %{
    "name" => "Reuben",
    "description" => "Roast beef, caramelized onions, horseradish, ...",
    "price" =>  "5.75",
    "categoryId" => category_id,
  }
  conn = build_conn()
  conn = post conn, "/api",
    query: @query,
    variables: %{"menuItem" => menu_item}

  assert json_response(conn, 200) == %{
    "data" => %{"createMenuItem" => nil},
    "errors" => [
      %{
        "locations" => [%{"column" => 0, "line" => 2}],
        "message" => "Could not create menu item",
        "details" => %{"name" => ["has already been taken"]},
        "path" => ["createMenuItem"]
      }
    ]
  }
end
```

Running it, we see that it still passes:

```
$ mix test test/plate_slate_web/schema/mutation/create_menu_item_test.exs
..

Finished in 0.2 seconds
2 tests, 0 failures
```

With this in place, we know that the error information is being extracted from the changeset and being returned correctly from the resolver to our users. It will be handy to keep it around to fend off any regressions in the future.

Now let's take a look at an alternate way to return errors.

Errors as Data

Sometimes, rather than returning errors in GraphQL's free-form errors portion of the result, it might make sense to model our errors as normal data—fully defining the structure of our errors as normal types to support introspection and better integration with clients.

If you recall, the mutation field that we created earlier returned a :menu_item:

```
mutation do
  field :create_menu_item, :menu_item do
    # «Contents»
  end
end
```

If we were to diagram the relationship between the resulting GraphQL types and fields, this is what it would look like:

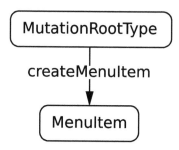

If we wanted to give our API clients more insight into the structure of the errors this mutation could return, we'd need to expand this modeling out a bit to make room for error types. What if, instead of returning the menu item directly, our mutation field returned an object type, :menu_item_result, that would sit in the middle?

```
05-chp.mutations/5-errorobjects/lib/plate_slate_web/schema/menu_types.ex
object :menu_item_result do
  field :menu_item, :menu_item
  field :errors, list_of(:input_error)
end
```

This result models each part of the output, the menu item, and the errors. The :errors themselves are an object, which we'll put in the schema because they're generic enough to be used in a variety of places:

```
05-chp.mutations/5-errorobjects/lib/plate_slate_web/schema.ex
@desc "An error encountered trying to persist input"
object :input_error do
  field :key, non_null(:string)
  field :message, non_null(:string)
end
```

The figure on page 93 shows how the resulting GraphQL type structure would look, once we modify the mutation field to declare its result to be a :menu_item_result.

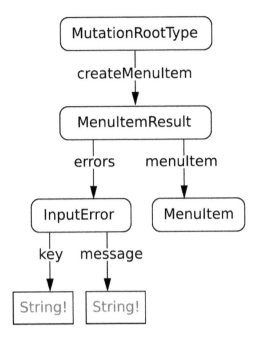

Let's do that, modifying the field resolver:

```
05-chp.mutations/5-errorobjects/lib/plate_slate_web/resolvers/menu.ex
def create_item(_, %{input: params}, _) do
  case Menu.create_item(params) do
    {:error, changeset} ->
➤      {:ok, %{errors: transform_errors(changeset)}}
    {:ok, menu_item} ->
➤      {:ok, %{menu_item: menu_item}}
  end
end

defp transform_errors(changeset) do
  changeset
  |> Ecto.Changeset.traverse_errors(&format_error/1)
  |> Enum.map(fn
    {key, value} ->
      %{key: key, message: value}
  end)
end

@spec format_error(Ecto.Changeset.error) :: String.t
defp format_error({msg, opts}) do
  Enum.reduce(opts, msg, fn {key, value}, acc ->
    String.replace(acc, "%{#{key}}", to_string(value))
  end)
end
```

It's important to notice that, regardless of error state, an :ok tuple is returned; it's just doing the work of translating database errors into values that can be transmitted back to clients.

GraphQL documents from the clients wouldn't look much different; they'd just be a level deeper. Let's modify the query we're using in our tests to support this new structure:

```
05-chp.mutations/5-errorobjects/test/plate_slate_web/schema/mutation/create_menu_item_test.exs
@query """
mutation ($menuItem: MenuItemInput!) {
  createMenuItem(input: $menuItem) {
    errors { key message }
    menuItem {
      name
      description
      price
    }
  }
}
"""
```

When clients receive responses for this document, they can interpret the success of the result by checking the value of menuItem and/or errors, then give feedback to users appropriately. Because the errors are returned as the result of specific fields, this means that, even in cases where the client sends multiple mutations in a single document, any errors encountered can be tied to the specific mutation that failed.

For our tests to work with the changes to the field and this new query, we need to update the assertions we make about the responses we expect.

We'll start with the case that successfully creates a menu item:

```
05-chp.mutations/5-errorobjects/test/plate_slate_web/schema/mutation/create_menu_item_test.exs
assert json_response(conn, 200) == %{
  "data" => %{
    "createMenuItem" => %{
      "errors" => nil,
      "menuItem" => %{
        "name" => menu_item["name"],
        "description" => menu_item["description"],
        "price" => menu_item["price"]
      }
    }
  }
}
```

We also need to update the error case:

```
05-chp.mutations/5-errorobjects/test/plate_slate_web/schema/mutation/create_menu_item_test.exs
assert json_response(conn, 200) == %{
  "data" => %{
    "createMenuItem" => %{
      "errors" => [
        %{"key" => "name", "message" => "has already been taken"}
      ],
      "menuItem" => nil
    }
  }
}
```

With the test assertions updated, your test assertions should pass. Let's run the tests for the field again:

```
$ mix test test/plate_slate_web/schema/mutation/create_menu_item_test.exs
..

Finished in 0.2 seconds
2 tests, 0 failures
```

This is a straightforward approach to modeling errors as data, and it's possible to take it a lot further—for example, supporting a fully fleshed out error code system using enums or setting a union as the result type—but it's important to make decisions about error modeling based on the needs of your API users. Remember, if users don't need to know the structure of your errors ahead of time, or if you don't think supporting introspection for documentation purposes is worth it, even this basic modeling is overkill; just return simple :error tuples instead. They're low ceremony and flexible enough to support most use cases.

Moving On

In this chapter, you learned how GraphQL draws a distinction between queries, which are used to retrieve information, and mutations used to change it. We worked through adding a root mutation type and a mutation field, discussed how to use input objects to model new records, and uncovered several strategies for returning error information if something goes wrong.

This chapter finishes up our work building the core pieces of a GraphQL API. Before we move on to some exciting near real-time features of GraphQL, here are some challenges you can tackle in the PlateSlate application to use your knowledge of the material in this chapter:

1. We added a :decimal scalar type in this chapter and used it as the type for the :price field of our :menu_item type. Back in Modeling Input Objects, on page 44, we added a :menu_item_filter type with price filters that use :float;

convert them to :decimal and make the changes necessary so the tests still pass. (Feel free to add more, too!)

2. Add a new mutation field, :update_menu_item, that takes a similar :input argument and an :id, but updates records instead of creating them.

3. Let's assume you've opted to include a :code value in your mutation errors to match up with some internationalized error messages in your client user interfaces. Think through how you might do this if returning simple :error tuples vs. :ok tuples with error objects.

4. Menu items belong to a category, and it would be useful to assign a menu item and create a new category on creation. How would you modify the :menu_item_input type to support providing a category name? If you're feeling ambitious, figure out how to use Ecto to create and associate the new category, too.

In the next chapter, you'll learn about subscriptions, GraphQL's approach to live data updates. Considering the near real-time performance of Elixir and Phoenix, it should be no surprise they're the perfect fit—with Absinthe's help—for this exciting capability.

## CHAPTER 6

Going Live with Subscriptions

In REST-oriented web frameworks, the need to have near real-time, live data streams still feels like a strange new world. It isn't necessarily that setting up a WebSocket connection is hard (particularly if you're using Phoenix), but rather that such connections don't fit into the REST API paradigm very easily. Setting up connections for specific data feeds and managing the communication across them is, to say the least, awkward in a world of "resources" tightly coupled to HTTP verbs. Consequently, even in frameworks that have fantastic near real-time support, whatever approach that's available doesn't feel like a first-class part of the API. When your API is built solidly around the semantics of HTTP requests, the needs of live data feeds can feel like an afterthought.

GraphQL, on the other hand, puts near real-time data at the same first-class level as queries or mutations with what are called *subscription operations*. It's these subscriptions that allow users to request data updates—using the same semantics as any other GraphQL request—and manage the life cycle of the data feed. Modern user interfaces using subscriptions can work with live data as a part of their normal conversation with a GraphQL server. Near real-time data updates are not a bolt-on, after-market component of a GraphQL API, but rather an intrinsic feature.

Over the last few chapters, we've built up the foundation of a GraphQL API for a restaurant menu and ordering system. Our example application, PlateSlate, is just crying out for user interfaces that use near real-time data. Whereas something like the restaurant menu is a relatively static set of information, orders are dynamic. From a screen in the restaurant's fast-moving kitchen that tells cooks when and what to prepare, to consumer mobile applications that support to-go and delivery ordering, it's important that information about changes to an order's status is distributed quickly and easily.

We'll spend this chapter building a simple system for tracking orders in a specific restaurant. The scenario will go like this:

- The customer goes to a cashier, orders and pays for items, and is handed a number.

- A user interface in the restaurant kitchen displays the order as it is placed, along with what items are in the order.

- A simple status screen is displayed in the seating area of the restaurant, letting the customer know when their order is ready for pickup.

- When their food is ready, the customer trades in the number for their food.

In this chapter, you'll learn how to model the related data operations and configure the subscriptions that will power these user interfaces. Let's get started by covering some important background about subscriptions.

Setting Up Subscriptions

Subscriptions let a client submit a GraphQL document that, instead of being executed immediately, is executed on the basis of some event in the system. From the perspective of the server, we need to be able to hold onto documents that clients have submitted so that we can run them at the right time, and we need a way to propagate events through the system. Finally, we need a way to have a persistent connection with the client so that we can push results up to them when their documents are executed.

This requires a little bit of setup. Fortunately, PlateSlate already has Phoenix as a dependency, and that will play the role of the publish-subscribe[1] and WebSocket system. This provides a number of handy features for free: clients will be able to use long polling or WebSockets, and the pubsub will work either over distributed Elixir or through any other adapter (like Redis) built to work with Phoenix pubsub. However, there are a few things you need to do to connect these capabilities to Absinthe.

The first order of business is to add an Absinthe.Subscription supervisor to the PlateSlate application's supervision tree by modifying the children list in the start/2 callback of application.ex.

06-chp.subscriptions/1-start/lib/plate_slate/application.ex
```
def start(_type, _args) do
  import Supervisor.Spec
```

---

1. https://en.wikipedia.org/wiki/Publish%E2%80%93subscribe_pattern

```
  children = [
    supervisor(PlateSlate.Repo, []),
    supervisor(PlateSlateWeb.Endpoint, []),
➤   supervisor(Absinthe.Subscription, [PlateSlateWeb.Endpoint]),
  ]
  opts = [strategy: :one_for_one, name: PlateSlate.Supervisor]
  Supervisor.start_link(children, opts)
end
```

This Absinthe.Subscription supervisor starts a number of processes that will handle broadcasting results and hold on to subscription documents. You pass the supervisor your PlateSlateWeb.Endpoint module because you're using the Phoenix endpoint as the underlying pubsub mechanism.

Phoenix Not Required

We're using Phoenix as the pubsub for our subscriptions in this chapter because it's a powerful system and easy to get started with. Absinthe's support for subscriptions is flexible enough to be used outside of WebSockets (or even the browser); we'll cover some ideas in later chapters.

Speaking of the Phoenix endpoint, we need to add a single line to its definition to provide a few extra callbacks that Absinthe expects:

06-chp.subscriptions/1-start/lib/plate_slate_web/endpoint.ex
```
defmodule PlateSlateWeb.Endpoint do
  use Phoenix.Endpoint, otp_app: :plate_slate
➤ use Absinthe.Phoenix.Endpoint

  # «Rest of file»
end
```

Here we see the first use of the Absinthe.Phoenix project. Much like Absinthe.Plug provides a way to use Absinthe from within a Plug pipeline, Absinthe.Phoenix provides a way to use Absinthe from within Phoenix-specific features like channels.[2]

With the actual pubsub stuff set up, we just need to configure our socket. Inside PlateSlateWeb.UserSocket, add:

06-chp.subscriptions/1-start/lib/plate_slate_web/channels/user_socket.ex
```
defmodule PlateSlateWeb.UserSocket do
  use Phoenix.Socket
➤ use Absinthe.Phoenix.Socket, schema: PlateSlateWeb.Schema

  # «Rest of file»
end
```

---

2. https://hexdocs.pm/phoenix/Phoenix.Channel.html

Last but not least, we need to configure GraphiQL to use this socket:

06-chp.subscriptions/1-start/lib/plate_slate_web/router.ex
```
forward "/graphiql", Absinthe.Plug.GraphiQL,
  schema: PlateSlateWeb.Schema,
  interface: :simple,
  socket: PlateSlateWeb.UserSocket
```

And with those four lines added, all the underlying mechanisms are wired up. Let's build an ordering system.

Event Modeling

Subscriptions push data in response to events or actions within your system, so it isn't enough to think of subscriptions as a purely API-related concern. A system that can't model change will have a very hard time communicating about changes to subscribers. Designing our application, we want to arrive at a model that lets us track the life cycle of an order as it is started, completed, and ultimately picked up by the customer. Along the way, each of these changes should be transmitted immediately to employees tasked with making the order, as well as to the hungry customer waiting for their food.

This part of the system is a bit more involved than the menu, so we're going to take it in pieces. The first piece just focuses on creating the orders and building your first simple subscription to be able to see those orders in real time. Then we'll circle back and expand these abilities to cover the full life cycle of the order.

Placing Orders

To jump-start this process, we're going to use the Phoenix context generator to rapidly build out the main files we need:

```
$ mix phx.gen.context Ordering Order orders \
  customer_number:integer \
  items:map \
  ordered_at:utc_datetime \
  state:string
```

This gets your core PlateSlate.Ordering.Order schema in place, and it provides a few useful functions in the PlateSlate.Ordering context that you'll expand on in a moment. You might be thinking that we'll need a join table connecting an order to the menu items included in the order, but doing so leads to some trouble. Menus change over time, but orders are historical. Future changes to the price of a menu item shouldn't retroactively affect the total of past orders, so directly and permanently tying order and menu item rows is problematic.

Instead, we're going to a use a different approach where a jsonb (PostgreSQL's binary JSON type[3]) column called items will store a snapshot of each item taken at the time the order is placed. This way, each order record is a nicely self-contained picture in time. If this were the real world, we'd be dealing with other similar issues such as taxes, payment modeling, and a host of other concerns. The point isn't to address every scenario, but just to show how we can easily use different underlying data approaches within our API.

The orders migration itself needs a few changes so that some database defaults are set correctly:

```
06-chp.subscriptions/2-ordering/priv/repo/migrations/20170826185436_create_orders.exs
defmodule PlateSlate.Repo.Migrations.CreateOrders do
  use Ecto.Migration

  def change do
    create table(:orders) do
      add :customer_number, :serial
      add :items, :map
      add :ordered_at, :utc_datetime, null: false, default: fragment("NOW()")
      add :state, :string, null: false, default: "created"

      timestamps()
    end

  end
end
```

The customer_number column will autogenerate by default, although if the store has a specific set of numbers it wants to use, it'll be able to override this when it creates the order.

Head over to your new Ordering.Order module to update the fields and changeset function:

```
06-chp.subscriptions/2-ordering/lib/plate_slate/ordering/order.ex
defmodule PlateSlate.Ordering.Order do
  use Ecto.Schema
  import Ecto.Changeset
  alias PlateSlate.Ordering.Order

  schema "orders" do
    field :customer_number, :integer, read_after_writes: true
    field :ordered_at, :utc_datetime, read_after_writes: true
    field :state, :string, read_after_writes: true

    embeds_many :items, PlateSlate.Ordering.Item

    timestamps()
  end
```

---

3. https://www.postgresql.org/docs/9.4/static/datatype-json.html

```
  @doc false
  def changeset(%Order{} = order, attrs) do
    order
    |> cast(attrs, [:customer_number, :ordered_at, :state])
    |> cast_embed(:items)
  end
end
```

We'll add PlateSlate.Ordering.Item, the embedded schema itself, in a separate file:

06-chp.subscriptions/2-ordering/lib/plate_slate/ordering/item.ex
```
defmodule PlateSlate.Ordering.Item do
  use Ecto.Schema
  import Ecto.Changeset

  embedded_schema do
    field :price, :decimal
    field :name, :string
    field :quantity, :integer
  end

  def changeset(item, attrs) do
    item
    |> cast(attrs, [:price, :name, :quantity])
    |> validate_required([:price, :name, :quantity])
  end
end
```

Before we build a test around ordering, you need to run migrations to add orders to the database schema:

```
$ mix ecto.migrate
«Running migration»
[info] create table orders
[info] == Migrated in 0.0s
```

With the core modeling in place, you now need to modify the create_order context function to actually build snapshots of the order. Let's set up a test case to capture the desired logic and then make the necessary changes to the create_order/1 function. The Phoenix generator you used will have already set up a test module, which you should essentially clear out in order to set up the following test case:

06-chp.subscriptions/2-ordering/test/plate_slate/ordering/ordering_test.exs
```
defmodule PlateSlate.OrderingTest do
  use PlateSlate.DataCase, async: true

  alias PlateSlate.Ordering

  setup do
    PlateSlate.Seeds.run()
  end
```

```
describe "orders" do
  alias PlateSlate.Ordering.Order

  test "create_order/1 with valid data creates a order" do
    chai = Repo.get_by!(PlateSlate.Menu.Item, name: "Masala Chai")
    fries = Repo.get_by!(PlateSlate.Menu.Item, name: "French Fries")
    attrs = %{
      ordered_at: "2010-04-17 14:00:00.000000Z",
      state: "created",
      items: [
        %{menu_item_id: chai.id, quantity: 1},
        %{menu_item_id: fries.id, quantity: 2},
      ]
    }
    assert {:ok, %Order{} = order} = Ordering.create_order(attrs)
    assert Enum.map(order.items,
      &Map.take(&1, [:name, :quantity, :price])
    ) == [
      %{name: "Masala Chai", quantity: 1, price: chai.price},
      %{name: "French Fries", quantity: 2, price: fries.price},
    ]
    assert order.state == "created"
  end
end
end
```

The idea here is that we pass in the menu items' IDs that the user wants to order, and then the create_order/1 function itself looks up the price to compute the total and build out the items snapshot.

From an implementation perspective, this is pretty straightforward:

```
06-chp.subscriptions/2-ordering/lib/plate_slate/ordering/ordering.ex
def create_order(attrs \\ %{}) do
  attrs = Map.update(attrs, :items, [], &build_items/1)

  %Order{}
  |> Order.changeset(attrs)
  |> Repo.insert()
end

defp build_items(items) do
  for item <- items do
    menu_item = PlateSlate.Menu.get_item!(item.menu_item_id)
    %{name: menu_item.name, quantity: item.quantity, price: menu_item.price}
  end
end
```

Now let's run our test to see if everything works:

```
$ mix test test/plate_slate/ordering/ordering_test.exs
.

Finished in 0.09 seconds
1 test, 0 failures
```

While it doesn't seem like much, the ordering schema with its state column goes a long way toward supporting meaningful events. We can already talk about placing orders, and the role column puts us in a great spot to track changes to that state as the order progresses.

Building the Ordering API

The context function we just built provides a pretty good indicator of what our GraphQL inputs should look like. We're expecting a list of items that we want to order, as well as an optional customer reference number. Notably, the items don't contain any price info, as that should always be looked up from the menu system (to make sure clients aren't doing anything funny with the prices). Add the following field to your mutation object:

06-chp.subscriptions/3-orderingapi/lib/plate_slate_web/schema.ex
```
import_types __MODULE__.OrderingTypes

# «Other schema content»

mutation do

  field :place_order, :order_result do
    arg :input, non_null(:place_order_input)
    resolve &Resolvers.Ordering.place_order/3
  end

  # «other types»
end
```

This field relies on types sourced via import_types/1 from a separate PlateSlate-Web.Schema.OrderingTypes module. We'll create the module, filling out all the ordering-related types that we'll need:

06-chp.subscriptions/3-orderingapi/lib/plate_slate_web/schema/ordering_types.ex
```
defmodule PlateSlateWeb.Schema.OrderingTypes do
  use Absinthe.Schema.Notation

  input_object :order_item_input do
    field :menu_item_id, non_null(:id)
    field :quantity, non_null(:integer)
  end
  input_object :place_order_input do
    field :customer_number, :integer
    field :items, non_null(list_of(non_null(:order_item_input)))
  end
```

```
object :order_result do
  field :order, :order
  field :errors, list_of(:input_error)
end
object :order do
  field :id, :id
  field :customer_number, :integer
  field :items, list_of(:order_item)
  field :state, :string
end
object :order_item do
  field :name, :string
  field :quantity, :integer
end
end
```

Non-Null Lists

The non_null(list_of(non_null(:order_item_input))) type we set for the :items field may seem a bit convoluted, but it makes sense when you break it down.

The outermost non_null indicates that the client can't leave out the :items field or make it null. The list_of just tells us that the value will be a list, and then the innermost non_null just tells the client that none of the items in the list can themselves be null.

Last but not least, we have our resolver, which—until we get to handling authentication concerns in Chapter 8, Securing with Authentication and Authorization, on page 139—has very little to do outside of managing errors.

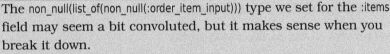
06-chp.subscriptions/3-orderingapi/lib/plate_slate_web/resolvers/ordering.ex

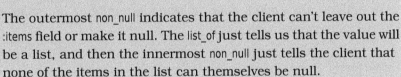

```
defmodule PlateSlateWeb.Resolvers.Ordering do
  alias PlateSlate.Ordering

  def place_order(_, %{input: place_order_input}, _) do
    case Ordering.create_order(place_order_input) do
      {:ok, order} ->
        {:ok, %{order: order}}
      {:error, changeset} ->
        {:ok, %{errors: transform_errors(changeset)}}
    end
  end
  defp transform_errors(changeset) do
    changeset
    |> Ecto.Changeset.traverse_errors(&format_error/1)
    |> Enum.map(fn
      {key, value} ->
        %{key: key, message: value}
    end)
  end
```

```
  @spec format_error(Ecto.Changeset.error) :: String.t
  defp format_error({msg, opts}) do
    Enum.reduce(opts, msg, fn {key, value}, acc ->
      String.replace(acc, "%{#{key}}", to_string(value))
    end)
  end
end
```

For the moment, we've just copied and pasted the error formatting logic that we put together in Errors as Data, on page 91. In the next chapter, we'll look at how we can use middleware to improve code reuse for resolvers (in a way that's even better than an Elixir use or import).

Let's pop open the GraphiQL user interface to play with our API a bit. First, start your server:

```
$ mix phx.server
[info] Running PlateSlateWeb.Endpoint with Cowboy using http://0.0.0.0:4000
```

Now, browse to http://localhost:4000/graphiql.

We're going to run a quick query so that we can figure out some menu item IDs. Here's the query we'll use:

```
{
  menuItems {
    id
    name
  }
}
```

Let's paste that into the left-side panel in GraphiQL and press "play." Here's what you should see:

We'll pick two of those IDs and use them in the following mutation:

```
mutation ($input: PlaceOrderInput!) {
  placeOrder(input: $input) {
    errors { message }
    order { id state }
  }
}
```

Use Variables!

 If you need to use values from a query in a subsequent mutation, copy and paste those values into the variables part of GraphiQL, and then reference those variables within your mutation document.

We used variables to define the inputs to the mutation, so we click on the "Query Variables" panel header at the bottom left of the GraphiQL interface to open up the variable entry panel.

GraphiQL expects variable input to be given in JSON format, so we enter an object that matches up with the structure of the :place_order_input type that we defined in our schema earlier. We pick a customer number, 4, and provide the two menu item IDs that we retrieved in our last query.

Once the variable values are ready to go, we press the "play" button to execute the mutation and see the following in the result panel:

```
GraphiQL  ▶  Prettify                                                    ‹ Docs

1 ▾ mutation ($input: PlaceOrderInput!) {           ▾ {
2 ▾   placeOrder(input: $input) {                        "data": {
3         errors {                                          "placeOrder": {
4           message                                           "order": {
5         }                                                     "state": "created",
6         order {                                               "id": "21"
7           id                                                },
8           state                                             "errors": null
9         }                                                 }
10      }                                                 }
11    }                                                 }
12

      QUERY VARIABLES

1 ▾ {
2 ▾   "input": {
3         "items": [
4           {"quantity": 1, "menuItemId": "4"},
5           {"quantity": 2, "menuItemId": "13"}
6         ],
7         "customerNumber": 4
8     }
9   }
```

Congratulations, an order has been placed!

Submitting Subscriptions

Now that we can create orders, we're at the perfect spot to introduce the first basic subscription that will support pushing these orders as they're created out to subscribed clients. You'll first need to define a subscription field in your schema, and then you'll also need a way to actually trigger this subscription when the :place_order mutation runs.

```
06-chp.subscriptions/4-publish/lib/plate_slate_web/schema.ex
subscription do
  field :new_order, :order do
    config fn _args, _info ->
      {:ok, topic: "*"}
    end
  end
end
```

For the most part, this is a pretty ordinary-looking field. We've got another top-level object, subscription, to house our subscription fields, and then the :new_order, which will return the :order object we're already familiar with. The fact that it returns a regular :order object is crucial, because this means that all the work we have done to support the output of the mutation can be reused immediately for real-time data.

What's new, however, is the config macro, and it's one of a couple macros that are specific to setting up subscriptions. The job of the config macro is to help us determine which clients who have asked for a given subscription field should receive data by configuring a *topic*. We'll talk more later about constructing topics, but the main thing to know is that topics are scoped to the field they're on, and they have to be a string. We're just going to use "*" to indicate that we care about all orders (but there's nothing special about "*" itself).

Set Up and Return Error

 The config function can also return {:error, reason}, which prevents the subscription from being created.

Let's see if we can subscribe with GraphiQL. First, let's make sure it's running again, but this time, inside an IEx session (you'll see why shortly):

```
$ iex -S mix phx.server
[info] Running PlateSlateWeb.Endpoint with Cowboy using http://0.0.0.0:4000
```

Then, browse to http://localhost:4000/graphiql and enter the following in the left-side panel (you can close the "Query Variables" panel if you have it open):

```
subscription {
  newOrder {
    customerNumber
    items { name quantity}
  }
}
```

When you hit "play," instead of getting a result, you'll get a message saying, "Your subscription data will appear here after server publication!":

What's happening here is that although the server has accepted the subscription document, the server is waiting on some kind of event that will trigger execution of the document and distribution of the result. Specifically, it's waiting for an event that targets the field of our subscription newOrder and the topic associated with this specific document "*".

The most direct way to make this trigger happen is with the Absinthe.Subscription.publish/3 function, which gives us manual control of the publishing mechanism. If you go into the IEx session in your console, you can trigger the subscription you just created in GraphiQL by running:

```
iex> order = PlateSlate.Ordering.Order |> PlateSlate.Repo.all |> List.last
«%PlateSlate.Ordering.Order{} displayed»
iex> Absinthe.Subscription.publish(
  PlateSlateWeb.Endpoint,
  order,
  new_order: "*"
)
:ok
```

If you look back to your GraphiQL page, you should see a result as shown in the figure on page 110.

The arguments to the publish/3 function are the module you're using as the pubsub, the value that you're broadcasting, and the field: topic pairs at which to broadcast the value. Concretely then, the function call you typed in IEx says to broadcast the last %Order{} struct to all clients subscribed to the :new_order field via the "*" topic.

You may have noticed when you set up the subscription field that you didn't specify a resolver, and this is why. Unlike a root query or root mutation resolver, which generally starts with no root value and has to start from scratch, the root value of a subscription document is the value that is passed to publish/3. You can see this for yourself if you add just an inspect resolver to the subscription field:

06-chp.subscriptions/4-publish/lib/plate_slate_web/schema.ex
```elixir
subscription do
  field :new_order, :order do

    config fn _args, _info ->
      {:ok, topic: "*"}
    end

    resolve fn root, _, _ ->
      IO.inspect(root)
      {:ok, root}
    end
  end
end
```

If you re-run the Absinthe.Subscription.publish/3 call in your IEx session, you will see printed into console the value you are broadcasting, nested under the :new_order key:

```elixir
%Ordering.Order{
  «Contents»
}
```

With this Absinthe.Subscription.publish/3 function at our disposal, it's clear then that one possibility for making our live interface is to put it inside the :place_order mutation resolver so that instead of triggering subscriptions from IEx, we'll trigger subscriptions every time a new order is placed.

06-chp.subscriptions/4-publish/lib/plate_slate_web/resolvers/ordering.ex

```elixir
def place_order(_, %{input: place_order_input}, _) do
  case Ordering.create_order(place_order_input) do
    {:ok, order} ->
➤     Absinthe.Subscription.publish(PlateSlateWeb.Endpoint, order,
➤       new_order: "*"
➤     )
      {:ok, %{order: order}}
    {:error, changeset} ->
      {:ok, %{errors: transform_errors(changeset)}}
  end
end
```

You could have some fun with this:

- In one window, open GraphiQL and enter the subscription document.
- In another window, also go to GraphiQL and enter the mutation document.
- Press "play" in the mutation window.
- Watch real-time events show up in the subscription window!

Play around with changing what parts of the subscription document you ask for, and play around with the values you put in the mutation document to get a feel for how the two documents relate to one another.

Testing Subscriptions

Testing your API is important, and subscriptions are no exception. We've been using helpers from the PlateSlate.ConnCase module in our test to ease building HTTP-based integration tests; you'll need a similar PlateSlate.SubscriptionCase module for managing the subscription integration tests via channels. While the ConnCase module gets generated by Phoenix when we first create the project, the SubscriptionCase module we'll need to make ourselves.

06-chp.subscriptions/4-publish/test/support/subscription_case.ex

```elixir
defmodule PlateSlateWeb.SubscriptionCase do
  @moduledoc """
  This module defines the test case to be used by
  subscription tests
  """

  use ExUnit.CaseTemplate

  using do
    quote do
      # Import conveniences for testing with channels
      use PlateSlateWeb.ChannelCase
      use Absinthe.Phoenix.SubscriptionTest,
        schema: PlateSlateWeb.Schema
```

```elixir
    setup do
      PlateSlate.Seeds.run()

      {:ok, socket} =
          Phoenix.ChannelTest.connect(PlateSlateWeb.UserSocket, %{})
      {:ok, socket} =
          Absinthe.Phoenix.SubscriptionTest.join_absinthe(socket)

      {:ok, socket: socket}
    end

    import unquote(__MODULE__), only: [menu_item: 1]
  end
end

# handy function for grabbing a fixture
def menu_item(name) do
  PlateSlate.Repo.get_by!(PlateSlate.Menu.Item, name: name)
end
end
```

This module sets up the socket we'll use in each of our test cases, and it also gives us a convenient function for getting menu items.

As far as the test case itself goes, much of the setup here is exactly the same as any other Phoenix channel test. Absinthe.Phoenix provides some helpers to instantiate a socket process with the configuration you added to the UserSocket.

06-chp.subscriptions/4-publish/test/plate_slate_web/schema/subscription/new_order_test.exs
```elixir
defmodule PlateSlateWeb.Schema.Subscription.NewOrderTest do
  use PlateSlateWeb.SubscriptionCase

  @subscription """
  subscription {
    newOrder {
      customerNumber
    }
  }
  """

  @mutation """
  mutation ($input: PlaceOrderInput!) {
    placeOrder(input: $input) { order { id } }
  }
  """

  test "new orders can be subscribed to", %{socket: socket} do
    # setup a subscription
    ref = push_doc socket, @subscription
    assert_reply ref, :ok, %{subscriptionId: subscription_id}

    # run a mutation to trigger the subscription
    order_input = %{"customerNumber" => 24,
      "items" => [%{"quantity" => 2, "menuItemId" => menu_item("Reuben").id}]
    }
```

```
    ref = push_doc socket, @mutation, variables: %{"input" => order_input}
    assert_reply ref, :ok, reply
    assert %{data: %{"placeOrder" => %{"order" => %{"id" => _}}}} = reply

    # check to see if we got subscription data
    expected = %{
      result: %{data: %{"newOrder" => %{"customerNumber" => 24}}},
      subscriptionId: subscription_id
    }
    assert_push "subscription:data", push
    assert expected == push
  end
end
```

If channels are pretty new to you, that's okay. The essential thing to keep in mind is that it's a lot like testing a GenServer. You've got the test process itself, which acts like the client, and you've got the socket process, which operates just as it does when connected to by an external client. You can push an event and params to the socket and then listen for a specific reply to that event, much like a GenServer call. Each push is asynchronous, so it's important to make sure to wait for a reply after each push. The socket can also send messages directly to the test process, which is what will happen when we trigger an event.

Testing a socket, then, is just a matter of sending it the data we need to configure our subscription, triggering a mutation, and then waiting for subscription data to get pushed to the test process.

So the first thing we do is push a "doc" event to the socket along with the parameters specifying our subscription document, and then we assert for a reply from the socket that returns a subscriptionId. This subscriptionId is important because a single socket can support many different subscriptions, and the subscriptionId is used to keep track of what data push belongs to what subscription.

The next thing we do is run a mutation to place an order. This operation is actually pushed over the socket as well; sockets support all the different operation types. While an explicit Absinthe.run would also work, it would require that we explicitly pass in the pubsub configuration, whereas that config is picked up automatically if the document is pushed through the socket.

Finally, all we have to do is assert that the test process gets a message containing the expected subscription data!

Let's go ahead and run our test to make sure everything is working as expected:

```
$ mix test test/plate_slate_web/schema/subscription/new_order_test.exs
«Debugging output»
.

Finished in 0.1 seconds
1 test, 0 failures
```

There we go! Not only did we get subscriptions working in GraphiQL, we were able to treat it like any other part of our API and write a proper integration test. Now that we have subscriptions working using a manual method, let's look at a mechanism that we can use to publish changes automatically as they occur.

Subscription Triggers

In the previous section, we only used a single hard-coded topic value, but when we start thinking about tracking the life cycle of a particular entity, we need to pay a lot more attention to how we're setting up our subscriptions and how we're triggering them. The challenge isn't just keeping track of how the topics are constructed; it can also be hard to make sense of where in your code base publish/3 calls may be happening. We're going to explore an alternative approach to trigger mutations as we expand on the order-tracking capabilities of the PlateSlate system.

Everything that has a beginning has an end, and for the hungry customer, orders are fortunately no exception. We need to complete the life cycle of an order by providing two mutations: one to indicate that it's ready, and one to indicate that it was picked up.

Fortunately, most of what we need to do this in our context and schema already exists, so we can just jump directly to building out the relevant mutation fields in the GraphQL schema and filling out each resolver.

06-chp.subscriptions/5-trigger/lib/plate_slate_web/schema.ex
```
mutation do

  field :ready_order, :order_result do
    arg :id, non_null(:id)
    resolve &Resolvers.Ordering.ready_order/3
  end
  field :complete_order, :order_result do
    arg :id, non_null(:id)
    resolve &Resolvers.Ordering.complete_order/3
  end

  # «Other fields»
end
```

Our :ready_order and :complete_order fields use new resolver functions from PlateSlateWeb.Resolvers.Ordering; let's add those:

06-chp.subscriptions/5-trigger/lib/plate_slate_web/resolvers/ordering.ex

```
def ready_order(_, %{id: id}, _) do
  order = Ordering.get_order!(id)
  with {:ok, order} <- Ordering.update_order(order, %{state: "ready"}) do
    {:ok, %{order: order}}
  else
    {:error, changeset} ->
      {:ok, %{errors: transform_errors(changeset)}}
  end
end

def complete_order(_, %{id: id}, _) do
  order = Ordering.get_order!(id)

  with {:ok, order} <- Ordering.update_order(order, %{state: "complete"}) do
    {:ok, %{order: order}}
  else
    {:error, changeset} ->
      {:ok, %{errors: transform_errors(changeset)}}
  end
end
```

So far, so good. This may start to feel pretty second nature at this point. If you are concerned that the changeset error handling here is seeming kind of redundant, hold on tight—that is covered in the very next chapter on middleware.

Subscribing to these events is just a little bit different than before, because now we're trying to handle events for specific orders based on ID. When the client is notified about new orders via a new_order subscription, we then want to give them the ability to subscribe to future updates for each of those subscriptions specifically.

We want to support a GraphQL document that looks like:

```
subscription {
  updateOrder(id: "13") {
    customerNumber
    state
  }
}
```

Notably, we want to use this one subscription field to get updates triggered by both the :ready_order and :complete_order mutation fields. While it's important to represent the mutations as different fields, it's often the case that you just need a single subscription that lets you get all the state changes for a particular entity that you want to watch.

```
06-chp.subscriptions/5-trigger/lib/plate_slate_web/schema.ex
subscription do
  field :update_order, :order do
    arg :id, non_null(:id)

    config fn args, _info ->
      {:ok, topic: args.id}
    end
  end

  # «Other fields»
end
```

The main difference is that we're now doing something more dynamic in our config function. Here we're using the arguments provided to the field to generate a topic that is specific to the ID of the order we care about.

Based on your previous experience with the Absinthe.Subscription.publish/3 function, you might be able to figure out the function call you could put in each mutation resolver to trigger this subscription field:

```
Absinthe.Subscription.publish(
  PlateSlateWeb.Endpoint, order,
  update_order: order.id
)
```

However, while we could use the publish/3 function here, we're going to explore a slightly different option. The issue with our approach thus far is that although our schema contains the :place_order mutation and also the :new_order subscription fields, there isn't any indicator in the schema that these two fields are connected in any way. Moreover, for subscription fields that are triggered by several different mutations, the topic logic is similarly distributed in a way that can make it difficult to keep track of.

This pattern of connecting mutation and subscription fields to one another is so common that Absinthe considers it a first-class concept and supports setting it as a trigger on subscription fields, avoiding the need to scatter publish/3 calls throughout your code base. Let's look at how we can use the trigger macro to connect the new subscription field to each mutation without touching our resolvers:

```
06-chp.subscriptions/5-trigger/lib/plate_slate_web/schema.ex
subscription do
  field :update_order, :order do
    arg :id, non_null(:id)

    config fn args, _info ->
      {:ok, topic: args.id}
    end
```

```
trigger [:ready_order, :complete_order], topic: fn
  %{order: order} -> [order.id]
  _ -> []
end

resolve fn %{order: order}, _ , _ ->
  {:ok, order}
end
end

# «Other fields»
end
```

The trigger macro takes two arguments: a mutation field name (or list of names) and a set of options that let you specify a topic function. This trigger topic function receives the output of the mutation as an argument, and should return a list of topics that are each used to find relevant subscriptions.

Let's think through how this works.

Two new orders are created with IDs "1" and "2". The UI client will send in two subscriptions. The first looks like this:

```
subscription {
  updateOrder(id: "1") {
    state
  }
}
```

The second looks like this:

```
subscription {
  updateOrder(id: "2") {
    state
  }
}
```

Even though they use the same field, each of these documents should only get events that are for the particular order ID specified in the arguments. The first document produces a topic of "1", and the second document produces a topic of "2".

Now order "2" is marked by the kitchen as ready to be picked up. The ready_order resolver returns {:ok, %{order: %Order{id: 2, ...}}}, and it's that value in that tuple that gets passed to the trigger function you've defined (where it's matched by the first pattern). This clause returns order.id, which, in the case of this specific order, produces a result of 2. As we noted earlier, topics are always strings, so Absinthe calls to_string/1 on whatever return, in this case producing "2".

We now have a value ("2") with which to look up subscriptions; when we do so, we get just the second document.

Triggering Many Topics

 Trigger topic functions can specify multiple topics by returning a list: ["topic1", "topic2"].

What about the other case that shows up in the trigger topic function: _, _ -> []? Remember that the mutation resolver can return error information from changesets. When this happens, we don't want to push out anything because the order wasn't actually updated. Returning [] prevents any publication from happening for this particular mutation, because we aren't returning any topics that we want to publish to.

What if the :ready_order and :complete_order mutation fields returned different values? A given subscription field can have many different triggers defined on it each with a different topic function. For example, suppose :ready_order returned %{ready: order}, and :completed_order returned %{completed: order}. We could handle this by doing:

```
trigger :ready_order, topic: fn
  %{ready: order}, _ -> [order.id]
  _, _ -> []
end
trigger :completed_order, topic: fn
  %{completed: order}, _ -> [order.id]
  _, _ -> []
end
```

Finally, you'll see that we're using a resolver here, whereas we didn't need to do so on the other subscription field. When we were calling publish/3 explicitly, we were passing the bare order record directly to publish. Now, however, we're getting the full result of the mutation, which in the success case is %{order: order}. The resolver can just pattern match on this to unwrap it.

Whether to use an explicit Absinthe.Subscription.publish/3 call or the trigger macro will depend on the scenario. In general, however, it's best to use triggers when there's a clear and sensible mapping of mutations to subscriptions because it helps place this information in a clear and central location. Placing the trigger topic functions next to the subscription topic function goes a long way toward keeping track of how each operation connects to the other.

No feature would be complete without a test, so let's encode this little narrative in a test case:

```elixir
defmodule PlateSlateWeb.Schema.Subscription.UpdateOrderTest do
  use PlateSlateWeb.SubscriptionCase

  @subscription """
  subscription ($id: ID! ){
    updateOrder(id: $id) { state }
  }
  """
  @mutation """
  mutation ($id: ID!) {
    readyOrder(id: $id) { errors { message } }
  }
  """
  test "subscribe to order updates", %{socket: socket} do
    reuben = menu_item("Reuben")
    {:ok, order1} = PlateSlate.Ordering.create_order(%{
      customer_number: 123, items: [%{menu_item_id: reuben.id, quantity: 2}]
    })
    {:ok, order2} = PlateSlate.Ordering.create_order(%{
      customer_number: 124, items: [%{menu_item_id: reuben.id, quantity: 1}]
    })

    ref = push_doc(socket, @subscription, variables: %{"id" => order1.id})
    assert_reply ref, :ok, %{subscriptionId: _subscription_ref1}

    ref = push_doc(socket, @subscription, variables: %{"id" => order2.id})
    assert_reply ref, :ok, %{subscriptionId: subscription_ref2}

    ref = push_doc(socket, @mutation, variables: %{"id" => order2.id})
    assert_reply ref, :ok, reply

    refute reply[:errors]
    refute reply[:data]["readyOrder"]["errors"]

    assert_push "subscription:data", push
    expected = %{
      result: %{data: %{"updateOrder" => %{"state" => "ready"}}},
      subscriptionId: subscription_ref2
    }
    assert expected == push
  end
end
```

This test case ultimately captures the story we're going for. You've got two distinct subscriptions, and then an update happens to just one of them; that's the one you get the update for, not any other. Let's run the test:

```
$ mix test test/plate_slate_web/schema/subscription/update_order_test.exs
.

Finished in 0.4 seconds
1 test, 0 failures
```

When you look back over the code in this chapter, you can see that nearly all of it just has to do with building out orders. At the end of the day, GraphQL subscriptions end up being rather simple, because with GraphQL, they're just another part of your normal API. The GraphQL type system binds each of these parts of the API together, so that all the work you do to support ordinary queries and mutations can simply get referenced from subscriptions.

Moving On

Although it's been a relatively simple system that we've built here, we've successfully built a basic menu and ordering application that provides flexible querying and near real-time data capabilities. More importantly, you learned about the significance of meaningful events in a system that supports subscriptions; GraphQL is able to naturally expose those events in a way that's in harmony with the way query and mutation operations are handled.

Here are a couple of ways to play around with subscriptions further:

1. Refactor the :place_order subscription to use the trigger macro.
2. Open GraphiQL in multiple browser windows and play around with subscribing to the same or different fields. Trigger values in your console and see them show up in real time.

In Part II of this book, we're going to cover some Absinthe-specific tools that you'll want to use as you take your application from the safe confines of your laptop to the real world. They'll help you control security, scalability, and maintainability concerns that are key to any production system.

Part II

Publish Your API

There's building something that works, then there's building something that's also solid, safe, and easy to maintain. In this part, you'll discover how to secure, scale, and simplify a GraphQL schema for long-term production use, turning your GraphQL API into one that's ready for the real world.

## CHAPTER 7

Resolution Middleware

Absinthe is built to be highly flexible. Even months prior to our first-class support for subscriptions, for example, people had put together their own implementations based on the tooling and support for extensions built into the framework. In this chapter, we're going to look at one of the most important of these mechanisms: *middleware*.

Even within the small API we've written over the last few chapters, we've seen some common patterns emerge within some of our resolvers. As you look forward toward error handling, authorization, and other concerns a real API would have, you'll want to become familiar with some tools that Absinthe provides for encapsulating these ideas into easier-to-use patterns.

We're going to start our exploration by looking at Absinthe middleware—a tool you can use to make resolvers shorter and more elegant by being able to reuse logic.

Our First Module

In Chapter 5, Making a Change with Mutations, on page 77, we added several resolution functions that all copied an error-handling function we first developed to power the :create_menu_item mutation field. This error-handling function enabled the system to give users feedback about errors that bubble up from the underlying database—from internal schema-validation problems like missing and badly formatted arguments to database constraint violations.

Let's take a look at that resolver again:

07-chp.middleware/1-start/lib/plate_slate_web/resolvers/menu.ex
```elixir
def create_item(_, %{input: params}, _) do
  case Menu.create_item(params) do
    {:error, changeset} ->
      {:ok, %{errors: transform_errors(changeset)}}
    {:ok, menu_item} ->
      {:ok, %{menu_item: menu_item}}
  end
end
```

The output of the resolver is a :menu_item_result type, which we've defined as part of our schema, and includes an :errors field:

07-chp.middleware/1-start/lib/plate_slate_web/schema/menu_types.ex
```elixir
object :menu_item_result do
  field :menu_item, :menu_item
  field :errors, list_of(:input_error)
end
```

Our resolver builds the error portion of the result using a transform_errors/1 function that turns %Ecto.Changeset{} structs into :input_error objects:

07-chp.middleware/1-start/lib/plate_slate_web/resolvers/menu.ex
```elixir
defp transform_errors(changeset) do
  changeset
  |> Ecto.Changeset.traverse_errors(&format_error/1)
  |> Enum.map(fn
    {key, value} ->
      %{key: key, message: value}
  end)
end

@spec format_error(Ecto.Changeset.error) :: String.t
defp format_error({msg, opts}) do
  Enum.reduce(opts, msg, fn {key, value}, acc ->
    String.replace(acc, "%{#{key}}", to_string(value))
  end)
end
```

This worked great when it was just the :create_menu_item mutation, but when we added more resolvers to power the ordering system, we just copied and pasted the same code into that resolver too. Clearly this isn't the approach we would want to take as the API expands. One option for cleaning this up is to just extract the transform_errors/1 function into its own module, which we could import into both resolvers.

If we take a step back, however, we can look at this problem a different way. We got to this point because functions within our Menu and Ordering contexts end up returning {:error, %Ecto.Changeset{}} when validations fail, and Absinthe doesn't really know what to do with a changeset. We might wonder, though, how Absinthe knows what to do with the existing {:ok, value} or {:error, error} tuples we've been using. If we knew what handled those tuples, we might be able to find a way to have Absinthe handle changesets, too.

Our first clue is to look closely at how the resolve macro is implemented:

```elixir
defmacro resolve(function_ast) do
  quote do
    middleware Absinthe.Resolution, unquote(function_ast)
  end
end
```

When you do something like this:

```elixir
resolve &Resolvers.Menu.menu_items/3
```

It expands to this in your schema:

```elixir
middleware Absinthe.Resolution, &Resolvers.Menu.menu_items/3
```

This Absinthe.Resolution middleware has been the driving force behind how our resolvers have operated this whole time, building the arguments to our resolvers, calling them, and then interpreting the result we've returned. However, we know more about our application than Absinthe does, so by building our own middleware, we can inform Absinthe about how to handle data that is more suited to our specific needs.

It's time to upgrade our app by building our first middleware module.

If we want to let Absinthe know how to handle changeset errors, we're going to need to build a middleware module to do so. Let's start by ripping the error transformation logic out of our resolver modules and putting it inside a new module that will serve as the base of our middleware.

07-chp.middleware/2-module/lib/plate_slate_web/schema/middleware/changeset_errors.ex
```elixir
defmodule PlateSlateWeb.Schema.Middleware.ChangesetErrors do
  @behaviour Absinthe.Middleware

  def call(res, _) do
    # «to be completed»
  end

  defp transform_errors(changeset) do
    changeset
    |> Ecto.Changeset.traverse_errors(&format_error/1)
    |> Enum.map(fn
      {key, value} ->
        %{key: key, message: value}
    end)
  end
```

```
  defp format_error({msg, opts}) do
    Enum.reduce(opts, msg, fn {key, value}, acc ->
      String.replace(acc, "%{#{key}}", to_string(value))
    end)
  end
end
```

So far, it's almost exactly what we had before, although we're also indicating that this module implements the Absinthe.Middleware behaviour. Modules that implement this behaviour are required to define a call/2 function that takes an %Absinthe.Resolution{} struct as well as some optional configuration. The resolution struct is packed with information about the field that's being resolved, including the results or errors that have been returned. We'll get to the middleware configuration in a bit; for the moment, we can ignore it.

Similarities to Plug

The %Absinthe.Resolution{} struct plays a role similar to the %Plug.Conn{} struct. Each gets passed through a sequence of functions that can transform it for some purpose and return it at the end.

The overall approach we're going to take with this call function is to look inside the resolution struct to see if we have a changeset error and, if we do, turn it into the structured error data we've been using.

07-chp.middleware/2-module/lib/plate_slate_web/schema/middleware/changeset_errors.ex
```
def call(res, _) do
  # «to be completed»
  with %{errors: [%Ecto.Changeset{} = changeset]} <- res do
    %{res |
      value: %{errors: transform_errors(changeset)},
      errors: [],
    }
  end
end
```

Here we're using the with pattern to check for this exact scenario. If this pattern doesn't match, the call/2 will just return the resolution struct unchanged.

This code block introduces us to two of the most significant keys inside resolution structs: :value and :errors. The :value key holds the value that will ultimately get returned for the field, and is used as the parent for any subsequent child fields. The :errors key is ultimately combined with errors from every other field and is used to populate the top-level errors in a GraphQL result.

When you return {:ok, value} from within a resolver function, the value is placed under the :value key of the %Absinthe.Resolution{} struct. If you return {:error,

error}, the error value is added to a list under the :errors key of the resolution struct.

Putting this knowledge together then, we can grasp the full picture of what our call/2 function is doing. We use the with macro to check for any changeset errors that would have been put there by a resolver returning {:error, changeset}. If we find one, we set the :value key to a map holding the transformed errors. We also clear out the :errors key, because we don't want any of this to bubble up to the top level.

Now that we have this middleware, we're going to look at how to place this on the schema so that it's used during resolution.

Applying Middleware

When it comes to applying middleware, we've got two different approaches available to us. Sometimes you have middleware that you want to apply to very specific fields, or even just one field. A logout mutation, for example, might use middleware to mutate the context, removing the current user.

Other times, you want to ensure that a particular middleware is always applied to every field in a certain object, or every field that has a particular name and return type. This is critical for something like authorization, where you want to protect against a programmer forgetting to specify that a field should be secured.

Absinthe provides two main approaches to handle these types of scenarios, which we'll examine in turn.

Macro Approach

When you have specific fields on which you want to place middleware, you'll want to reach for the middleware/2 macro. As we hinted at earlier, you've already been using this macro indirectly via the resolve/1 macro. To recap how it works:

```
defmacro resolve(function_ast) do
  quote do
    middleware Absinthe.Resolution, unquote(function_ast)
  end
end
```

All we've been doing with resolve is placing a single piece of middleware on our field, Absinthe.Resolution, and giving it the function we want to execute. With this piece of knowledge, we're ready to place our newly minted ChangesetErrors middleware on the :create_menu_item field.

```
07-chp.middleware/3-macro/lib/plate_slate_web/schema.ex
alias PlateSlateWeb.Schema.Middleware
# «Other schema content»
mutation do
  # «Other mutation fields»
  field :create_menu_item, :menu_item_result do
    arg :input, non_null(:menu_item_input)
    resolve &Resolvers.Menu.create_item/3
    middleware Middleware.ChangesetErrors
  end

end
```

Notice how we've placed it after the resolve/1 call. When it comes time to execute the :create_menu_item field, Absinthe goes through each piece of middleware in order. We want our ChangesetErrors code to process errors that happen during resolution, so we need to place it after the resolve call. If we had it prior, there would never be any errors to transform yet!

You can have as many middleware/1,2 calls on a field as you like, and a few different varieties are supported. In addition to the module-based calls you've seen, you can also do inline functions, refer to specific remote functions, or even refer to local functions. You can also provide a configuration value that will be passed as the second argument during all middleware call/2 invocations.

With this logic extracted into middleware now, we can drastically simplify our :create_menu_item resolver:

```
07-chp.middleware/3-macro/lib/plate_slate_web/resolvers/menu.ex
def create_item(_, %{input: params}, _) do
  with {:ok, item} <- Menu.create_item(params) do
    {:ok, %{menu_item: item}}
  end
end
```

No longer do we need to worry about the error case at all, much less worry about transforming errors.

Running the tests confirms that we are still getting the right results back, even in the error case.

```
$mix test test/plate_slate_web/schema/mutation/create_menu_item_test.exs
..

Finished in 0.2 seconds
2 tests, 0 failures
```

We've taught Absinthe how to handle changesets!

Differences from Plug

The way you add middleware to a field with the macro and the way each of these functions work on a common struct may remind you a lot of how Plug[a] works. While Plug was definitely an inspiration for this API, there is at least one major difference: all Absinthe middleware is always run.

In Plug, if you halt the connection struct, no further plugs are executed. A consequence of this is that it's hard to use plugs to do stuff after your controller actions, because controller actions will frequently send a result to the client, which halts the connection. This is why Phoenix had to add action_fallback as a separate mechanism to do what we're doing here with just a single underlying behavior.

---

a. https://hex.pm/packages/plug

Callback Approach

As we look at our schema as a whole at this point, we can clearly see some other places where we want this error handling to happen. In fact, every field in our mutation object so far can return Ecto changeset errors, and those resolvers would be a lot cleaner if they could use this middleware instead. If we took the macro-based approach we have covered so far, that might look like this:

```
mutation do

  field :ready_order, :order_result do
    arg :id, non_null(:id)
    resolve &Resolvers.Ordering.ready_order/3
➤   middleware Middleware.ChangesetErrors
  end
  field :complete_order, :order_result do
    arg :id, non_null(:id)
    resolve &Resolvers.Ordering.complete_order/3
➤   middleware Middleware.ChangesetErrors
  end

  field :place_order, :order_result do
    arg :input, non_null(:place_order_input)
    resolve &Resolvers.Ordering.place_order/3
➤   middleware Middleware.ChangesetErrors
  end

  field :create_menu_item, :menu_item_result do
    arg :input, non_null(:menu_item_input)
    resolve &Resolvers.Menu.create_item/3
➤   middleware Middleware.ChangesetErrors
  end
end
```

Not only does this seem like unnecessary duplication of code, it's also a bit of an error-prone approach because as your schema grows, it could become easy to miss a field. Even if you have tests to catch it (everyone always tests the error case, right?), what you really want is a schema-wide rule that says something to the effect of, "All fields on the mutation object should run this middleware after resolution." Fortunately, we have a way to do just that and more. Meet the middleware/3 callback:

07-chp.middleware/4-callback/lib/plate_slate_web/schema.ex
```elixir
defmodule PlateSlateWeb.Schema do
  use Absinthe.Schema

  alias PlateSlateWeb.Resolvers
  alias PlateSlateWeb.Schema.Middleware

  def middleware(middleware, _field, _object) do
    middleware
  end
end
```

When you use Absinthe.Schema in your schema module, it injects a middleware/3 function that looks just like the previous one, which you can override if you want to do some dynamic logic. This function is called for every field in the schema, passing the list of middleware already configured for the field—set using the resolve/1 macro or a middleware/1,2 macro call elsewhere in the schema—as well as the actual field and object structs themselves.

We took a look at these %Absinthe.Type.Field{} and %Absinthe.Type.Object{} structs back at the very beginning, in Chapter 2, Building a Schema, on page 15. If you remember, they both have an :identifier key that's set when the field and object are defined in our schema. Let's take a closer look at what's going on here. We'll modify the function and insert a bit of inspection code, and then run a simple query against our API:

```elixir
def middleware(middleware, field, object) do
  IO.inspect [
    object: object.identifier,
    field: field.identifier,
  ]
  middleware
end
```

If we compile our program with iex -S mix and then run this:

```elixir
iex(1)> Absinthe.run("""
{ search(matching: \"Reuben\") { name } }
""", PlateSlateWeb.Schema)
[object: :query, field: :menu_items]
[object: :query, field: :search]
[object: :menu_item, field: :added_on]
[object: :menu_item, field: :description]
```

```
[object: :menu_item, field: :id]
[object: :menu_item, field: :name]
[object: :menu_item, field: :price]
{:ok, %{data: %{"search" => [%{"name" => "Reuben"}]}}}
```

We get a lot of output! You also probably got even more output at compile time. What's going on here? If you run the query again, there's no output at all. What's going on?

The middleware/3 callback is run on every field for an object whenever that object is loaded from the schema. The compile-time output happens because Absinthe does a lot of compile-time checking of your schema, which involves loading every object out of it to make sure it's valid.

Then when we run the GraphQL query, Absinthe has to load the root query object and the menu item object out of the schema in order to execute the document. What about the lack of output if you run the query again? In the current version of Absinthe, there is some in-memory caching that happens on loaded schema objects. If you run the same query twice, it's just going to re-use the in-memory cache for the second run, so no loading happens. In that case, the middleware/3 callback doesn't need to be run.

Back to our goal: we want to apply error-handling middleware on the mutation object, but not elsewhere. With middleware/3, this becomes nice and easy!

07-chp.middleware/4-callback/lib/plate_slate_web/schema.ex
```
def middleware(middleware, _field, %{identifier: :mutation}) do
  middleware ++ [Middleware.ChangesetErrors]
end
def middleware(middleware, _field, _object) do
  middleware
end
```

We've got two middleware/3 clauses: one that pattern matches for an object with the identifier :mutation, and another that is just a fallback. In the :mutation clause, we're taking whatever existing middleware is already specified on the field like a resolver, and we're appending our ChangesetErrors module to the end.

Much like when we had a sequence of middleware/1,2 calls in our schema earlier in the chapter, the middleware placed in this list is executed in order. Remove the middleware callback :create_menu_item field and re-run the tests, confirming that our changeset handling is being applied correctly by our callback.

```
$mix test test/plate_slate_web/schema/mutation/create_menu_item_test.exs
..

Finished in 0.2 seconds
2 tests, 0 failures
```

We can also significantly improve the ordering resolver as well now. Here's just one particular resolver function by way of example:

```
07-chp.middleware/4-callback/lib/plate_slate_web/resolvers/ordering.ex
def ready_order(_, %{id: id}, _) do
  order = Ordering.get_order!(id)
  with {:ok, order} <- Ordering.update_order(order, %{state: "ready"}) do
    {:ok, %{order: order}}
  end
end
```

The middleware/3 callback is incredibly powerful. At the end of the day, all we had to do was add a single function and a few lines of code to our schema in order to educate Absinthe about how to handle changesets coming back from our mutation resolvers, which gave us big wins in readability.

Setting Defaults

Now that we feel comfortable with def middleware, we're in a good place to address an important question: how do fields without specific resolvers actually resolve anything? Throughout the entire book so far, we've had stuff in our schema like this:

```
object :menu_item do
  field :name, :string
  # ... other fields
end
```

Despite the fact that the :name field has no obvious resolver, we nonetheless can include it in a GraphQL query and we get a result. What we need to do is look at what actually happens here because what you'll find is not only a feature you can use yourself, but more importantly, a tool you can customize as necessary when the default behavior doesn't suit the data you are working with.

As you might remember from Making a Query, on page 21, what happens at this point is that the default resolution logic does something equivalent to this:

```
field :name, :string do
  resolve fn parent, _, _ ->
    {:ok, Map.get(parent, :name)}
  end
end
```

Any time a def middleware callback returns an empty list of middleware for a field, Absinthe adds the incredibly simple middleware spec [{Absinthe.Middleware.MapGet, field.identifier}]. Here it is in full:

```
def call(%{source: source} = resolution, key) do
  %{resolution | state: :resolved, value: Map.get(source, key)}
end
```

This is handy when the parent entity in question is a map with atom keys, but it isn't what we want in every scenario.

It's increasingly common that an API will expose data from a variety of data sources, only some of which may have a fully structured schema on hand that will give you nice maps with atom keys. Whether you're hitting a NoSQL database or calling out to a third-party API for JSON data, you're going to eventually run into a situation where the data that you want to expose via GraphQL has string keys or keys that aren't quite what you want.

We can get some of this NoSQL experience without even changing databases, as PostgreSQL has significantly expanded its NoSQL features, and now offers a JSONB column type with which we can store a JSON blob. We're going to add a column to our items table that uses this JSONB type and in it we'll store allergy information about the menu items.

Start by creating the database migration:

```
$ mix ecto.gen.migration add_allergy_info_to_menu_item
```

Add the column in the migration file:

```
07-chp.middleware/5-default/priv/repo/migrations/20170828023859_add_allergy_info_to_menu_item.exs
defmodule PlateSlate.Repo.Migrations.AddAllergyInfoToMenuItem do
  use Ecto.Migration

  def change do
    alter table(:items) do
      add :allergy_info, :map
    end
  end
end
```

Then expose it in Elixir by adding the field in the schema module:

```
07-chp.middleware/5-default/lib/plate_slate/menu/item.ex
field :allergy_info, {:array, :map}
```

That's it as far as the underlying data schema is concerned. Let's run the database migration, and then add a menu item with allergy information:

```
$ mix ecto.migrate
```

In the book code for this chapter, we've added a new item, "Thai Salad," that contains some allergy information. If you don't want to reset your database, you can just copy and paste this into an iex -S mix session:

```
07-chp.middleware/5-default/dev/support/seeds.ex
alias PlateSlate.{Menu, Repo}
category = Repo.get_by(Menu.Category, name: "Sides")
%Menu.Item{
  name: "Thai Salad",
  price: 3.50,
  category: category,
  allergy_info: [
    %{"allergen" => "Peanuts", "severity" => "Contains"},
    %{"allergen" => "Shell Fish", "severity" => "Shared Equipment"},
  ]
} |> Repo.insert!
```

Otherwise, a mix ecto.reset will clear everything out and re-run the seeds. Now that everything is here, let's take a look at what the menu item actually looks like:

```
iex> PlateSlate.Menu.Item |> PlateSlate.Repo.get_by(name: "Thai Salad")
%PlateSlate.Menu.Item{__meta__: #Ecto.Schema.Metadata<:loaded, "items">,
 added_on: ~D[2017-08-27],
 allergy_info: [%{"allergen" => "Peanuts", "severity" => "Contains"},
  %{"allergen" => "Shell Fish", "severity" => "Shared Equipment"}],
 category: #Ecto.Association.NotLoaded<association :category is not loaded>,
 category_id: 2, description: nil, id: 9,
 inserted_at: ~N[2017-08-28 02:39:37.300521], name: "Thai Salad",
 price: #Decimal<3.5>,
 tags: #Ecto.Association.NotLoaded<association :tags is not loaded>,
 updated_at: ~N[2017-08-28 02:39:37.300525]}
```

As you can see, there is an allergy_info key in our Menu.Item struct now, and it contains a list of maps. Each map describes a particular allergen, giving its name and severity information. Some people only care if a particular allergen is an ingredient in the dish, whereas others must avoid anything that shares even preparation surfaces with that allergen.

Notice how the map on the allergy_info: key of the Thai salad is full of string keys and not atom keys—for example, "allergen" instead of :allergen. All we told Ecto is that the :allergy_info column is a :map, and since it can't know anything about its internal structure, it just gives us plain, deserialized JSON. Let's see how this messes up our default resolver, and what we can do to fix it.

Modeling this in our Absinthe schema starts off pretty simply. We need to add the allergy_info field to our menu_item object, and then we need to create a new object to model the information found there:

07-chp.middleware/5-default/lib/plate_slate_web/schema/menu_types.ex

```
object :menu_item do

  interfaces [:search_result]

  field :id, :id
  field :name, :string
  field :description, :string
  field :price, :decimal
  field :added_on, :date
➤ field :allergy_info, list_of(:allergy_info)
end

➤ object :allergy_info do
➤   field :allergen, :string
➤   field :severity, :string
➤ end
```

We run into trouble, though, if we actually try to query this information in GraphiQL:

```
mix phx.server
```

```
{
  menuItems(filter: {name: "Thai Salad"}) {
    allergyInfo { allergen severity }
  }
}
```

All of the allergen and severity fields came back null!

What's going on? We didn't get any errors back from the server, and our code certainly looks valid. If we think back to how the default resolution behavior works, though, this makes sense. Our :allergen field, for example, is going to do a Map.get(parent, :allergen) call on the map inside the JSONB column, but of course there isn't any such key there. :allergen is an atom, but all the keys in that map are strings. We can make this work by doing this:

```
object :allergy_info do
  field :allergen, :string do
    resolve fn parent, _, _ ->
      {:ok, Map.get(parent, "allergen")}
    end
  end
  field :severity, :string do
    resolve fn parent, _, _ ->
      {:ok, Map.get(parent, "severity")}
    end
  end
end
```

This is a bit tedious and verbose. Really what we want to do is change the default resolver for the fields defined on this object:

```
07-chp.middleware/5-default/lib/plate_slate_web/schema.ex
def middleware(middleware, field, %{identifier: :allergy_info} = object) do
  new_middleware = {Absinthe.Middleware.MapGet, to_string(field.identifier)}
  middleware
  |> Absinthe.Schema.replace_default(new_middleware, field, object)
end
def middleware(middleware, _field, %{identifier: :mutation}) do
  middleware ++ [Middleware.ChangesetErrors]
end
def middleware(middleware, _field, _object) do
  middleware
end
```

We'll add an additional function head for middleware/3 that pattern matches for fields where the object definition's identifier matches :allergy_info.

This new code sets up a new specification using the Absinthe.Middleware.MapGet middleware, and passes as its option a stringified version of our field identifier. The middleware will then use the string identifier (instead of an atom) to retrieve the correct value from the map. With this new middleware definition, we call the Absinthe.Schema.replace_default/4 function, which handles swapping it in for the existing default in the list.

We could just return [{Absinthe.Middleware.MapGet, to_string(field.identifier)}] from the function and be done with it, but the replace_default/4 function is more future-proof. This is both from the perspective of Absinthe itself, which may decide to change its default somewhere down the line, and also from the perspective of your own schema. In Chapter 9, Tuning Resolution, on page 167, we'll add some tracing middleware, and this function makes sure we don't end up ignoring that.

Now if we try our query in GraphiQL again:

```
GraphiQL    ▶    Prettify                                                    〈 Docs

1 ▾ {                                          ▾ {
2     menuItems(filter: {name:"Thai Salad"}) {    ▾  "data": {
3        allergyInfo { allergen severity }       ▾    "menuItems": [
4     }                                          ▾      {
5  }                                             ▾        "allergyInfo": [
                                                            {
                                                              "severity": "Contains",
                                                              "allergen": "Peanuts"
                                                            },
                                                            {
                                                              "severity": "Shared Equipment",
                                                              "allergen": "Shell Fish"
                                                            }
                                                          ]
                                                        }
                                                      ]
                                                    }
                                                  }

   QUERY VARIABLES
```

We get the expected result!

Middleware is an enormously important tool for keeping your resolvers focused, giving you an incredible amount of control over what happens when executing a document. It's also a great feature for third-party packages that want to augment Absinthe's resolution logic; the middleware/3 callback is a handy integration point.

Moving On

During this chapter, you've learned an important new skill: how to build and use middleware that can modify the way fields are resolved during document execution. You know how to configure middleware on an individual basis, using the middleware/1,2 macros, and at the schema level, using middleware/3. Armed with this knowledge and an understanding of the MapGet middleware that's used as Absinthe's default resolution logic, you're ready to build much more interesting patterns in your Absinthe schemas.

In the next chapter, we're going to look at a critical use of middleware: securing your application behind authentication and authorization checks.

Before we move on, however, give this challenge a shot:

1. Build some middleware that can be used to measure how long it takes to resolve a field. It should print how long it took and the current path. Hint: you may need to have the same middleware appear more than once in the middleware list. Consult the Absinthe.Resolution module docs to see what data is available to you in middleware.
2. Apply the middleware to a specific field in our schema using the middleware/1,2 macro.
3. Apply the middleware to all the fields in the schema that are running custom resolvers/middleware.

Once you're feeling comfortable with the mechanics of building and applying middleware, let's move on to how to use that knowledge to secure our API.

## CHAPTER 8

Securing with Authentication and Authorization

With some basic functionality squared away and Absinthe tools ready at hand, we're all set to take the API live. When any API goes live, even internally within an organization, there is generally a need to secure portions of the API behind authentication and authorization checks.

In this chapter, we'll cover how to add these checks to an Absinthe schema, continuing to build on the restaurant ordering system, PlateSlate. Along the way, you'll discover how to tailor mechanisms that you're probably already familiar with, like token-based authentication, to work within the greater flexibility of a GraphQL API.

Let's start by giving our hungry restaurant customers access to our system to create orders.

Logging In

Online ordering is all the rage right now, as customers look to beat the lines by placing an order online and then picking it up shortly afterward. The (theoretical) mobile team has been hard at work on a mobile application that customers can use to place orders from the comfort of their homes, so we need to provide a way to do this securely.

So far, when we've been responding to API requests, we haven't been concerned with who is making those requests; we've been focused on how to deal with the data itself. Both menu updates and the orders themselves have come from within the restaurant, so we could just accept whatever it sent us. If we're going to accept orders from the customers themselves, however, not only do we need to keep track of who has ordered what, but we also need to give each customer the ability to view and subscribe to their orders (and no one else's).

Authentication

Tracking customers also entails tracking employees, because we need a way to permit employees to carry out actions that are forbidden for customers, like editing the menu or completing an order. In fact, most of the operations in the system at the moment ought only to be carried out by employees.

The first step then is being able to identify whether someone is an employee or a customer. From there, we'll see how we can use this information to perform authentication and authorization checks within our schema.

Our goal is to support a simple mutation like the following:

```
mutation Login($email: String!, $password: String!) {
  login(role: EMPLOYEE, email: $email, password: $password) {
    token
  }
}
```

This should return an API token valid for this particular employee if the supplied email address and password are correct. The response from our API should look something like this:

```
{
  "data": {
    "login": {
      "token": "EMPLOYEE-TOKEN-HERE"
    }
  }
}
```

To do this, though, we need to make a few additions to our database and Ecto schemas in order to have the data on hand. We'll get those changes in, and then we'll build out the code necessary to integrate the data with our API.

There are many different ways to model users, but we don't need something particularly complicated for our use case. We're going to use a single users table that will hold the user's name, email address, and password. We'll also have a role column to indicate whether they're an employee or a customer.

Our first order of business is to create the schema and migration we need to manage these users. We can use a Phoenix generator to get some of the basics going:

```
$ mix phx.gen.schema Accounts.User users \
  name:string \
  email:string \
  password:string \
  role:string
```

Make a small change to the generated migration to add a unique index on the user email and role:

08-chp.auth/1-start/priv/repo/migrations/20170828175714_create_users.exs
```
defmodule PlateSlate.Repo.Migrations.CreateUsers do
  use Ecto.Migration

  def change do
    create table(:users) do
      add :name, :string
      add :email, :string
      add :password, :string
      add :role, :string

      timestamps()
    end

➤    create unique_index(:users, [:email, :role])

  end
end
```

There's a useful package called :comeonin_ecto_password that we're going to use to hash the password for us. Let's add it with a compatible hash algorithm dependency to our mix.exs file:

08-chp.auth/1-start/mix.exs
```
defp deps do
  [
➤    {:comeonin_ecto_password, "~> 2.1"},
➤    {:pbkdf2_elixir, "~> 0.12.0"},
    # «Other deps»
  ]
end
```

Here's all we need to make a small tweak to the User schema to set that up:

08-chp.auth/1-start/lib/plate_slate/accounts/user.ex
```
schema "users" do
  field :email, :string
  field :name, :string
➤  field :password, Comeonin.Ecto.Password
  field :role, :string

  timestamps()
end
```

Additionally, we're going to put a couple of extra columns on the orders table that we can use to relate a given order to the customer who ordered it.

```
$ mix ecto.gen.migration AddCustomerToOrders
```

08-chp.auth/1-start/priv/repo/migrations/20170828180804_add_customer_to_orders.exs
```elixir
defmodule PlateSlate.Repo.Migrations.AddCustomerToOrders do
  use Ecto.Migration

  def change do
    alter table(:orders) do
      add :customer_id, references(:users)
    end
  end
end
```

After we run our migrations, we'll be all set up:

```
$ mix ecto.migrate
Compiling 1 file (.ex)
Generated plate_slate app
[info] == Running Migrations.CreateUsers.change/0 forward
[info] create table users
[info] create index users_email_role_index
[info] == Migrated in 0.0s
[info] == Running Migrations.AddCustomerToOrders.change/0 forward
[info] == Migrated in 0.0s
```

The column we've added to the orders table needs a corresponding line in the order schema module, and the addition of the :customer_id to the changeset function's cast list:

08-chp.auth/1-start/lib/plate_slate/ordering/order.ex
```elixir
schema "orders" do
➤   field :customer_id, :integer
    # «other schema fields»
end
def changeset(%Order{} = order, attrs) do
  order
➤   |> cast(attrs, [:customer_id, :customer_number, :ordered_at, :state])
  |> cast_embed(:items)
end
```

We can use the new "users" table to build out a basic PlateSlate.Accounts module and authenticate/3 function:

08-chp.auth/1-start/lib/plate_slate/accounts/accounts.ex
```elixir
defmodule PlateSlate.Accounts do
  @moduledoc """
  The Accounts context.
  """
```

```
  import Ecto.Query, warn: false
  alias PlateSlate.Repo
  alias Comeonin.Ecto.Password

  alias PlateSlate.Accounts.User

  def authenticate(role, email, password) do
    user = Repo.get_by(User, role: to_string(role), email: email)

    with %{password: digest} <- user,
    true <- Password.valid?(password, digest) do
      {:ok, user}
    else
      _ -> :error
    end
  end
end
```

We're using a pretty simple authentication mechanism here: just role, email, and password. Our function looks up a customer by role and email address, and then the password the customer supplies is compared against the stored password. If the email belongs to a user, and if the password is valid, our function here will return {:ok, user}. You can find a variety of authentication and user management systems on Hex,[1] and you may well find that one of those suits your particular needs very well. The way you'd integrate this with Absinthe will be almost exactly the same in each case.

Before we integrate authentication into PlateSlate's API, fire up iex -S mix and get a feel for using authenticate/3. Here's an example of creating employee and customer users and then successfully authenticating them:

```
iex(1)> alias PlateSlate.Accounts
iex(2)> %Accounts.User{} |>
Accounts.User.changeset(%{role: "employee", name: "Becca Wilson",
  email: "foo@example.com", password: "abc123"}) |> PlateSlate.Repo.insert!
#=> %Accounts.User{...}

iex(3)> %Accounts.User{} |>
Accounts.User.changeset(%{role: "customer", name: "Joe Hubert",
  email: "bar@example.com", password: "abc123"}) |> PlateSlate.Repo.insert!
#=> %Accounts.User{...}

iex(4)> Accounts.authenticate("employee", "foo@example.com", "abc123")
{:ok,
 %Accounts.User{
   email: "foo@example.com", id: 1, inserted_at: ~N[2017-08-28 18:14:15.785375],
   name: "Becca Wilson",
   password: "$pbkdf2-sha512$16...",
   role: "employee", updated_at: ~N[2017-08-28 18:14:15.786666]}}
```

---

1. https://hex.pm

If you try to log in with either an invalid email/password or with the wrong role, you'll get an :error atom as the result:

```
iex(5)> alias PlateSlate.Accounts
iex(6)> Accounts.authenticate("customer", "foo@example.com", "abc123")
:error
iex(7)> Accounts.authenticate("employee", "foo@example.com", "123")
:error
iex(8)> Accounts.authenticate("employee", "bad@example.com", "abc123")
:error
```

While simple, this user modeling accomplishes a lot. The role column lets us distinguish employees from customers, and this makes it easy to write code that handles both as we move forward.

Login API

With the underlying database work all set, the next task is to define the mutation for your API. Head over to your Absinthe schema and add a :login mutation field to the root mutation type:

```
08-chp.auth/2-login/lib/plate_slate_web/schema.ex
mutation do

  field :login, :session do
    arg :email, non_null(:string)
    arg :password, non_null(:string)
    arg :role, non_null(:role)
    resolve &Resolvers.Accounts.login/3
  end
  # «Other mutation fields»
end
```

The mutation requires an email address, password, and role, and it returns a :session type. We'll be creating a new type module to house this type and the others like it:

```
08-chp.auth/2-login/lib/plate_slate_web/schema/accounts_types.ex
defmodule PlateSlateWeb.Schema.AccountsTypes do
  use Absinthe.Schema.Notation

  object :session do
    field :token, :string
    field :user, :user
  end

  enum :role do
    value :employee
    value :customer
  end
```

```
  interface :user do
    field :email, :string
    field :name, :string
    resolve_type fn
      %{role: "employee"}, _ -> :employee
      %{role: "customer"}, _ -> :customer
    end
  end
  object :employee do
    interface :user
    field :email, :string
    field :name, :string
  end

  object :customer do
    interface :user
    field :email, :string
    field :name, :string
    field :orders, list_of(:order)
  end
end
```

There are a couple of interesting types here. At the top, we've got the :session object returned from the :login mutation, which contains an API token and a user field. This user field is an interface, which you learned about back in Chapter 4, Adding Flexibility, on page 59. Both employee and customer objects have email and name fields. However, we still want to keep them as separate objects because, as our API grows, there will be fields that only apply to one but not the other. In a bit, we'll be filling out the orders field on the customer, but this field doesn't make much sense on an employee.

The resolution function for the login field is Resolvers.Accounts.login/3. We'll add it in a new resolver module:

```
08-chp.auth/2-login/lib/plate_slate_web/resolvers/accounts.ex
defmodule PlateSlateWeb.Resolvers.Accounts do
  alias PlateSlate.Accounts

  def login(_, %{email: email, password: password, role: role}, _) do
    case Accounts.authenticate(role, email, password) do
      {:ok, user} ->
        token = PlateSlateWeb.Authentication.sign(%{
          role: role, id: user.id
        })
        {:ok, %{token: token, user: user}}
      _ ->
        {:error, "incorrect email or password"}
    end
  end
end
```

Here we're using the Accounts.authenticate/3 function we built earlier, and if it's successful, creating a token using the PlateSlateWeb.Authentication module. This module is really just a small wrapper about the token generation abilities we get from Phoenix.Token.

```elixir
08-chp.auth/2-login/lib/plate_slate_web/authentication.ex
defmodule PlateSlateWeb.Authentication do
  @user_salt "user salt"

  def sign(data) do
    Phoenix.Token.sign(PlateSlateWeb.Endpoint, @user_salt, data)
  end

  def verify(token) do
    Phoenix.Token.verify(PlateSlateWeb.Endpoint, @user_salt, token, [
      max_age: 365 * 24 * 3600
    ])
  end

end
```

The token encodes information about the type of session, as well as who the session belongs to, by including the employee.id. We'll need this information to know what role (customers or employees) to use when we want to look up the user record later.

Now we're ready to write some basic tests to ensure our mutation is built and behaves correctly. The first thing we'll do is create a small helper module for generating users so that we can have some on hand in this and any future tests:

```elixir
08-chp.auth/3-context/test/support/factory.ex
defmodule Factory do
  def create_user(role) do
    int = :erlang.unique_integer([:positive, :monotonic])
    params = %{
      name: "Person #{int}",
      email: "fake-#{int}@example.com",
      password: "super-secret",
      role: role
    }

    %PlateSlate.Accounts.User{}
    |> PlateSlate.Accounts.User.changeset(params)
    |> PlateSlate.Repo.insert!
  end
end
```

With that out of the way, we can look at the login test itself:

```elixir
08-chp.auth/2-login/test/plate_slate_web/schema/mutation/login_test.exs
defmodule PlateSlateWeb.Schema.Mutation.LoginEmployeeTest do
  use PlateSlateWeb.ConnCase, async: true
```

```
@query """
mutation ($email: String!) {
  login(role: EMPLOYEE, email:$email,password:"super-secret") {
    token
    user { name }
  }
}
"""
test "creating an employee session" do
  user = Factory.create_user("employee")
  response = post(build_conn(), "/api", %{
    query: @query,
    variables: %{"email" => user.email}
  })
  assert %{"data" => %{ "login" => %{
    "token" => token,
    "user" => user_data
  }}} = json_response(response, 200)

  assert %{"name" => user.name} == user_data
  assert {:ok, %{role: :employee, id: user.id}} ==
    PlateSlateWeb.Authentication.verify(token)
  end
end
```

We use the employee's information in our test to ensure that, given the correct credentials, the correct token is returned from our :login mutation. Let's run the test:

```
$ mix test test/plate_slate_web/schema/mutation/login_test.exs
.

Finished in 0.1 seconds
1 test, 0 failures
```

We can also see this working in GraphiQL because of the user we created in IEx earlier, so let's give that a shot by starting the server:

```
mix phx.server
```

```
mutation {
  login(role: CUSTOMER, email:"bar@example.com",password:"abc123") {
    token
    user { name __typename }
  }
}
```

It worked! As shown in the figure on page 148, we got back an auth token and some information about the employee we just authenticated. Now we just take that authentication token and...do what with it? Is it something that should get passed to future GraphQL fields?

This is the next thing we need to figure out.

Using the Execution Context

Now that we have a way to identify users, we need to figure out how to integrate this information with the processing of GraphQL requests so that fields that need to be secured have access to the relevant data.

One option would be to just make each field resolution function responsible for authenticating the user and have the token passed as normal arguments, but this causes two problems. If we need this information in several fields, we require the user to pass in the token in many places—not a very nice API for clients. It wouldn't be very nice for the server, either; it would need to look up the same user in each field even though the information returned would be the same each time.

The Absinthe feature that addresses this problem is called the *execution context*. It's a place where we can set values that will be available to all of our resolvers.

Handily, the final argument passed to the resolver function is an Absinthe.Resolution struct, which includes the context. Here's a basic example of using a context and how the context is provided to Absinthe:

```
defmodule ContextExample.Schema do
  use Absinthe.Schema

  query do
    field :greeting, :string do
      resolve fn _, _, %{context: context} ->
        {:ok, "Welcome #{context.current_user.name}"}
      end
    end
  end
end
```

```
# Our document
doc = "{ greeting }"

# Our context
context = %{current_user: %{name: "Alicia"}}

# Running Absinthe manually
Absinthe.run(doc, ContextExample.Schema, context: context)
```

If you paste this into iex -S mix, you'll see this result:

```
{:ok, %{data: %{"greeting" => "Welcome Alicia"}}}
```

The context that you passed into the Absinthe.run/3 call is the same context you accessed in the third argument to the resolution function of the greeting field. After that, you're just accessing the values you placed inside of it earlier.

Context Is Everywhere

 Whatever we pass into the context is always made available as is in the resolution functions. Importantly, the context is always available in every field at every level, and it's this property that gives it its name: it's the "context" in which execution is happening.

Our application code, however, does not explicitly call Absinthe.run/3 but instead uses Absinthe.Plug, which executes the GraphQL documents that we receive over HTTP. We need to make sure that the context is set up ahead of time so that it has what it needs to execute documents.

Storing Auth Info in Context with a Plug

To recap the relationship between Absinthe and Plug, remember that we placed an Absinthe.Plug in our router at the API path, which looks like this:

```
08-chp.auth/1-start/lib/plate_slate_web/router.ex
scope "/" do
  pipe_through :api

  forward "/api", Absinthe.Plug,
    schema: PlateSlateWeb.Schema

  forward "/graphiql", Absinthe.Plug.GraphiQL,
    schema: PlateSlateWeb.Schema,
    interface: :simple,
    socket: PlateSlateWeb.UserSocket
end
```

We've got a root scope that pipes requests through the :api Phoenix router pipeline, which is basically just a sequence of plugs that operate on the connection. Within this scope, we're just passing along the conn to one of the two Absinthe.Plug plugs, which will run any query document sent to us with the specified schema.

Thankfully, Absinthe.Plug knows how to extract certain values from the connection automatically for use in the context. All we need to do is write a plug that inserts the appropriate values into the connection first.

Let's build it! We'll start by adding the reference to the new plug in our :api pipeline:

```
08-chp.auth/3-context/lib/plate_slate_web/router.ex
pipeline :api do
  plug :accepts, ["json"]
  plug PlateSlateWeb.Context
end
```

We added the PlateSlateWeb.Context plug so that it will run prior to Absinthe.Plug and give us a place to set up our context.

```
08-chp.auth/3-context/lib/plate_slate_web/context.ex
defmodule PlateSlateWeb.Context do
  @behaviour Plug
  import Plug.Conn

  def init(opts), do: opts

  def call(conn, _) do
    context = build_context(conn)
    IO.inspect [context: context]
    Absinthe.Plug.put_options(conn, context: context)
  end

  defp build_context(conn) do
    with ["Bearer " <> token] <- get_req_header(conn, "authorization"),
         {:ok, data} <- PlateSlateWeb.Authentication.verify(token),
         %{} = user <- get_user(data) do
      %{current_user: user}
    else
      _ -> %{}
    end
  end

  defp get_user(%{id: id, role: role}) do
    PlateSlate.Accounts.lookup(role, id)
  end
end
```

If you're unfamiliar with the Plug framework, that's okay; the core idea is pretty straightforward. Let's walk through it.

We have an init callback, which receives any options that get passed to our module (but we're not using any of those, so we just pass them through).

The core functionality of the plug is the call/2 callback, which takes a %Plug. Conn{} struct. Inside this struct is a private key, which is a place for libraries like Absinthe to place values for later use. We use the call/2 function to return another %Plug.Conn{} struct, with our current user helpfully placed behind a context key in the private absinthe namespace. It turns out that this namespace is exactly where Absinthe.Plug looks for a prebuilt context.

We get the user in the build_context/1 function by looking up the header to get the Phoenix token sent with the request, and then using that token to find the related user (whether they're a customer or employee). If there is no "authorization" header or if there is no user for a given API key, with will simply fall through to its else clause, where we'll return the context without a :current_user specified.

The Accounts.lookup/2 is just a little helper function we're going to use to help keep account-related responsibilities out of the plug itself, so it doesn't need to worry about implementation details.

08-chp.auth/3-context/lib/plate_slate/accounts/accounts.ex
```
def lookup(role, id) do
  Repo.get_by(User, role: to_string(role), id: id)
end
```

With the context placed in the connection, Absinthe.Plug is properly set up to pass this value along when it runs the document, and it will be available to our resolvers. Note that we've got a little debugging going on with the IO.inspect [context: context]. This gives us a cheap and easy way to look at what our context is until we have something more real in place.

The final question is how to use this from within GraphiQL, because there isn't any place in the GraphiQL interface we've been using to configure headers. It's time to break out the advanced GraphiQL interface. Head over to your router and remove the interface: :simple option on the Absinthe.Plug.Graphiql plug:

08-chp.auth/3-context/lib/plate_slate_web/router.ex
```
forward "/graphiql", Absinthe.Plug.GraphiQL,
  schema: PlateSlateWeb.Schema,
  socket: PlateSlateWeb.UserSocket
```

Now start your server (mix phx.server), browse to http://localhost:4000/graphiql, and behold GraphiQL Workspace as shown in the figure on page 152.

There's a lot more here! Let's run the same mutation we did earlier:

This operates as it did before, but now we have the ability to configure GraphiQL to use the token that was just returned as a header to authorize future requests.

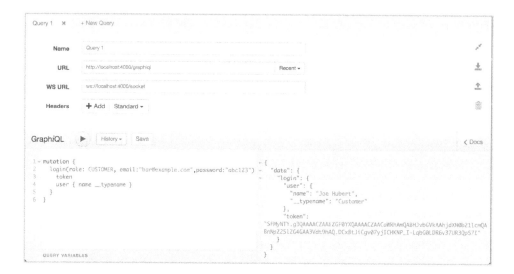

Select the token string value (without quotes) in the response box and copy it. Click the Standard drop-down, select "OAuth 2 Bearer Token," and paste the token after Bearer.

After clicking OK, you should see that you've got a header configured in the upper right-hand part of the GraphiQL Workspace.

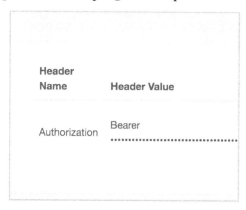

Let's see if this header is being used to set our context correctly. Run a simple GraphQL query like this:

```
{
  menuItems { name }
}
```

In your console logs, you should see something like the following (we've cleaned it up a bit here for readability):

```
[
  context: %{
    current_user: %PlateSlate.Accounts.User{
      __meta__: #Ecto.Schema.Metadata<:loaded, "users">,
      email: "bar@example.com",
      id: 2,
      inserted_at: ~N[2017-08-29 01:23:15.743144],
      name: "Joe Hubert",
      password: "$pbkdf2-sha512$160...",
      role: "customer",
      updated_at: ~N[2017-08-29 01:23:15.744546]
    }
  }
]
```

This means it worked! The essence of an authentication system is the ability to verify that someone is who they say they are, and that's exactly what we have here. The next step is to sort out what exactly that person is permitted to do, now that we know who they are.

Securing Fields

Now that we have a way to get the current user, we have what we need to enforce authorization on particular fields: we can just check the context. Having the current user also gives us the ability to retrieve associated records in our resolvers, returning information specific to the user.

Inline Authorization

Before we let customers anywhere near this API, we need to put some authorization checks between the current user and the variety of important actions our API can perform. Just as we did before, the most direct way to do this is to use the third argument to each resolver to pattern match for the desired case.

Let's start by securing the :create_menu_item resolver, as we really don't want to let customers run wild with that one.

```
08-chp.auth/3-context/lib/plate_slate_web/resolvers/menu.ex
def create_item(_, %{input: params}, %{context: context}) do
  case context do
    %{current_user: %{role: "employee"}} ->
      with {:ok, item} <- Menu.create_item(params) do
        {:ok, %{menu_item: item}}
      end
    _ ->
      {:error, "unauthorized"}
  end
end
```

In the function head, we pattern match the context out of the resolution struct in the third argument. Then we're just wrapping the contents of the function in a `case` expression, carrying on as normal if the context contains an employee as the current user, or returning an error otherwise.

If we run our tests right now, we'll get two errors!

```
$ mix test test/plate_slate_web/schema/mutation/create_menu_item_test.exs
Compiling 5 files (.ex)

# ... test output elided

Finished in 0.2 seconds
2 tests, 2 failures
```

This makes sense, of course, because we aren't doing anything in our tests to set up a context that might permit the creation of menu items. Let's change that. We just need to generate a user and put an "authorization" header on the conn.

```
08-chp.auth/3-context/test/plate_slate_web/schema/mutation/create_menu_item_test.exs
test "createMenuItem field creates an item", %{category_id: category_id} do
  menu_item = %{
    "name" => "French Dip",
    "description" => "Roast beef, caramelized onions, horseradish, ...",
    "price" => "5.75",
    "categoryId" => category_id,
  }
  user = Factory.create_user("employee")
  conn = build_conn() |> auth_user(user)
  conn = post conn, "/api",
    query: @query,
    variables: %{"menuItem" => menu_item}

  assert json_response(conn, 200) == %{
    "data" => %{
      "createMenuItem" => %{
        "errors" => nil,
        "menuItem" => %{
          "name" => menu_item["name"],
          "description" => menu_item["description"],
```

```
              "price" => menu_item["price"]
            }
          }
        }
      }
    }
  end

➤ defp auth_user(conn, user) do
➤   token = PlateSlateWeb.Authentication.sign(%{role: user.role, id: user.id})
➤   put_req_header(conn, "authorization", "Bearer #{token}")
➤ end
```

In essence, this is exactly what we did in GraphiQL. Fixing the next test is easy too, as you can just reuse the auth_user helper function we've got there. Consider extracting it to the ConnCase module for easy use in other tests.

While it's good that we've fixed these test regressions, we really ought to also add a test demonstrating what happens if a user is unauthorized.

08-chp.auth/3-context/test/plate_slate_web/schema/mutation/create_menu_item_test.exs

```
test "must be authorized as an employee to do menu item creation",
%{category_id: category_id} do
  menu_item = %{
    "name" => "Reuben",
    "description" => "Roast beef, caramelized onions, horseradish, ...",
    "price" =>  "5.75",
    "categoryId" => category_id,
  }
  user = Factory.create_user("customer")
  conn = build_conn() |> auth_user(user)
  conn = post conn, "/api",
    query: @query,
    variables: %{"menuItem" => menu_item}
➤   assert json_response(conn, 200) == %{
➤     "data" => %{"createMenuItem" => nil},
➤     "errors" => [%{
➤       "locations" => [%{"column" => 0, "line" => 2}],
➤       "message" => "unauthorized",
➤       "path" => ["createMenuItem"]
➤     }]
➤   }
  end
```

Now that you know resolvers can check the current user for authorization, you might be asking yourself if you're going to be forced to add authorization checks to every single field that you want to secure. This is going to get pretty tedious if you have to do that, for there's already a handful of top-level resolvers you need to secure. Fortunately, there's a tool you can apply here to extract common logic: middleware!

Authorization Middleware

Adding authorization checks inside all of our resolvers is going to produce a lot of clutter, so let's build some middleware to handle this problem once and for all.

As you recall, we have two choices for how to apply middleware: the middleware/2 macro for configuring individual fields, and the middleware/3 callback function for taking a pattern-based approach. Different fields each have slightly different authorization conditions, so we're going to use the middleware/2 macro to annotate them individually. Using this middleware should look something like this:

08-chp.auth/4-middleware/lib/plate_slate_web/schema.ex
```
field :create_menu_item, :menu_item_result do
  arg :input, non_null(:menu_item_input)
  middleware Middleware.Authorize, "employee"
  resolve &Resolvers.Menu.create_item/3
end
```

Then in the resolver, we can just go back to how it was before we had the authorization check:

08-chp.auth/4-middleware/lib/plate_slate_web/resolvers/menu.ex
```
def create_item(_, %{input: params}, _) do
  with {:ok, item} <- Menu.create_item(params) do
    {:ok, %{menu_item: item}}
  end
end
```

Note that we no longer need to check the type of the current_user in the resolution function or handle the possibility that there is no current_user at all. The middleware will handle all of this for us!

Let's take a look:

08-chp.auth/4-middleware/lib/plate_slate_web/schema/middleware/authorize.ex
```
Line 1  defmodule PlateSlateWeb.Schema.Middleware.Authorize do
   -      @behaviour Absinthe.Middleware
   -
   -      def call(resolution, role) do
   5        with %{current_user: current_user} <- resolution.context,
   -        true <- correct_role?(current_user, role) do
   -          resolution
   -        else
   -          _ ->
  10            resolution
   -            |> Absinthe.Resolution.put_result({:error, "unauthorized"})
   -      end
   -    end
   -
```

```
15  defp correct_role?(%{}, :any), do: true
    defp correct_role?(%{role: role}, role), do: true
    defp correct_role?(_, _), do: false
  end
```

By specifying @behaviour Absinthe.Middleware, the compiler will make sure that we provide a call/2 callback function. The function takes an %Absinthe.Resolution{} struct and will also need to return one, as described in the previous chapter.

The %Absinthe.Resolution{} struct should feel familiar; it's the same value passed as the last argument to our resolution functions, and it contains our :context so that it's accessible to resolvers and middleware. It's useful in resolvers—in a read-only sense—but middleware can manipulate resolution structs to enhance how documents are executed.

The call/2 function also takes a second argument, which is whatever additional value was supplied to the middleware/2 call in our schema. In the previous :create_menu_item field example, we added the middleware with an argument, "employee", which means that role on line 4 is "employee". We check this type against the context's current user and if they match, we pass the resolution onward, unchanged. There's also an option for specifying middleware Authenticate, :any, which permits any user to view the page, whether they're a customer or an employee, but it does still require that the user is logged in.

If the types don't match or if there is no current user at all, we use the Absinthe.Resolution.put_result/2 function to stick an error on the resolution struct, and if there are any errors on the resolution struct, the Absinthe.Resolution middleware will not call our resolve function.

You can now annotate any fields that need to be authenticated with the middleware/1,2 macro prior to the resolve/1 macro, and Absinthe will handle the authentication check prior to doing any resolution.

This is handy now that we want to turn to the central task of letting customers themselves place orders. This has two components to it. There's an authorization component where we only want to allow an order to be placed by a logged-in customer or employee, and then there's also a data component where if the person placing the order is a customer, their ID needs to be associated with the record. The first of these can be handled by the newly minted middleware:

```
08-chp.auth/4-middleware/lib/plate_slate_web/schema.ex
field :place_order, :order_result do
  arg :input, non_null(:place_order_input)
➤ middleware Middleware.Authorize, :any
  resolve &Resolvers.Ordering.place_order/3
end
```

To configure the params, though, we'll need to head over to the place_order/3 resolver function and conditionally add a value to the place_order_input if the current user is a customer:

```
08-chp.auth/4-middleware/lib/plate_slate_web/resolvers/ordering.ex
def place_order(_, %{input: place_order_input}, %{context: context}) do
  place_order_input = case context[:current_user] do
    %{role: "customer", id: id} ->
      Map.put(place_order_input, :customer_id, id)
    _ ->
      place_order_input
  end
  with {:ok, order} <- Ordering.create_order(place_order_input) do
    Absinthe.Subscription.publish(PlateSlateWeb.Endpoint, order,
      new_order: "*"
    )
    {:ok, %{order: order}}
  end
end
```

With this change, we've officially got a customer-based ordering system! Let's place a couple via GraphiQL:

```
mutation {
  placeOrder(input:{items:[{quantity: 2, menuItemId:"1"}]}) {
    order {
      customerNumber
    }
    errors { key message }
  }
}
```

After you've run this mutation, head to IEx and look up the last order:

```
iex(3)> PlateSlate.Ordering.Order |> Ecto.Query.last |> PlateSlate.Repo.one
%PlateSlate.Ordering.Order{__meta__: #Ecto.Schema.Metadata<:loaded, "orders">,
  customer_id: 1, id: 3,
  ...}
```

It's got a customer ID! Online ordering is live. However, if we run our tests at this point, we'll see that we've got a failing case:

```
ben:plate_slate ben$ mix test
.......................
  1) test new orders can be subscribed to (...)
     test/plate_slate_web/schema/subscription/new_order_test.exs:16
     ...
     stacktrace:
       test/plate_slate_web/schema/subscription/new_order_test.exs:27: (test)

Finished in 2.1 seconds
26 tests, 1 failure
```

We've broken our subscriptions test! This isn't actually that surprising if you think about it, because this test places an order, and we've just put authentication checks in the middle of that process. There are a couple ways to fix this. We could simply refactor how we connect to the socket, passing in and parsing some token as we do with the headers in our PlateSlateWeb.Context plug. There's a Absinthe.Phoenix.Socket.put_options/2[2] function that we can use to set the context exactly like we did with Plug.

There's a slightly more interesting option, however. Unlike HTTP requests, a Phoenix channel connection is stateful. If a GraphQL document makes a change to the context, this will affect other subsequent documents that are executed by that client.

To enable this, we need to modify our login mutation to persist a change to the context, and then we'll need to add a login mutation call to the subscription test:

```
08-chp.auth/4-middleware/lib/plate_slate_web/schema.ex
field :login, :session do
  arg :email, non_null(:string)
  arg :password, non_null(:string)
  arg :role, non_null(:role)
  resolve &Resolvers.Accounts.login/3
  middleware fn res, _ ->
    with %{value: %{user: user}} <- res do
      %{res | context: Map.put(res.context, :current_user, user)}
    end
  end
end
```

This is an example of some inline middleware, where we've just got a simple anonymous function inline with the field definition. What we're doing is pattern matching via with on the resolution struct to see if the value returned by the resolver includes a user. If it does, we're logged in, so we can update the context accordingly. Not only does this help with subscription fields, but it also ensures that any sub-selections on the login field are authorized properly.

To get the test back to green, we just need to log in:

```
08-chp.auth/4-middleware/test/plate_slate_web/schema/subscription/new_order_test.exs
@login """
mutation ($email: String!, $role: Role!) {
  login(role: $role, password: "super-secret", email:$email) {
    token
  }
}
"""
```

2. https://hexdocs.pm/absinthe_phoenix/Absinthe.Phoenix.Socket.html#put_options/2

```
➤  test "new orders can be subscribed to", %{socket: socket} do
➤    # login
➤    user = Factory.create_user("employee")
➤    ref = push_doc socket, @login, variables: %{
➤      "email" => user.email,
➤      "role" => "EMPLOYEE",
➤    }
➤    assert_reply ref, :ok, %{data: %{"login" => %{"token" => _}}}, 1_000

      # setup a subscription
      ref = push_doc socket, @subscription
      assert_reply ref, :ok, %{subscriptionId: subscription_id}
      # «Rest of test case»
  end
```

Note that we're providing a slightly longer timeout value (1_000) to the assert_reply call. Login mutations will generally take slightly longer because of the password hashing that happens.

Running mix test again shows the tests are green.

Authorizing Subscriptions

While we're on the subject, subscriptions pose some interesting challenges with respect to authorization. For example, we straight away run into some trouble with the new_order field because it uses a "*" topic. The way it's built right now, every customer who subscribes is going to get pushed information about everyone else's order. This is probably not good.

Fixing this isn't simply a matter of adding authorization middleware to the new_order field. Middleware runs when the document is executed, but the document won't be executed until an actual order is placed and published. In other words, we'd still be letting clients create the subscription, but then instead of an order, they'd get "unauthorized" when an event happens. What we want to do is scope new_order so that when a subscription is created by a customer, we only route that customer's orders to that subscription.

Let's capture this problem in a test case:

08-chp.auth/5-subscriptions/test/plate_slate_web/schema/subscription/new_order_test.exs
```
test "customers can't see other customer orders", %{socket: socket} do
  customer1 = Factory.create_user("customer")
  # login as customer1
  ref = push_doc socket, @login, variables: %{
    "email" => customer1.email,
    "role" => "CUSTOMER"
  }
  assert_reply ref, :ok, %{data: %{"login" => %{"token" => _}}}, 1_000
```

```
  # subscribe to orders
  ref = push_doc socket, @subscription
  assert_reply ref, :ok, %{subscriptionId: _subscription_id}

  # customer1 places order
  place_order(customer1)
  assert_push "subscription:data", _

  # customer2 places order
  customer2 = Factory.create_user("customer")
  place_order(customer2)
  refute_receive _
end
defp place_order(customer) do
  order_input = %{"customerNumber" => 24,
    "items" => [%{"quantity" => 2, "menuItemId" => menu_item("Reuben").id}]
  }
  {:ok, %{data: %{"placeOrder" => _}}} = Absinthe.run(@mutation,
    PlateSlateWeb.Schema, [
      context: %{current_user: customer},
      variables: %{"input" => order_input},
  ])
end
```

This test case starts off just like our other test in this module. We create a customer, log them in, and then subscribe to new_order. We affirm that we get messages when customer1 places an order. Then we create an additional user and place an order under that user. At this point, the socket we're testing shouldn't receive anything, since this isn't an order by customer1.

However, running this test gives us the error we expect:

```
$ mix test test/plate_slate_web/schema/subscription/new_order_test.exs

  1) test customers can't see other customer orders (...)
     test/plate_slate_web/schema/subscription/new_order_test.exs:61
     Unexpectedly received message %Phoenix.Socket.Message{
      event: "subscription:data", join_ref: nil,
      payload: %{
        result: %{data: %{"newOrder" => %{"customerNumber" => 24}}},
        subscriptionId: "__absinthe__:doc:128181748"
      }, ref: nil, topic: "__absinthe__:doc:128181748"} (which matched _)
     code: refute_receive _
     stacktrace:
       test/plate_slate_web/schema/subscription/new_order_test.exs:85: (test)
.

Finished in 1.9 seconds
2 tests, 1 failure
```

Let's tweak our subscription topics to fix this security issue, while still preserving the ability for employees to watch for everything:

```
08-chp.auth/5-subscriptions/lib/plate_slate_web/schema.ex
subscription do
  # «Other fields»
  field :new_order, :order do
    config fn _args, %{context: context} ->
      case context[:current_user] do
        %{role: "customer", id: id} ->
          {:ok, topic: id}
        %{role: "employee"} ->
          {:ok, topic: "*"}
        _ ->
          {:error, "unauthorized"}
      end
    end
  end
end
```

At the heart of our solution is the ability to retrieve the current user from within the config function. If the current user is a customer, we're going to use the customer ID as the topic. Employees still get the "*" topic, and everyone else gets an unauthorized message. This does prevent customers from listening on the "*" topic, but we also need to update how we publish orders if we're to make the id topic useful.

This happens back in the place_order resolver:

```
08-chp.auth/5-subscriptions/lib/plate_slate_web/resolvers/ordering.ex
with {:ok, order} <- Ordering.create_order(place_order_input) do
  Absinthe.Subscription.publish(PlateSlateWeb.Endpoint, order,
    new_order: [order.customer_id, "*"]
  )
  {:ok, %{order: order}}
end
```

The change here is very small. When we publish an order, we're now publishing on two topics: "*" and the ID of the customer that ordered it. If we run our test again, we'll see it's all been cleared up.

Subscriptions and authorization are all about topic design. Topics are extremely cheap and should be used readily to help scope published data to precisely the clients that should be able to see it.

Structuring for Authorization

Some authorization concerns can be handled by the very structure of the data within our application, and we can use this when we design our schema.

The idea is that a single field can authenticate for fields deeper down in our query. After all, a GraphQL document is a tree; if we can have a single field act as a gatekeeper for any data that requires authorization, it could simplify our code and the amount of mental overhead involved in trying to remember what's public and what isn't.

A good example of some data in our application that is structured this way is the orders that are associated with a particular customer record. Based on what we've done so far, if we're logged in as a customer and want to get our orders as well as the current menu, we might expect to use a document like this:

```
{
  orders {
    id
    items { name quantity}
  }
  menuItems {
    name
  }
}
```

We saw how by using the context, we could restrict the values that are returned to only those that belong to the current user, but this produces a small problem. The menuItems field always shows the same thing no matter who is looking at that field, and the orders field always shows different things depending on who is looking at the field, but there's nothing in the document that might hint that this is what will happen.

The me pattern is an approach where fields that always depend on whoever is viewing the API are placed on some object representing the current user so that the document's structural hierarchy makes that dependency clear.

Here's how it might be used in our GraphQL query:

```
{
  me {
    orders {
      id
      items { name quantity}
    }
  }
  menuItems {
    name
  }
}
```

The menuItems field still happens at the top level because its values are the same regardless of the current user, whereas the orders field has been placed under me. The shape of the document itself helps communicate what is going on.

History of a Pattern

This pattern has its roots in the Relay[3] v1 implementation—the original GraphQL framework, now called "Relay Classic"—where the field was called viewer. It served to provide both authorization and an easy way to ensure that certain data is always loaded in the context of the current user. We're using the field name me, which is the general convention within the broader GraphQL community at this point.

We're already in a pretty good place to support this pattern. The :user interface type we created in the AccountTypes module already encapsulates the possibilities of a "current user" in our system, so we can just go ahead and add the requisite field to our schema:

```
08-chp.auth/6-me/lib/plate_slate_web/schema.ex
query do
  field :me, :user do
    middleware Middleware.Authorize, :any
    resolve &Resolvers.Accounts.me/3
  end
  # «Other query fields»
end
```

The resolver itself couldn't be simpler; we just need to grab the current user out of the context and return it:

```
08-chp.auth/6-me/lib/plate_slate_web/resolvers/accounts.ex
def me(_, _, %{context: %{current_user: current_user}}) do
  {:ok, current_user}
end
def me(_, _, _) do
  {:ok, nil}
end
```

We can complete the authorization story by filling out the orders field on the :customer object, which we had previously just stubbed:

```
08-chp.auth/6-me/lib/plate_slate_web/schema/accounts_types.ex
object :customer do
  # «Other fields»
  field :orders, list_of(:order) do
```

---

3.   https://facebook.github.io/relay/

```
    resolve fn customer, _, _ ->
      import Ecto.Query

      orders =
        PlateSlate.Ordering.Order
        |> where(customer_id: ^customer.id)
        |> PlateSlate.Repo.all

      {:ok, orders}
    end
  end
end
```

What we end up with is a GraphQL query that looks like this:

```
{
  me {
    name
    ... on Customer { orders { id } }
  }
  menuItems { name }
}
```

This tells us a lot. We know that the customer has a name, we know that customers have orders, and we know that those orders are going to be specific to that customer and not include somebody else's. We also can reasonably expect that the menu items are global values and won't be different if our friend checks it. In situations where "authorization" boils down to scoping data under other data, it's often best to express that scope via the GraphQL document itself.

Moving On

We covered quite a bit in this chapter! We delved into how the client can request a token from the server and how that token is used in subsequent requests. You discovered the Absinthe context and how values placed inside of it are available in resolution functions. We also had an opportunity to see how middleware can be used ahead of resolvers to prevent unauthorized resolution, and how the structure of our schema itself can be used to manage authorization in a more user-friendly way.

Before moving to the next chapter:

1. We've added some basic authorization to the API; review the rest of the schema and add authorization rules on the remaining mutations. Lock them down!

2. Imagine that you want to create a way for employees to look up the order history of a customer. How would you do it? How could you secure it?

3. We updated the new_order subscription to prevent security holes. Make similar updates to the other subscription fields to prevent customers from subscribing to orders that don't belong to them.

With our API secured, we're about ready to expose it to the Internet as a whole. Before we do so, though, we need to look at the tools and patterns Absinthe provides to support high-performance data access.

## CHAPTER 9

Tuning Resolution

As your knowledge of GraphQL grows and you start to imagine how your APIs might need to scale and deal with different problems, you're bound to have questions that go beyond basic field resolvers and middleware.

Resolvers (as we've been using them so far in the book) execute one after another, serially. What if we want to have some of them happen concurrently instead? If several fields on the same object need to retrieve the same data, how could we execute those fields together so that we don't calculate the same value more than once, negatively affecting performance? How do we make decisions by looking at the whole GraphQL document, rather than just field by field, to efficiently execute a query, mutation, or subscription?

In this chapter, we're going to explore the last major tool that Absinthe provides for tweaking the execution of a document: *plugins*. We'll walk through Absinthe's core built-in plugins, and we'll make a new one ourselves: a plugin that can use the associations we've defined with Ecto to easily and efficiently power associations in our GraphQL schemas without violating context boundaries.

Before we jump into plugins, though, we're going to take a quick glance at the underlying engine that powers Absinthe, the *pipeline*. The pipeline is at the heart of how Absinthe works, and manipulating the parts that make up the pipeline—*phases*—is key to many of the advanced features that Absinthe offers. You don't need to know much about the pipeline to build plugins, and you generally don't need to know anything at all to use them. Still, it's worth taking a quick moment to get familiar with the pipeline so that as we move forward, we have the right context to understand what's going on.

Absinthe is a lot like an interpreter. When you pass it a GraphQL document, it's parsed into an abstract syntax tree, converted into an intermediate structure we call a *blueprint* that houses additional metadata, and fed through configured validation and preprocessing logic before being ultimately executed. At a high level, this is what the process looks like:

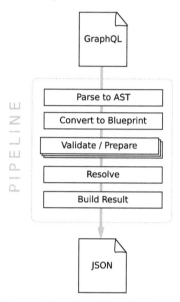

This is the Absinthe pipeline, and each of the steps in the process—represented by a rectangle in the diagram—is called a *phase*. A phase is simply a module that has a run/2 function, accepting an input and options, and returning an output.

After the %Absinthe.Blueprint{} struct is created, the rest of the document processing pipeline centers on the manipulation of the blueprint, passed from phase to phase. Phases are the real workhorses of Absinthe and have names like Phase.Document.Validation.NoFragmentCycles and Phase.Document.Arguments.Normalize.

Broadly speaking, Absinthe phases fall into three categories:

- Preparation phases
- Execution phases
- Result building phases

All the Phases

 At the time of writing, the default pipeline has forty-one phases!

As you've followed along with the examples in the book, this pipeline has been working behind the scenes for every document you've submitted, returning results and providing the error messages when you make mistakes. All of the code that you've written within your resolvers and middleware happens within the Phase.Document.Execution.Resolution phase, which takes a validated document and starts walking through it to run your code.

A plugin then is essentially an upgraded middleware module that has some specific hooks into this Resolution phase. These hooks let us run some stuff before and after resolution, as well as give us the ability to control whether additional phases need to happen. Combined with the middleware behaviour, they are the perfect building blocks to craft the right execution model for our domain, whatever it may be.

Understanding the Problem

Anytime we need to do something like load an Ecto schema has_many association in a resolver, then query child values, we can quickly find ourselves mired in what's referred to as the "N + 1 problem" and performing more database work than we expect. Let's say you want to get the category for a bunch of menu items. The best way to go is to collate all the category_id values found within your set of menu items and then do a single SQL query for categories with those IDs. The N+1 problem happens when instead, you do an SQL query for each individual menu item's category; this is where the problem gets its name. There's 1 query to get the menu items themselves, and then N queries afterward, where N is the number of menu items.

To illustrate this, let's review how a document is executed with a naive example and see what happens. We'll add a small piece of middleware to our schema that will print out each field that executes. To do so, we need to reorganize how we apply middleware a little so that we can more easily compose different options. Start with the def middleware refactor:

```
09-chp.performance/1-start/lib/plate_slate_web/schema.ex
def middleware(middleware, field, object) do
  middleware
  |> apply(:errors, field, object)
  |> apply(:get_string, field, object)
end

defp apply(middleware, :errors, _field, %{identifier: :mutation}) do
  middleware ++ [Middleware.ChangesetErrors]
end
defp apply([], :get_string, field, %{identifier: :allergy_info}) do
  [{Absinthe.Middleware.MapGet, to_string(field.identifier)}]
end
defp apply(middleware, _, _, _) do
  middleware
end
```

Functionally, this is exactly the same, but it gives us a little more flexibility. Previously, we were pattern matching for objects or fields within the middleware/3 function heads, which meant each situation was handled totally separately. If we wanted to apply common middleware to all fields, we'd need to add it to every clause of the middleware/3 block.

With this refactor in place, we can trivially add a debug middleware to every field. In order to make it easy to turn on and off, we'll only run it if we do DEBUG=true when starting our IEx session. We want the debugger to print at the start of every field's resolution, and also at the end. One option for doing this is to put the middleware at both the beginning and the end:

```
[{Middleware.Debug, :start}] ++ middleware ++ [{Middleware.Debug, :finish}]
```

Instead, though, we're going to just put it at the beginning with a :start option, and then add the :finish part inside the middleware itself, which is a trick that will be useful to know later on:

```
09-chp.performance/1-start/lib/plate_slate_web/schema.ex
def middleware(middleware, field, object) do
  middleware
  |> apply(:errors, field, object)
  |> apply(:get_string, field, object)
  |> apply(:debug, field, object)
end

defp apply(middleware, :errors, _field, %{identifier: :mutation}) do
  middleware ++ [Middleware.ChangesetErrors]
end
defp apply([], :get_string, field, %{identifier: :allergy_info}) do
  [{Absinthe.Middleware.MapGet, to_string(field.identifier)}]
end
defp apply(middleware, :debug, _field, _object) do
  if System.get_env("DEBUG") do
    [{Middleware.Debug, :start}] ++ middleware
  else
    middleware
  end
end
defp apply(middleware, _, _, _) do
  middleware
end
```

Let's take a look at the Middleware.Debug module:

```
09-chp.performance/1-start/lib/plate_slate_web/schema/middleware/debug.ex
defmodule PlateSlateWeb.Schema.Middleware.Debug do

  @behaviour Absinthe.Middleware
```

```
  def call(resolution, :start) do
    path = resolution |> Absinthe.Resolution.path |> Enum.join(".")
    IO.puts """
    ======================
    starting: #{path}
    with source: #{inspect resolution.source}\
    """
    %{resolution |
      middleware: resolution.middleware ++ [{__MODULE__, {:finish, path}}]
    }
  end
  def call(resolution, {:finish, path}) do
    IO.puts """
    completed: #{path}
    value: #{inspect resolution.value}
    ======================\
    """
    resolution
  end
end
```

Here we've got two call function clauses where we're pattern matching on our option argument, :start or :finish. The first corresponds to the option we specified in our schema middleware callback. In this clause, we get the current path in the document and then print out a message providing info about the field we've started resolving.

Now the cool part: we can actually change what future middleware will run on this specific field. One of the keys under the %Absinthe.Resolution{} struct is :middleware, and it contains a list of all remaining middleware queued up to run on this field. By adding the Debug module at the end of the list with the :finish option, we ensure that it will be called again after everything else. While we're at it, we also pass along the path variable we've calculated, just so that we don't need to compute it again.

When Debug is called the second time with the {:finish, path} option, we can print some info about the value that's been resolved. Let's give this a try! We'll open up an IEx session (don't forget DEBUG=true) and run a query:

```
$ DEBUG=true iex -S mix
iex> Absinthe.run("""
...> {
...>   menuItems(filter: {name: "Reu"}) {
...>     name
...>     id
...>   }
...> }
...> """, PlateSlateWeb.Schema)
```

```
======================
starting: menuItems
with source: %{}
[debug] QUERY OK source="items" db=3.3ms
SELECT i0."id", i0."added_on", ...
FROM "items" AS i0 WHERE (i0."name" ILIKE $1) ORDER BY i0."name" ["%Reu%"]
completed: menuItems
value: [%PlateSlate.Menu.Item{...}]
======================
======================
starting: menuItems.0.name
with source: %PlateSlate.Menu.Item{...}
completed: menuItems.0.name
value: "Reuben"
======================
======================
starting: menuItems.0.id
with source: %PlateSlate.Menu.Item{...}
completed: menuItems.0.id
value: 1
======================
{:ok, %{data: %{"menuItems" => [%{"id" => "1", "name" => "Reuben"}]}}}
```

There's a decent bit of output here, but most of that is just from inspecting the menu item itself (which we have omitted from the book for space reasons). As you might expect, our tracing middleware indicates that Absinthe starts at the :menu_items field, then moves to the :name and :id fields. At the :menu_items field, the source value is just an empty map, because there isn't any data yet at the top level. That field returns a list with a single menu item. When Absinthe moves to the :name and :id fields, it does so using that specific menu item struct as the source value.

You May Need to Use env

 If you're using a non-standard shell like the friendly interactive shell (fish)[1] and didn't see the expected output, remember that you may need to prefix commands that use ad hoc environment variables with env—for example, env DEBUG=true iex -S mix.

If we do a slightly broader search and just match for "on", we get two results: "Croque Monsieur" and "Lemonade."

```
iex> Absinthe.run("""
...> {
...>   menuItems(filter: {name: "on"}) {
...>     name
...>     id
```

---

1. https://fishshell.com/

```
...>   }
...> }
...> """, PlateSlateWeb.Schema)
=====================
starting: menuItems
with source: %{}
[debug] QUERY OK source="items" db=3.5ms
SELECT i0."id", i0."added_on", ...
FROM "items" AS i0 WHERE (i0."name" ILIKE $1) ORDER BY i0."name" ["%on%"]
completed: menuItems
value: [
  %PlateSlate.Menu.Item{name: "Croque Monsieur", ...},
  %PlateSlate.Menu.Item{name: "Lemonade", ...}
]
=====================
=====================
starting: menuItems.0.name
with source: %PlateSlate.Menu.Item{name: "Croque Monsieur", ...}
completed: menuItems.0.name
value: "Croque Monsieur"
=====================
=====================
starting: menuItems.0.id
with source: %PlateSlate.Menu.Item{name: "Croque Monsieur", ...}
completed: menuItems.0.id
value: 2
=====================
=====================
starting: menuItems.1.name
with source: %PlateSlate.Menu.Item{name: "Lemonade", ...}
completed: menuItems.1.name
value: "Lemonade"
=====================
=====================
starting: menuItems.1.id
with source: %PlateSlate.Menu.Item{name: "Lemonade", ...}
completed: menuItems.1.id
value: 12
=====================
{:ok,
 %{data: %{"menuItems" => [%{"id" => "2", "name" => "Croque Monsieur"},
       %{"id" => "12", "name" => "Lemonade"}]}}}
```

The menu items field once again starts with an empty map as the source, but now it returns a list of two different menu items. When we look at the next lines of tracing output, we see that Absinthe goes through each in turn and executes the :name and :id fields our query document selected. It gets the name and ID field on the "Croque Monsieur" item, and then the name and ID field from the "Lemonade" item. All of this happens in a single process, one item and one field after another. If we return N items from the menu_items field, the name and ID field resolvers will each run N times.

This is both the simplest and most optimal way to proceed when all those fields do is a Map.get on their source, but this approach won't serve if we need to execute fields in parallel, or if we want to work with a group of fields all together. A good example of the latter situation is if we're doing a database call. Every menu item belongs to a category, and if we want to let people query the category on a menu item, we really want to do a single database query to get all of those categories, instead of N.

Let's start by creating the problem we want to fix: a naive implementation where we directly get the category for each menu item. We'll start by making sure we have the correct fields and objects set up in our menu_types.ex file.

```
09-chp.performance/2-naive/lib/plate_slate_web/schema/menu_types.ex
alias PlateSlateWeb.Resolvers
object :menu_item do

  interfaces [:search_result]

  field :id, :id
  field :name, :string
  field :description, :string
  field :price, :decimal
  field :added_on, :date
  field :allergy_info, list_of(:allergy_info)
  field :category, :category do
    resolve &Resolvers.Menu.category_for_item/3
  end
end
```

We already have a :category object from all the way back in Chapter 2, Building a Schema, on page 15, so all we need to do is add in the field on our :menu_item object connecting it to a category, then give it a resolver.

```
09-chp.performance/2-naive/lib/plate_slate_web/resolvers/menu.ex
def items_for_category(category, _, _) do
  query = Ecto.assoc(category, :items)
  {:ok, PlateSlate.Repo.all(query)}
end

def category_for_item(menu_item, _, _) do
  query = Ecto.assoc(menu_item, :category)
  {:ok, PlateSlate.Repo.one(query)}
end
```

In the resolver, we just use the Ecto.assoc/2 function to build an Ecto query, which is then run by our Repo. If we run some queries and pay attention to the [debug] database logging, we'll see that for each menu item in the result, we're having to do a lookup in the categories table:

```
iex> Absinthe.run("""
...> {
...>   menuItems(filter: {name: "on"}) {
...>     name
...>     category { name }
...>   }
...> }
...> """, PlateSlateWeb.Schema)
======================
starting: menuItems
with source: %{}
[debug] QUERY OK source="items" db=7.4ms
SELECT i0."id", i0."added_on", ...
FROM "items" AS i0 WHERE (i0."name" ILIKE $1) ORDER BY i0."name" ["%on%"]
completed: menuItems
value: [
  %PlateSlate.Menu.Item{name: "Croque Monsieur", ...},
  %PlateSlate.Menu.Item{name: "Lemonade", ...}
]
======================
======================
starting: menuItems.0.name
with source: %PlateSlate.Menu.Item{name: "Croque Monsieur", ...}
completed: menuItems.0.name
value: "Croque Monsieur"
======================
======================
starting: menuItems.0.category
with source: %PlateSlate.Menu.Item{name: "Croque Monsieur", ...}
[debug] QUERY OK source="categories" db=1.5ms
SELECT c0."id", ...
FROM "categories" AS c0 WHERE (c0."id" = $1) [1]
completed: menuItems.0.category
value: %PlateSlate.Menu.Category{name: "Sandwiches", ...}
======================
======================
starting: menuItems.0.category.name
with source: %PlateSlate.Menu.Category{name: "Sandwiches", ...}
completed: menuItems.0.category.name
value: "Sandwiches"
======================
======================
starting: menuItems.1.name
with source: %PlateSlate.Menu.Item{name: "Lemonade", ...}
completed: menuItems.1.name
value: "Lemonade"
======================
```

```
=======================
starting: menuItems.1.category
with source: %PlateSlate.Menu.Item{name: "Lemonade", ...}
[debug] QUERY OK source="categories" db=1.4ms
SELECT c0."id", ...
FROM "categories" AS c0 WHERE (c0."id" = $1) [3]
completed: menuItems.1.category
value: %PlateSlate.Menu.Category{name: "Beverages", ...}
=======================
=======================
starting: menuItems.1.category.name
with source: %PlateSlate.Menu.Category{name: "Beverages", ...}
completed: menuItems.1.category.name
value: "Beverages"
=======================
{:ok,
 %{data: %{"menuItems" => [%{"category" => %{"name" => "Sandwiches"},
        "name" => "Croque Monsieur"},
      %{"category" => %{"name" => "Beverages"}, "name" => "Lemonade"}]}}}
```

If we look at our tracing, it isn't hard to see why: we're fully resolving the category field on each menu item before moving on. Given how we've built our resolver, this isn't surprising. The solutions we're going to look at next make use of Absinthe plugins to alter how each of these fields are executed, providing us opportunities to load this data more efficiently.

Using Built-in Plugins

As we noted at the start, a plugin in Absinthe is any module that implements the Absinthe.Plugin behaviour. It is not uncommon for a plugin module to also implement the Absinthe.Middleware behaviour, because the two behaviours work together. The middleware callbacks handle changes that need to happen to each individual field, and the plugin callbacks operate at the document level.

We'll start by looking at two simple plugins built into Absinthe itself. These will help us get the hang of how plugins work, and each has use cases where they're the perfect tool for the job.

Async

A step in the direction of efficient execution would be to run each field concurrently. It doesn't get rid of the N+1 query, but it does mean that by doing all the N at the same time, we can improve our response time. While obviously not the optimal solution for SQL-based data, async execution is a useful tool when dealing with external APIs. Async is one of the simplest plugins, so let's give it a look as a way to get our feet wet.

Let's head back to our category_for_item/3 resolver function and make it async. To do this, we'll make use of a helper built into Absinthe—async/1—which we'll import from the Absinthe.Resolution.Helpers module.

```
09-chp.performance/3-async/lib/plate_slate_web/resolvers/menu.ex
import Absinthe.Resolution.Helpers, only: [async: 1]
# «Rest of file»
def category_for_item(menu_item, _, _) do
  async(fn ->
    query = Ecto.assoc(menu_item, :category)
    {:ok, PlateSlate.Repo.one(query)}
  end) |> IO.inspect
end
```

The change to the resolution function is very small; we're wrapping the body of the function in an 0-arity anonymous function and then passing that to async/1, much like you would with Task.async. You'll notice that we've added an IO.inspect after our async call, and if we run a query, we'll see a return value that we've never seen before:

```
$ iex -S mix
iex> query = """
{menuItems(filter: {name: "Reu"}) { category { name } id } }
"""
iex> Absinthe.run(query, PlateSlateWeb.Schema)

{:middleware, Absinthe.Middleware.Async, {
  #Function<0.33547832/0 in PlateSlateWeb.Resolvers.Menu.category_for_item/3>,
  []
}}
```

This is new! Every resolver we've written so far has returned either an {:ok, value} or {:error, error} tuple. Here, though, we're seeing the third and final tuple, which has the form {:middleware, MiddlewareModule, options} and amounts to telling Absinthe, "Hey, hand off the execution of this field to this middleware with these options." In our specific case then, Absinthe is going to call the Absinthe.Middleware.Async.call function with the field's resolution struct, and then pass it the options tuple we see at the end there. It houses the function we have in our category_for_item/3 and an empty list of options.

In fact, the entire contents of the async/1 helper is just:

```
def async(fun, opts \\ []) do
  {:middleware, Middleware.Async, {fun, opts}}
end
```

Run a query that gets all the menu items, paying attention to the tracing output this time.

```
$ DEBUG=true iex -S mix
iex> Absinthe.run("{menuItems { category { name } id }}",
  PlateSlateWeb.Schema)
```

The menuItems field returns the full list of items, and then you can see it
starting the category field on the first item. However, instead of completing,
the next thing you see is it starting and finishing the id field. Then it starts
the category field of the next menu item! As you keep going down, you'll actually begin to see database output as the function happens in the background
while Absinthe is still processing the document.

Only after all the category fields have been started do you see Absinthe completing any of them with values. Nothing in the async helper seems to be doing
anything to spawn processes though, so the work has to be done inside the
Middleware.Async module. Let's dive in:

```elixir
defmodule Absinthe.Middleware.Async do
  @behaviour Absinthe.Middleware
  @behaviour Absinthe.Plugin

  def before_resolution(exec) do
    put_in(exec.context[__MODULE__], false)
  end

  def call(%{state: :unresolved} = res, {fun, opts}) do
    task_data = {Task.async(fun), opts}

    %{res |
      state: :suspended,
      context: Map.put(res.context, __MODULE__, true),
      middleware: [{__MODULE__, task_data} | res.middleware]
    }
  end
  def call(%{state: :suspended} = res, {task, opts}) do
    result = Task.await(task, opts[:timeout] || 30_000)
    Absinthe.Resolution.put_result(res, result)
  end

  def after_resolution(exec), do: exec

  def pipeline(pipeline, exec) do
    case exec.context do
      %{__MODULE__ => true} ->
        [Absinthe.Phase.Document.Execution.Resolution | pipeline]
      _ ->
        pipeline
    end
  end
end
```

There's a lot going on here! Notably, this module is implementing both the Absinthe.Middleware and the Absinthe.Plugin behaviours. The first makes sure we can hook into individual fields when they need to use Async, and the other provides us before and after resolution callbacks. We're going to walk through this step by step, keeping in mind our GraphQL query:

```
{
  menuItems {
    category { name }
    id
  }
}
```

The first thing that happens, as the name suggests, is the before_resolution/1 callback. The value passed to this function is an %Absinthe.Blueprint.Execution{} struct, from which every field's %Absinthe.Resolution{} struct is derived. The before_resolution/1 callback is a good place to set up values we may need later. In this case, we just set a flag to false within our context. This context is the exact same one we've been using to store the current user for authentication. The flag will be used later to figure out whether any processes are running in the background or not. Since we just started, none are.

As execution proceeds, Absinthe will hit our :category field, which hands off to this middleware's call function via the :middleware tuple we saw inside the async/1 function. This is 100% the same def call callback that we looked at when we were doing the error handling or authorization middleware.

Notably, we actually have two clauses here. The first one we'll hit immediately at the end of our resolver; since no result has been placed on our field, the state is still :unresolved. Here we find where the actual asynchronous action happens! This clause does four things: calls Task.async/1 with our function, suspends resolution, sets our context flag to true, and then updates the field's middleware to re-run this module when the field is unsuspended. The context part is pretty simple, in that now that there is definitely a process running in the background, we need to set the flag to true so that we know about it later.

The other two changes are a bit less simple. When you suspend the resolution struct, Absinthe stops doing any further processing to that field and moves on to the next sibling field. If you suspend the category field, it stops doing work on that field and moves on to the id field. The name field is unreachable until after category has finally resolved. After doing the id field of the first menu item, it would move to the next menu item to begin its category field (which also pushes a value into the loader) and then suspend.

This makes sense of the tracing output we saw earlier, where :category fields kept being started, but then Absinthe would just move on to the next field. When Absinthe comes back to this field, it needs a way to turn this task back into an actual value that it can continue resolution with, so we use the same trick we learned in the Debug module to re-enqueue our middleware. This time though, instead of adding it at the end, we add the middleware and our task to the beginning so that it will be the very next thing to run. When Absinthe comes back to the field, it'll run this module again, and we'll have the opportunity to Task.await/1 and get a value.

After Absinthe has completed this particular walk through the document, it runs the after_resolution callback. This is an opportunity to do any extra transformations or loading, but for our purposes, we don't need to do anything.

The Absinthe.Phase.Document.Execution.Resolution phase we've been inside this whole time only does a *single* walk through the document. Now that we're executing certain fields asynchronously, however, this is a problem, because we need to go back and get values out of each task. This brings us to the last and most interesting callback: pipeline. Based on the execution struct we returned from after_resolution, our plugin has the option to tell Absinthe to run additional phases on the document. We're putting that flag in our context we've been tracking to good use; if it's been set to true, then we know there are async fields happening, and we need to go back to await them. If the flag is false, then as far as this plugin is concerned, there's nothing more to be done, so we leave the pipeline alone.

Graphically, this execution flow looks like this:

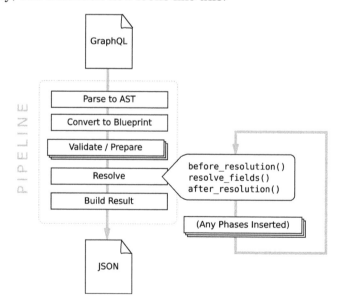

With this additional phase specified, Absinthe knows it has more work to do, effectively starting the whole process over again. As Absinthe walks through the document, it will come across the first suspended field, calling whatever remaining middleware exists on that field. Of course, that's just Middleware.Async clause number two because that's what we set up the first time around. All we need to do is just Task.await on our process and put the result on the field.

Batch

The problem with async, of course, is that while it's faster than serial database queries, we're still doing N of them to get N categories when we could really be doing just one database query to get *all* the categories. We need a way to aggregate values, a function that can use those aggregated values to run an SQL query, and then the ability to get those values back into individual fields.

Fortunately, the Absinthe.Middleware.Batch plugin has our backs. Let's see how it looks in our resolver:

```
09-chp.performance/4-batching/lib/plate_slate_web/resolvers/menu.ex
import Absinthe.Resolution.Helpers, only: [batch: 3]
# «Rest of file»
def category_for_item(menu_item, _, _) do
  batch({PlateSlate.Menu, :categories_by_id}, menu_item.category_id, fn
    categories ->
      {:ok, Map.get(categories, menu_item.category_id)}
  end) |> IO.inspect
end
```

As before, we've got an Absinthe helper function we're importing to provide a nice API, as well as an |> IO.inspect at the end, so we'll be able to see in a second what this function returns. The function takes three arguments: a module and function tuple indicating what function will actually run the batch, a value to be aggregated, and then a function for retrieving the results specific to this field.

The function specified, PlateSlate.Menu.categories_by_id/2, looks like this:

```
09-chp.performance/4-batching/lib/plate_slate/menu/menu.ex
def categories_by_id(_, ids) do
  Category
  |> where([c], c.id in ^Enum.uniq(ids))
  |> Repo.all
  |> Map.new(fn category ->
    {category.id, category}
  end)
end
```

The body of this function gives us a pretty good idea of what's going to happen. The resolver function is aggregating menu_item.category_ids, and those will get passed in as the second arg of the categories_by_id function. Within that function, we have a simple Ecto query that grabs all the categories with the ids we want, and then we make a map of category IDs to the associated category for easy lookup later. Let's give this a whirl:

```
$ DEBUG=true iex -S mix
iex> Absinthe.run("""
...> {menuItems(filter: {name: "on"}) { category {name} } }
...> """, PlateSlateWeb.Schema)
======================
starting: menuItems
with source: %{}
[debug] QUERY OK source="items" db=7.7ms decode=1.5ms
SELECT i0."id", i0."added_on", ...
FROM "items" AS i0 WHERE (i0."name" ILIKE $1) ORDER BY i0."name" ["%on%"]
completed: menuItems
value: [%PlateSlate.Menu.Item{...}, %PlateSlate.Menu.Item{...}]
======================
======================
starting: menuItems.0.category
with source: %PlateSlate.Menu.Item{...}
{:middleware, Absinthe.Middleware.Batch,
 {{PlateSlate.Menu, :categories_by_id}, 1,
  #Function<0.54233969/1 in PlateSlateWeb.Resolvers.Menu.category_for_item/3>,
  []}}
======================
starting: menuItems.1.category
with source: %PlateSlate.Menu.Item{...}
{:middleware, Absinthe.Middleware.Batch,
 {{PlateSlate.Menu, :categories_by_id}, 3,
  #Function<0.54233969/1 in PlateSlateWeb.Resolvers.Menu.category_for_item/3>,
  []}}
======================
[debug] QUERY OK source="categories" db=1.9ms
SELECT c0."id", c0."description", c0."name", c0."inserted_at", c0."updated_at"
FROM "categories" AS c0 WHERE (c0."id" = ANY($1)) [[3, 1]]
completed: menuItems.0.category
value: %PlateSlate.Menu.Category{name: "Sandwiches", ...}
======================
======================
starting: menuItems.0.category.name
with source: %PlateSlate.Menu.Category{name: "Sandwiches", ...}
completed: menuItems.0.category.name
value: "Sandwiches"
======================
completed: menuItems.1.category
value: %PlateSlate.Menu.Category{name: "Beverages", ...}
======================
```

```
=======================
starting: menuItems.1.category.name
with source: %PlateSlate.Menu.Category{name: "Beverages", ...}
completed: menuItems.1.category.name
value: "Beverages"
=======================
{:ok,
 %{data: %{"menuItems" => [%{"category" => %{"name" => "Sandwiches"}},
       %{"category" => %{"name" => "Beverages"}}]}}}
```

This is looking good! As with async, we see that when we get to the first menuItems.0.category field, we start it but then immediately move on to the menuItems.1.category field. Our debug Ecto output shows that we do a single SQL query for two categories, IDs 3 and 1, and then each category field completes without any further database querying.

Logger Prints Asynchronously

Depending on your computer, you may see the SQL debug output show up at different points amid the output from your Debug middleware. This is because Elixir's Logger maintains a small buffer for performance reasons, so output may be delayed. We're using IO.puts in our debugger, which outputs immediately. If you see the SQL query show up after one of the category fields shows as complete, that's the reason why!

We aren't going to dive into the actual code of the Absinthe.Middleware.Batch because the code for managing the batches is a little too much to fit into a book. From what we saw within the Async plugin, though, we can see that a similar process is at work. The fact that we started each category field before we completed any of them tells us that the plugin is suspending each field as it internally builds up a batch under each function, and the fact that each field ultimately completes tells us it's doing the trick of modifying the middleware to come back. Then, each batch is run during the after_resolution callback. If there were any batches to run, the resolution phase happens once more, and results can be filtered into the proper fields.

The Absinthe.Middleware.Batch achieves a lot and, with some helpers, was the standard way to solve this problem for a long time. While batch still has a place, it has a few limitations that have driven the development of the final approach we'll look at in this chapter. There are small-scale annoyances like the limitation of only being able to batch one thing at a time in a field, or the fact that the API can get very verbose.

There are also some larger-scale issues. Ecto has a fair number of quirks that make it a difficult library to abstract access to. If you want the concurrent testing feature to work, you need to add self() to all the batch keys and do Repo.all(caller: pid) in every batch function so that it knows which sandbox to use. It gets easy for your GraphQL functions to become full of direct database access, inevitably going around important data access rules you may want to enforce in your Phoenix contexts. Alternatively, your context functions can end up with dozens of little functions that only exist to support batching items by ID.

In time, people involved in larger projects were able to build some abstractions, helpers, and conventions around the Absinthe.Middleware.Batch plugin that did a good job of addressing these issues. That effort has been extracted into the project *Dataloader*, which, while a generic tool not tied to GraphQL, is the perfect fit for what we're trying to accomplish here.

Discovering Dataloader

The challenge here is getting the data we want efficiently without coupling our GraphQL API tightly to the SQL structure of our data, and without stuffing our contexts full of tons of functions that exist just for GraphQL purposes. We want to respect the idea that our contexts define a boundary, and if we start just doing Ecto queries in all of our resolvers, we'll be violating that boundary. At the same time, GraphQL's flexibility means that without a little bit of help, we're going to end up with dozens of functions within our context to handle every scenario.

Dataloader is a small package that defines a minimalist API for getting data in batches. We can use it within our contexts to keep all the SQL details nicely packed away, while still providing flexibility. It also won't require us to have a lot of context boilerplate either. Although Dataloader is managed under the absinthe-graphql GitHub organization, it really is entirely separate from GraphQL itself, and actually has utilities for conveniently retrieving values inside ordinary Phoenix controllers.

Credit Where Credit Is Due

 Dataloader was first created in JavaScript by the developers at Facebook to handle similar situations.[2] The Elixir package is inspired by its JavaScript counterpart, but is built to better suit Elixir conventions and capabilities.

---

2.   https://github.com/facebook/dataloader

We'll start by using Dataloader in an explicit and manual kind of way, and then gradually build some helper functions so that within our schemas we'll eventually get something as easy as this:

```
field :category, :category, resolve: dataloader(Menu)
```

Let's get a basic Dataloader up and running, and then we'll walk through what it does.

First let's add it to our mix.exs file:

```
09-chp.performance/5-dataloader/mix.exs
defp deps do
  [
    {:dataloader, "~> 1.0.0"},
    # «Other deps»
  ]
end
```

Then in our Menu context, we're going to define a Dataloader source:

```
09-chp.performance/5-dataloader/lib/plate_slate/menu/menu.ex
def data() do
  Dataloader.Ecto.new(Repo, query: &query/2)
end

def query(queryable, _) do
  queryable
end
```

Let's hop into iex -S mix and play with this new library. First we'll create ourselves a Dataloader with a source:

```
iex> alias PlateSlate.Menu
iex> source = Menu.data()
iex> loader = Dataloader.new |> Dataloader.add_source(Menu, source)
```

With that in place, we'll queue up some items to be loaded:

```
iex> loader = (
...>    loader
...>    |> Dataloader.load(Menu, Menu.Item, 1)
...>    |> Dataloader.load(Menu, Menu.Item, 2)
...>    |> Dataloader.load(Menu, Menu.Item, 3)
...> )
```

This doesn't actually run any queries against the database yet. If we try to get one of those items out of the Dataloader, we'll just get nil.

```
iex> loader |> Dataloader.get(Menu, Menu.Item, 2)
nil
```

To retrieve all queued-up batches, we use Dataloader.run/1:

```
iex> loader = loader |> Dataloader.run
[debug] QUERY OK source="items" db=17.2ms
SELECT i0."id", ...
FROM "items" AS i0 WHERE (i0."id" = ANY($1)) [[3, 2, 1]]
```

When we run that function, we can see that a single SQL query runs to grab all the items we've queued up so far. Now if we use Dataloader.get/3 again, we'll see that our items are here. We can also use Dataloader.get_many/3 to conveniently grab several items at once:

```
iex> menu_item = loader |> Dataloader.get(Menu, Menu.Item, 2)
%PlateSlate.Menu.Item{...}
iex> menu_items = loader |> Dataloader.get_many(Menu, Menu.Item, [1,2,3])
[%PlateSlate.Menu.Item{...}, ...]
```

The idea here is that we can load up one or more batches' worth of data we want to retrieve, on one or more sources, delaying the actual execution of any SQL queries until we actually need the results. When we call Dataloader.run, each data source is run concurrently, and within each data source each batch is run concurrently. It doesn't just work for IDs either; we can also use Ecto association names:

```
iex> loader = (
...>   loader
...>   |> Dataloader.load_many(Menu, :category, menu_items)
...>   |> Dataloader.run
...> )
[debug] QUERY OK source="categories" db=5.6ms
SELECT c0."id", ...
FROM "categories" AS c0 WHERE (c0."id" = $1) [1]

iex> categories = loader |> Dataloader.get_many(Menu, :category, menu_items)
[%PlateSlate.Menu.Category{...}, ...]
```

With the basics of Dataloader under our belt, let's see how we can wire it in to GraphQL. To start with, we're going to place a loader struct inside of the Absinthe context. This will make it readily available in all of our resolvers, so that each one can efficiently load data if desired.

Right now, we set up our context within a plug, and we could definitely add our Dataloader there. Annoyingly, though, we would also need to add it to our UserSocket, because the plug we set up doesn't affect sockets. While it's useful to be able to run specific code for plugs and sockets, this is a common concern for both, so we want a common place for it to live.

Helpfully, the schema itself supports a context/1 callback that's perfect for setting up values that you want to be around no matter how you run GraphQL queries.

Head on over to your PlateSlateWeb.Schema module and do this:

09-chp.performance/5-dataloader/lib/plate_slate_web/schema.ex
```elixir
def dataloader() do
  alias PlateSlate.Menu
  Dataloader.new
  |> Dataloader.add_source(Menu, Menu.data())
end

def context(ctx) do
  Map.put(ctx, :loader, dataloader())
end
```

The dataloader/0 function here is nothing special, just a handy way to organize our code and make it easy to grab a Dataloader in IEx if we ever want to. The context/1 callback gets passed the existing context value, and then we have the opportunity to make any adjustments to it that we want. This function runs after code in our PlateSlateWeb.Context plug, so, for example, if there's a current user configured we'll find that in the ctx map that's passed in.

We're almost done with integrating Dataloader into Absinthe. One thing we haven't addressed so far is how Absinthe knows it needs to run the before_resolution callbacks of the Absinthe.Middleware.Async and Absinthe.Middleware.Batch plugins we looked at earlier in the chapter. No resolution functions have happened at that point in the execution process, so it needs an external way of knowing what plugins to run callbacks for. The data source it uses is a plugins/0 function on your schema module, which simply defaults to Async and Batch if you don't supply a custom one. Let's add one to include the Dataloader plugin:

09-chp.performance/5-dataloader/lib/plate_slate_web/schema.ex
```elixir
def plugins do
  [Absinthe.Middleware.Dataloader | Absinthe.Plugin.defaults]
end
```

Return once more to the :category field resolver, and let's put Dataloader to work:

09-chp.performance/5-dataloader/lib/plate_slate_web/resolvers/menu.ex
```elixir
import Absinthe.Resolution.Helpers, only: [on_load: 2]
# «Rest of file»
def category_for_item(menu_item, _, %{context: %{loader: loader}}) do
  loader
  |> Dataloader.load(Menu, :category, menu_item)
  |> on_load(fn loader ->
    category = Dataloader.get(loader, Menu, :category, menu_item)
    {:ok, category}
  end)
end
```

Not too bad! We grab our loader and load a batch exactly like we were doing in IEx previously. New to the helper team is on_load, which we're importing from Absinthe.Resolution.Helpers. The callback function we pass to on_load is a lot like the callback function we pass to the batch helper. Similar to batch, on_load hands off control to the Absinthe.Middleware.Dataloader module, which arranges to run our callback after the Dataloader batches have been run.

This resolver handles going from an item to its category, but we also ought to handle the association going the other way as well, from a category to the items on it. This direction is a bit more complicated though, because we probably ought to support ordering, filtering, and other query customization options.

The Dataloader.Ecto source we're using makes this easy by accepting a tuple as the third argument, where the first element is the association or queryable, and the second element is a map of params it passes down to our context. This looks like:

```
loader |> Dataloader.get_many(Menu, {:items, %{order: :asc}}, categories)
```

As you recall, we set up our Menu Dataloader source with a query/2 function we had stubbed out inside of our Menu context. This function lets you alter the Ecto query used by Dataloader to enforce access rules or apply filters. Let's hook it up to the existing filtering options we have for our menu items. We'll refactor the list_items/1 function so the query building part is extracted into its own function:

09-chp.performance/5-dataloader/lib/plate_slate/menu/menu.ex
```
def list_items(args) do
  args
  |> items_query
  |> Repo.all
end

defp items_query(args) do
  Enum.reduce(args, Item, fn
    {:order, order}, query ->
      query |> order_by({^order, :name})
    {:filter, filter}, query ->
      query |> filter_with(filter)
  end)
end
```

Now add a clause to the query/2 function pattern matching on Menu.Item, and apply arguments:

09-chp.performance/5-dataloader/lib/plate_slate/menu/menu.ex
```
def query(Item, args) do
  items_query(args)
end
```

```
def query(queryable, _) do
  queryable
end
```

Now, every time Dataloader queries a Menu.Item, the query/2 function will pattern match on the first arg Item and apply the arguments specific for that queryable. We can use this to easily wire efficient and flexible loading into the :items field of our :category object, with the same kind of filtering we do at the top level.

09-chp.performance/5-dataloader/lib/plate_slate_web/schema/menu_types.ex

```
object :category do

  interfaces [:search_result]

  field :name, :string
  field :description, :string
  field :items, list_of(:menu_item) do
➤    arg :filter, :menu_item_filter
➤    arg :order, type: :sort_order, default_value: :asc
    resolve &Resolvers.Menu.items_for_category/3
  end
end
```

All we're doing here is just adding two arguments to the :items field. We can easily support this inside of our items_for_category/3 resolver function by using Dataloader and passing in the arguments as part of the batch key.

09-chp.performance/5-dataloader/lib/plate_slate_web/resolvers/menu.ex

```
def items_for_category(category, args, %{context: %{loader: loader}}) do
  loader
  |> Dataloader.load(Menu, {:items, args}, category)
  |> on_load(fn loader ->
    items = Dataloader.get(loader, Menu, {:items, args}, category)
    {:ok, items}
  end)
end
```

Let's play around with this in GraphiQL with the following GraphQL query (see figure on page 190):

```
{
  search(matching:"es") {
    name
    ... on Category {
      items(filter: {name: "F"}) {
        name
      }
    }
  }
}
```

```
GraphiQL    ▶    History ▼   Save                                                      ‹ Docs

1 ▾ {                                              ▾ {
2 ▾   search(matching:"es") {                        "data": {
3       name                                            "search": [
4 ▾     ... on Category {                                 {
5         items(filter: {name:"F"}) {                       "name": "French Fries"
6           name                                          },
7         }                                               {
8       }                                                   "name": "Sandwiches",
9     }                                                     "items": [
10  }                                                         {
                                                              "name": "Muffuletta"
                                                            }
                                                          ]
                                                        },
                                                        {
                                                          "name": "Sides",
                                                          "items": [
                                                            {
                                                              "name": "French Fries"
                                                            }
                                                          ]
                                                        },
                                                        {
                                                          "name": "Beverages",
                                                          "items": [
                                                            {
                                                              "name": "Soft Drink"
                                                            }
        QUERY VARIABLES                                   }
```

We start by doing a basic search so that we can get some categories. Then on each category, we're retrieving items, filtering down to just those items with the matching the letter "F". Fields on the :category object work exactly like fields on the root :query object, so just as we could have arguments on the root menuItems field, we can also have them on the items field of the :category object.

Looking at our logs, we can see that Dataloader is handling both the filtering as well as the batching:

```
SELECT i0."id", ...
FROM "items" AS i0
WHERE (i0."name" ILIKE $1) AND (i0."category_id" = ANY($2))
ORDER BY i0."category_id", i0."name" ["%F%", [1, 2, 3]]
```

If we look at the :items_for_category and :category_for_item resolver functions, we can begin to sense a pattern here. In both cases, we're just grabbing the parent item, loading an association on it, and then pulling the result out in the on_load callback.

This is such a common pattern that Absinthe provides a helper that lets you turn both of these resolvers into a nice one-liner:

09-chp.performance/6-final/lib/plate_slate_web/schema/menu_types.ex
```
import Absinthe.Resolution.Helpers
alias PlateSlate.Menu
# «Rest of file»
  field :items, list_of(:menu_item) do
    arg :filter, :menu_item_filter
    arg :order, type: :sort_order, default_value: :asc
    resolve dataloader(Menu, :items)
  end
```

There's no magic here. It's no different than what we've already been doing. Here is the dataloader/2 helper from within Absinthe itself:

```
def dataloader(source, key) do
  fn parent, args, %{context: %{loader: loader}} ->
    loader
    |> Dataloader.load(source, {key, args}, parent)
    |> on_load(fn loader ->
      result = Dataloader.get(loader, source, {key, args}, parent)
      {:ok, result}
    end)
  end
end
```

In essence, the dataloader function is simply building exactly the same resolver functions we have been doing. With this in place, we do not even need the two dedicated functions within the Resolvers.Menu module at all, and we can remove them.

Dataloader is an incredibly powerful tool that strikes a balance between flexible querying and having strict code boundaries. We've seen how with a few functions, we can make it easy to walk associations within our GraphQL schema, finally providing users with all the potential data that they need.

Moving On

If your head is spinning a bit about when to use each of these plugins, don't fear—we're going to take a moment and recap what we covered in this chapter. The linear "one field at a time" approach that Absinthe takes when executing your documents is a great default, but it isn't what you want all the time. When you want things to go differently, you combine middleware's ability to suspend fields with plugins, which give you before and after resolution callbacks. We looked at three built-in plugins that Absinthe supplies: Async, Batch, and Dataloader.

- Dataloader: Use this library when it makes sense to get data in aggregate out of sources. It ships with integrations with Ecto and some flexible modules for making more sources. It provides the easiest, cleanest integration with Phoenix's bounded context, and it should be your first choice for efficiently loading fields from external sources.

- Batch: Use this plugin when you need to be very hands on with how to actually get the data for a batch. Whether it's a particularly gnarly SQL query that you can't sensibly handle with Dataloader, or any situation where you need field-by-field control over how to get the data, Batch will have your back.

- Async: Use this plugin as a quick and easy way to get asynchronous execution when the thing you're executing isn't sensibly batched. In most cases, the Batch or Dataloader plugins are a superior approach. However, the Async plugin is written to be a tutorial, and it's a great place to start if you want to look into making your own plugins.

With these tools at your disposal, you are fully equipped to build flexible, secure, and efficient GraphQL servers with Elixir and Absinthe. Although the helpers you use at the end should cover 99% of your day-to-day Absinthe development needs, you've also got a firm foundation for understanding what's going on behind the one-liner that will support you no matter how you need Absinthe to run.

To wrap up our PlateSlate server, here are some additional exercises you can now do efficiently with the features you learned in this chapter:

1. Use the helper functions Absinthe provides or ones you create yourself to fill out other relevant fields associating different objects together.
2. In particular, play around with retrieving the current menu item for a given order's order item. This one is tricky, since it crosses contexts and order_item in an embedded schema.
3. There's actually a helper that only requires that you pass in the Dataloader source, which looks like dataloader(Menu). See if you can figure out how it knows what field it's on.

In the final part, we're going to look at some features Absinthe provides for integrating with clients.

Part III

Use Your API

In this third and final part of the book, you'll learn how to use your Absinthe-based GraphQL APIs, both from the server and the client.

## CHAPTER 10

Driving Phoenix Actions with GraphQL

As you've learned in the previous chapters, the foundation of a GraphQL API is the definition of its schema, which models the domain and provides a cohesive interface for accessing and modifying its data.

GraphQL APIs are commonly used (and in fact, GraphQL was originally developed) to support data fetching for user interfaces that aren't co-located with the server code. Mobile applications and single-page JavaScript applications are the conventional clients for a web-facing GraphQL API. But it doesn't need to be that way. You can use the power of GraphQL directly from other parts of your Elixir application too.

You can even use GraphQL to build more traditional, server-side, rendered user interfaces, and in this chapter, we're going to show you how.

We're going to work on building out a basic administrative interface for our example application, PlateSlate. We'll add features so that administrators can list and get the details of menu items, and we'll do this all by using—and improving—our existing GraphQL schema.

We'll be building the user interface on top of Phoenix's controllers and templating. If you've never used Phoenix to build a UI, don't worry; we'll work through it step by step.

Along the way, you're going to learn about an advanced GraphQL feature, *directives*, which are special annotations that you can use to customize GraphQL execution. You'll see that they're a pretty handy feature to have around.

Let's jump right in and start building our first GraphQL-driven Phoenix action, complete with a user interface!

Building an Action

The first thing we'll need is a simple way to list all the menu items that we have in our system so that we can then take further action upon them. If you aren't super familiar with doing server-side rendering with Phoenix, don't worry; we'll cover everything you need to know here. In order to avoid writing a ton of HTML boilerplate, we'll use one of the Phoenix generators and then we'll replace the generated controller contents as needed. Run this in your shell:

```
$ mix phx.gen.html --no-context --no-schema Menu Item items
$ rm test/plate_slate_web/controllers/item_controller_test.exs
```

The first command generates some boilerplate HTML for us, and the second removes a test case we won't be needing. Up next is our router. We'll be making use of the :browser pipeline that's been sitting around unused this whole time by creating an "/admin" scope inside of which we'll be setting up our controller:

10-chp.serverui/1-start/lib/plate_slate_web/router.ex
```
scope "/admin", PlateSlateWeb do
  pipe_through :browser

  resources "/items", ItemController
end
```

We can confirm that that our router is properly set up by using the handy mix phx.routes command:

```
$ mix phx.routes
*          /api                      Absinthe.Plug [schema: PlateSlateWeb.Schema]
*          /graphiql                 Absinthe.Plug.GraphiQL [...]
item_path  GET     /admin/items              PlateSlateWeb.ItemController :index
item_path  GET     /admin/items/:id/edit  PlateSlateWeb.ItemController :edit
item_path  GET     /admin/items/new       PlateSlateWeb.ItemController :new
item_path  GET     /admin/items/:id          PlateSlateWeb.ItemController :show
item_path  POST    /admin/items              PlateSlateWeb.ItemController :create
item_path  PATCH   /admin/items/:id          PlateSlateWeb.ItemController :update
PUT        /admin/items/:id       PlateSlateWeb.ItemController :update
item_path  DELETE  /admin/items/:id          PlateSlateWeb.ItemController :delete
```

With that out of our way, we can turn our attention to the controller, where we should replace its existing contents entirely with the following:

10-chp.serverui/1-start/lib/plate_slate_web/controllers/item_controller.ex
```
defmodule PlateSlateWeb.ItemController do
  use PlateSlateWeb, :controller
  use Absinthe.Phoenix.Controller,
    schema: PlateSlateWeb.Schema

end
```

Now for the fun part. The way that Absinthe.Phoenix.Controller works is that it gives you a way to associate a GraphQL query with a controller action, and use the data looked up from that query in your controller. We won't be replacing the controller actions but rather augmenting them by utilizing all the lookup ability we've already written, letting our controller focus on just managing the HTTP connection. Start with something basic:

```
10-chp.serverui/1-start/lib/plate_slate_web/controllers/item_controller.ex
@graphql """
{
  menu_items {
    name
  }
}
"""
def index(conn, result) do
  result |> IO.inspect
  render(conn, "index.html", items: result.data["menu_items"] || [])
end
```

Let's break this down. At the top of this snippet is a @graphql module attribute on which we're putting a string with a GraphQL query. Beneath that there's a relatively ordinary-looking Phoenix controller callback index/2, which gets the HTTP conn and some params, and then renders an index.html.

At a high level, the controller action is acting as a GraphQL *client*. Instead of looking up menu items by directly hitting the database or PlateSlate.Menu context, it submits a GraphQL query to Absinthe, and then it receives the results of that query as the second argument to the index/2 function. The controller then can go about whatever it would normally do with data; in this case, we're using it to render an HTML template, and we're providing that template with some :assigns.

By way of Phoenix review, :assigns is a key on the connection struct that holds a map where you can just "assign" values. Those values propagate along with the connection itself and are made available to you inside of templates.

Head over to the template briefly so that you can make sure it will actually show you something interesting:

```
10-chp.serverui/1-start/lib/plate_slate_web/templates/item/index.html.eex
<h2>Listing Items</h2>

<table class="table">
  <thead>
    <tr>
      <th>Menu Item</th>
    </tr>
  </thead>
```

```
  <tbody>
<%= for item <- @items do %>
    <tr>
      <td><%= item["name"] %></td>
    </tr>
<% end %>
  </tbody>
</table>
```

This is all 100% totally normal EEx (Embedded Elixir[1]) template code. As with other templates in Phoenix, we can access values that we place on the connection assigns (from within our controller) as usual via @. We put all of the items that we got back from GraphQL under the items: assign in the controller, so we can access it in the template as @items. Then we can just loop over each item and build out the HTML table.

Before we go deeper, let's get this running a bit so we can get some hands-on familiarity. Start your server:

```
$ iex -S mix phx.server
```

Then browse to http://localhost:4000/admin/items.

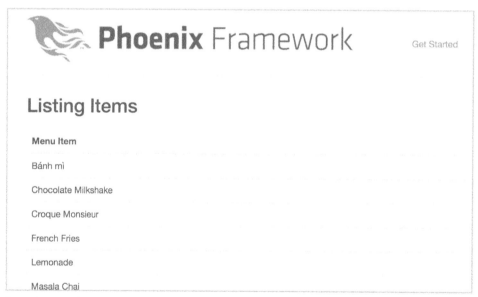

It isn't much, but we've got items!

Now let's take a look at the logs. The IO.inspect line from our controller will show us the result of our GraphQL query:

1.   https://hexdocs.pm/eex

```
[info] GET /admin/items
[debug] Processing with PlateSlateWeb.ItemController.index/2
  Parameters: %{}
  Pipelines: [:browser]
[debug] QUERY OK source="items" db=2.4ms decode=0.1ms
SELECT ... FROM "items" AS i0 ORDER BY i0."name" []
%{data: %{"menu_items" => [%{"name" => "Bánh mì"},
     %{"name" => "Chocolate Milkshake"}, %{"name" => "Croque Monsieur"},
     %{"name" => "French Fries"}, %{"name" => "Lemonade"},
     %{"name" => "Masala Chai"}, %{"name" => "Muffuletta"},
     %{"name" => "Papadum"}, %{"name" => "Pasta Salad"}, %{"name" => "Reuben"},
     %{"name" => "Soft Drink"}, %{"name" => "Thai Salad"},
     %{"name" => "Vada Pav"}, %{"name" => "Vanilla Milkshake"},
     %{"name" => "Water"}]}}
]}}
```

No surprises here. The result that we get in the second argument to our index/2 function is essentially the output you'd get from using Absinthe.run manually. The only difference is that here we're doing menu_items instead of menuItems, so we get keys that are a bit more idiomatic to Elixir.

The response could be easier to use. If we were getting this data directly from a Menu.list_items/1 function call, we'd have nice atom keys to work with, and what we want is a way to get the same kind of result from GraphQL too. In fact, if we want to use Phoenix path or form helpers, we really need to be able to get the entire MenuItem struct back, because Phoenix uses some internal information in Ecto structs to make certain markup decisions.

In other words, if we wanted to link to each menu item in our template, we'd do something like <%= link "Show", to: item_path(@conn, :show, item) %>. Right now, however, item is just %{"name" => "Reuben"} and, understandably, Phoenix doesn't know how to build a link from that. It needs a fully fleshed out %Menu.Item{} struct and all of its data.

Here's where directives come into play.

A directive is a type that's defined in our schema, just like an object or a scalar, and we can use these types to annotate parts of our GraphQL documents for special handling.

Absinthe.Phoenix ships with a couple of directives, which we can get access to by importing them into our own schema:

10-chp.serverui/2-action/lib/plate_slate_web/schema.ex
```
import_types __MODULE__.MenuTypes
import_types __MODULE__.OrderingTypes
import_types __MODULE__.AccountsTypes
import_types Absinthe.Phoenix.Types
```

With this in place, we have access to the :action directive, which we can use to annotate GraphQL queries in our controller. Directives are placed in GraphQL documents prefixed with a @ sigil. Let's see it at work:

10-chp.serverui/2-action/lib/plate_slate_web/controllers/item_controller.ex

```
@graphql """
query Index @action(mode: INTERNAL) {
```

Here you can see the :action directive placed in the GraphQL document via @action, marking the query operation. Much like a field, directives can take arguments. The mode: INTERNAL bit isn't a strange new syntax; this is a totally ordinary argument with an enum value that tells Absinthe.Phoenix that we want to have it adjust the results of executing the query to suit internal Elixir usage.

If we do just this one change and reload our controller, we won't get the list anymore, since our code still expects string keys, but we do get some interesting IO.inspect output:

```
%{data: %{menu_items: [%{name: "Bánh mì"}, %{name: "Chocolate Milkshake"},
    %{name: "Croque Monsieur"}, %{name: "French Fries"}, %{name: "Lemonade"},
    %{name: "Masala Chai"}, %{name: "Muffuletta"}, %{name: "Papadum"},
    %{name: "Pasta Salad"}, %{name: "Reuben"}, %{name: "Soft Drink"},
    %{name: "Thai Salad"}, %{name: "Vada Pav"}, %{name: "Vanilla Milkshake"},
    %{name: "Water"}]}}
```

Because we placed the @action directive on our query, flagging the query as something we want to run in the INTERNAL mode, we get atom keys. When Absinthe.Phoenix ran the query, it used special phases that looked for these flags to adjust the output for us.

While atom keys are nice, they aren't enough to give us a first-class, server-side experience. We need to be able to get the full structs of each menu item so that we can have the full Phoenix.HTML experience. Thankfully, @action has our back.

10-chp.serverui/2-action/lib/plate_slate_web/controllers/item_controller.ex

```
@graphql """
query Index @action(mode: INTERNAL) {
  menu_items
}
"""
def index(conn, result) do
  result |> IO.inspect
  render(conn, "index.html", items: result.data.menu_items)
end
```

The most important thing to notice here is that our GraphQL query now just has a bare menu_items field instead of the previous menu_items { name }. When using @action, this bears special significance: it will return the bare data from field resolvers. With this and the change we make to the render line (to use the atom keys), a controller reload will give us back our list.

Take a look at the debug output:

```
%{data: %{menu_items: [
    %PlateSlate.Menu.Item{name: "Bánh mì", ...},
    %PlateSlate.Menu.Item{name: "Chocolate Milkshake", ...],
    ...
```

The GraphQL document on the controller is returning regular Elixir structs! This is the power of directives. By giving you a flexible way to annotate your document, GraphQL clients and servers have the ability to make deep customizations to their APIs.

Let's put this new struct data to use:

```
10-chp.serverui/2-action/lib/plate_slate_web/templates/item/index.html.eex
<%= for item <- @items do %>
    <tr>
      <td><%= item.name %></td>
      <td class="text-right">
        <span><%= link "Show", to: item_path(@conn, :show, item),
          class: "btn btn-default btn-xs" %>
        </span>
        <span><%= link "Edit", to: item_path(@conn, :edit, item),
          class: "btn btn-default btn-xs" %>
        </span>
        <span><%= link "Delete", to: item_path(@conn, :delete, item),
          method: :delete,
          data: [confirm: "Are you sure?"],
          class: "btn btn-danger btn-xs" %>
        </span>
      </td>
    </tr>
<% end %>
```

The index page here is a jumping-off point to other pages that will let us view more details or edit particular items on the menu. The chunk of code we've added to the table contains various links to those pages that make use of Phoenix path helpers.

Phoenix path helpers are pretty cool. At compile time, the routes that you set up in your router are compiled into a bunch of functions within the PlateSlate-Web.Router.Helpers module, which get imported for us inside of templates. Together with the Phoenix.Param protocol, which builds a URL parameter out of a struct, we can use handy functions like item_path(@conn, :show, item).

The real value of the @action directive is that we can treat our GraphQL API as a first-class Elixir data source. With that kind of support, it frees us to go back to writing completely ordinary server-side UI code. The effort you expend to build your GraphQL API for a mobile or JavaScript application can be immediately reused to power backend UIs, and vice versa.

Let's wrap up this first pass at our index by including the name of the category that each menu item belongs to. Here we face a small challenge. If we do the ordinary { menu_items { category { name }}}, we would no longer have a bare menu_items field, so the result would no longer include the full structs. What we want to have happen here is for the contents of the category resolver to simply get placed into the results we were getting before. To accomplish this, we'll use another directive, :put:

```
10-chp.serverui/3-put/lib/plate_slate_web/controllers/item_controller.ex
@graphql """
query Index @action(mode: INTERNAL) {
  menu_items @put {
    category
  }
}
"""
def index(conn, result) do
  render(conn, "index.html", items: result.data.menu_items)
end
```

The use of @put in our document indicates to Absinthe.Phoenix that instead of narrowing down the results of the menu_items field to only the fields in the selection set, we want to put those values into the previous result.

Now that we're loading our category, we can update our template:

```
10-chp.serverui/3-put/lib/plate_slate_web/templates/item/index.html.eex
<table class="table">
  <thead>
    <tr>
      <th>Menu Item</th>
➤     <th>Category</th>
➤     <th></th>
    </tr>
  </thead>
  <tbody>

<%= for item <- @items do %>
    <tr>
      <td><%= item.name %></td>
➤     <td><%= item.category.name %></td>
```

Reload your server to see it all come together:

Listing Items

Menu Item	Category			
Bánh mì	Sandwiches	Show	Edit	Delete
Chocolate Milkshake	Beverages	Show	Edit	Delete
Croque Monsieur	Sandwiches	Show	Edit	Delete
French Fries	Sides	Show	Edit	Delete
Lemonade	Beverages	Show	Edit	Delete

At the end of the day, our controller is hardly doing anything at all, which is how it should be. The controller can focus on managing the HTTP connection itself, which, in the case of an index page, is essentially just a matter of sending a rendered template over the wire. Our Absinthe schema already knows how to do all the heavy lifting to get our data, so we just tell it what the controller needs and pass it along to the template.

Directives Are Safe

When using normal GraphQL documents, all values that the client will receive are noted explicitly in the schema. This means that clients to the API will only get exactly the data that we're willing to give them; they can't get data that might be sensitive. When using @action, however, extra Elixir values are making their way to our templates, even if they aren't in the schema.

Fortunately, this isn't unsafe at all. Directives can't force the server to do anything; they just ask nicely. The :action and :put directives we're using here are ignored completely unless run through Absinthe.Phoenix.Controller. This means that if someone uses them in a normal API, they are ignored completely, and any sensitive values remain safely on the server.

Handling Input

The main administrative feature we want is to be able to look at the order history for each of the menu items that we have listed here. This isn't the kind of thing that should be visible to just anyone, though, so we need to take some steps to secure the UI. You already know how to secure portions of your GraphQL schema, but you'll learn how to hook that up to the kinds of session mechanisms you use when doing server-driven UIs. It'll also be a good first intro to handling input that comes from the forms.

When working with normal browser-based interfaces, we'll need a way to put authentication information into the session cookie that Plug manages. After a successful login, user information will be placed into the cookie, and then that cookie will get pushed along in every subsequent request. Back in Chapter 8, Securing with Authentication and Authorization, on page 139, we created a plug to handle retrieving auth information from headers, and we'll create a similar plug for our admin scope. It's possible to refactor the existing plug to handle both the API and the admin interface, but there's enough distinct logic that it's cleaner to create a new one.

```
10-chp.serverui/4-login/lib/plate_slate_web/admin_auth.ex
defmodule PlateSlateWeb.AdminAuth do
  @behaviour Plug
  import Plug.Conn

  def init(opts), do: opts

  def call(conn, _) do
    with id when not is_nil(id) <- get_session(conn, :employee_id),
      %{} = user <- PlateSlate.Accounts.lookup("employee", id) do
        conn
        |> Plug.Conn.assign(:current_user, user)
        |> Absinthe.Plug.put_options(context: %{current_user: user})
    else
      _ ->
        conn
        |> clear_session
        |> Phoenix.Controller.redirect(to: "/admin/session/new")
    end
  end
end
```

Instead of looking at the headers, we're using the get_session/2 function provided by the Plug.Conn module to check the user-provided cookie for an :employee_id. If there is such an ID and it matches up to a user, we put that user in the connection :assigns so that the user is available broadly within our UI, and we put it in the Absinthe.Plug context so that our GraphQL queries have access to it too. If the user isn't authenticated, they'll just be redirected to the login page, and whatever session info they have is cleared out just in case it's erroneous.

The trick in the router is that you want this to be applied to the item routes but not the session routes. Otherwise, you'd have the catch 22 of requiring authentication to log in. You can achieve this by having two "/admin" scopes in the router:

```
10-chp.serverui/4-login/lib/plate_slate_web/router.ex
pipeline :admin_auth do
  plug PlateSlateWeb.AdminAuth
end

scope "/admin", PlateSlateWeb do
  pipe_through :browser

  resources "/session", SessionController,
    only: [:new, :create, :delete],
    singleton: true
end

scope "/admin", PlateSlateWeb do
  pipe_through [:browser, :admin_auth]

  resources "/items", ItemController
end
```

The first bit here is a Phoenix router pipeline with our brand-new AdminAuth module plugged in. Then we've got the "/admin" scope holding the session paths, and it only uses the :browser pipeline so that anyone can view the login page. Afterward, there's another admin clause that we run through both the :browser and the :admin_auth pipeline, and it locks down the item routes we defined previously.

At this point, we've really handled the most complicated Phoenix bits. Let's fill out the session view and template, then turn our attention to the interesting part: the controller.

Our view couldn't be simpler:

```
10-chp.serverui/4-login/lib/plate_slate_web/views/session_view.ex
defmodule PlateSlateWeb.SessionView do
  use PlateSlateWeb, :view
end
```

When we created the ItemController, we used a Phoenix generator, so the ItemView was created for us. We aren't using generators this time, so we need to create it ourselves, but this isn't a lot of trouble given its size.

The login template is pretty simple too:

```
10-chp.serverui/4-login/lib/plate_slate_web/templates/session/new.html.eex
<h2>Login</h2>

<%= form_for @conn, session_path(@conn, :create), fn f -> %>
  <div class="form-group">
    <label>
      Email: <%= text_input f, :email %>
    </label>

    <label>
      Password: <%= password_input f, :password %>
    </label>

    <%= submit "Submit", class: "btn btn-primary" %>
  </div>
<% end %>
```

We're using the Phoenix form_for helper just to minimize the HTML boilerplate, and with it we set up a basic form with email and password inputs. When we submit this form, it'll do a POST to the session_path, which evaluates out to /admin/sessions.

Looking Up Your Paths

 Remember, if you need to check what the name for a route is, use the mix phx.routes task.

Last but not least, let's get a basic controller action going so we can render this.

```
10-chp.serverui/4-login/lib/plate_slate_web/controllers/session_controller.ex
defmodule PlateSlateWeb.SessionController do
  use PlateSlateWeb, :controller
  use Absinthe.Phoenix.Controller,
    schema: PlateSlateWeb.Schema

  def new(conn, _) do
    render(conn, "new.html")
  end
end
```

At this point, we've got enough in place that we can start our server and head over to the login page. If we head to the items page that we were looking at before at /admin/items instead, we should be redirected to the login page, since we've locked that down now.

Start your server and browse to http://localhost:4000/admin/session/new.

```
$ iex -S mix phx.server
```

It's a form!

Login

Email: Password: Submit

If we try to submit this form at the moment, it's going to raise an error, since we haven't configured a create/2 function in the session controller yet. Let's do it anyway, though, just so that we can see the parameter output in the logs:

```
[info] POST /admin/session
[debug] Processing with PlateSlateWeb.SessionController.create/2
  Parameters: %{
    "_csrf_token" => ...,
    "_utf8" => "✓",
    "email" => "user@localhost",
    "password" => "[FILTERED]"
  }
```

We can hook these parameters up to a GraphQL document by naming variables within a document after their corresponding parameter. All of the actual validation logic already exists in our login_employee mutation, so we just need to write a GraphQL document that maps these parameters to that mutation field.

```
10-chp.serverui/4-login/lib/plate_slate_web/controllers/session_controller.ex
@graphql """
mutation ($email: String!, $password: String!) @action(mode: INTERNAL) {
  login(role: EMPLOYEE, email: $email, password: $password)
}
"""
def create(conn, %{data: %{login: result}}) do
  case result do
    %{user: employee} ->
      conn
      |> put_session(:employee_id, employee.id)
      |> put_flash(:info, "Login successful")
      |> redirect(to: "/admin/items")
    _ ->
      conn
      |> put_flash(:info, "Wrong email or password")
      |> render("new.html")
  end
end
```

To recap, the login_employee mutation field returns an :employee_session object, which consists of an employee field and a token field. If the login information isn't correct, it adds a GraphQL error and returns nil. The login field requires two arguments, email and password, which we're passing in via variables. Those variable names match up the parameter names set in our form, so when we submit the form, Absinthe.Phoenix.Controller grabs those parameters and uses them as GraphQL variable inputs.

Our controller logic is focused on what to do with the HTTP connection depending on the result of the mutation. If the login is successful, we need to add the employee information to the session via put_session so that the data is available in future requests for the AdminAuth plug's get_session function. With the session configured, the controller can redirect to the items page, which should now render happily for us.

Give it a go first with a bad username and password:

Wrong email or password

Login

Email: **user@localhost**   Password: •••••   Submit

If you still have the user we created back in Chapter 8, Securing with Authentication and Authorization, on page 139, you should be able to log in with email: foo@example.com, password: abc123. If not, let's create one here in your console:

```
$ iex -S mix phx.server
iex(1)> %PlateSlate.Accounts.User{} |>
PlateSlate.Accounts.User.changeset(%{
  role: "employee",
  name: "Becca Wilson",
  email: "foo@example.com",
  password: "abc123"}) |> PlateSlate.Repo.insert!
```

Head back to http://localhost:4000/admin/sessions/new and give it a whirl!

Logging out is just a matter of clearing out the session cookie, which doesn't really involve our GraphQL API. All we need is a basic delete action in the controller:

```
10-chp.serverui/4-login/lib/plate_slate_web/controllers/session_controller.ex
def delete(conn, _) do
  conn
  |> clear_session
  |> redirect(to: "/admin/session/new")
end
```

And we need a link to it on the UI:

```
10-chp.serverui/4-login/lib/plate_slate_web/templates/layout/app.html.eex
<nav role="navigation">
  <ul class="nav nav-pills pull-right">
    <li><a href="http://www.phoenixframework.org/docs">Get Started</a></li>
➤   <%= if @conn.assigns[:current_user] do %>
➤   <li><%= link "Logout", to: session_path(@conn, :delete),
➤     method: :delete,
➤     class: "btn btn-danger btn-xs" %>
➤   </li>
➤   <% end %>
  </ul>
</nav>
```

Reload the page and look to the top right-hand corner:

At the end of the day, getting data into our GraphQL queries is pretty simple. Absinthe.Phoenix just does a one-to-one mapping of parameters to variables, and then all the usual logic takes over.

Complex Queries

Now that we have a session management story for our admin UI, we can tackle exposing more sensitive information. What we want to do is provide an order history that we'll display on each menu item show page. We'll have to start by adding some fields to our GraphQL schema in order to connect menu items over to the orders, and we'll need to do a few tweaks at the database and context level to make pulling the data out easy.

What we'll get for this effort, though, is pretty cool. Not only will it give us the ability to show this information on the show page, but we'll also suddenly have the ability to display a subset of the information back on the index page, and we'll have set up everything the next chapter needs to do the same thing in JavaScript. A little bit of effort goes a long way.

Connecting Items to Orders

Let's start with thinking about how we want to get the orders for a menu item, because the database design we came up with in Chapter 6, Going Live with Subscriptions, on page 97 does not make that quite as easy as we'd like. As you recall, when an order is placed, there is a snapshot taken of the orders at the time of ordering, so that any future price or name changes to the menu won't affect our historical record. It also gives us an opportunity to experiment with how embedded schemas work with GraphQL.

What this means, however, is that the snapshots don't reference menu items by ID but rather by name, and they're inside of a JSONB column on the orders table. If this were a production system, we'd probably normalize this into a significantly more complicated setup with a half dozen join tables, but for our purposes, we can do something a bit simpler.

In the code provided for this book, you'll find a database migration that creates a PostgreSQL view. A view is basically a table powered by an SQL query. You can treat it exactly like a table from within Ecto, which is a perfect way to expose an Elixir-friendly interface for certain database operations that might otherwise be less ergonomic. We've included the code that creates this database view here for reference:

```
10-chp.serverui/5-history/priv/repo/migrations/20171108213102_create_order_item_view.exs
defmodule PlateSlate.Repo.Migrations.CreateOrderItemView do
  use Ecto.Migration

  def up do
    execute("""
    CREATE VIEW order_items AS
      SELECT i.*, o.id as order_id
      FROM orders AS o, jsonb_to_recordset(o.items)
        AS i(name text, quantity int, price float, id text)
    """)
  end

  def down do
    execute("DROP VIEW order_items")
  end
end
```

We're not going to worry too terribly much about the SQL query itself here. The point to take away is that we've created a view we can query as "order_items" and it has the columns name, quantity, price, id, order_id.

With that in place, we're in a good spot to turn to our GraphQL schema and think about how we want to represent the history. When we think about an order history, we often want to do more than merely list the orders, we also want to know certain aggregate information about the span of time we're querying. In our case, we're going to show the total quantity of the menu item sold, as well as the total revenue we've earned from it over time.

Here's how we model this in our GraphQL schema:

```
10-chp.serverui/5-history/lib/plate_slate_web/schema/menu_types.ex
alias PlateSlateWeb.Resolvers
alias PlateSlateWeb.Schema.Middleware
# «Rest of file»
object :menu_item do
# «Rest of menu item object»
  field :order_history, :order_history do
    arg :since, :date
    middleware Middleware.Authorize, "employee"
    resolve &Resolvers.Ordering.order_history/3
  end
end

object :order_history do
  field :orders, list_of(:order) do
    resolve &Resolvers.Ordering.orders/3
  end

  field :quantity, non_null(:integer) do
    resolve Resolvers.Ordering.stat(:quantity)
  end

  @desc "Gross Revenue"
  field :gross, non_null(:float) do
    resolve Resolvers.Ordering.stat(:gross)
  end
end
```

Instead of doing something like field :order_history, list_of(:order), we have this interstitial :order_history object, and what it does is provide us a place to expose metadata alongside the actual orders themselves. In a way, it's a lot like what we did in Chapter 4, Adding Flexibility, on page 59 when we created a :menu_item_result object to manage error information. This pattern of creating intermediate objects to provide metadata is a good one to keep in mind, and we'll see it again in the next chapter when we look at pagination.

We're also doing something new with the :gross and :quantity fields. On the :orders field, the resolve: key is provided an anonymous function literal, but on these two statistics fields, we're actually *calling* a function to build a resolver function dynamically.

Last but not least, in our schema we need to add a top-level way to get a menu item by ID:

10-chp.serverui/5-history/lib/plate_slate_web/schema.ex
```
query do
  # «Other query fields»
  field :menu_item, :menu_item do
    arg :id, non_null(:id)
    resolve &Resolvers.Menu.get_item/3
  end
end
```

And the corresponding resolver:

10-chp.serverui/5-history/lib/plate_slate_web/resolvers/menu.ex
```
import Absinthe.Resolution.Helpers
# «Other resolvers»

def get_item(_, %{id: id}, %{context: %{loader: loader}}) do
  loader
  |> Dataloader.load(Menu, Menu.Item, id)
  |> on_load(fn loader ->
    {:ok, Dataloader.get(loader, Menu, Menu.Item, id)}
  end)
end
```

While Dataloader isn't mandatory here since it isn't super common to have a large number of top-level queries by ID, it makes the resolver function a bit more versatile, and we could use the same function on any other field that needs to look up an item by ID in the future.

This will enable queries like this:

```
{
  menu_item(id: "1") {
    name
    order_history(since: "2017-01-01") {
      quantity
      gross
      orders { orderedAt customerNumber }
    }
  }
}
```

One challenge our resolvers will need to sort out is that while it makes sense to place the since: argument on the order_history field itself, we really need that value in all three resolvers underneath it. We'll find all of them inside the Resolvers.Ordering file, so let's give them a look:

```
10-chp.serverui/5-history/lib/plate_slate_web/resolvers/ordering.ex
import Absinthe.Resolution.Helpers

def order_history(item, args, _) do
  one_month_ago = Date.utc_today |> Date.add(-30)
  args = Map.update(args, :since, one_month_ago, fn date ->
    date || one_month_ago
  end)
  {:ok, %{item: item, args: args}}
end
```

Each resolver here is doing something a bit different. The resolver for the order_history field itself simply grabs the arguments and the menu_item and it passes those through as a map. This is how we can get access to those values within the :quantity and :orders fields, because the order_history return value is used as the parent value for each of their resolvers.

```
10-chp.serverui/5-history/lib/plate_slate_web/resolvers/ordering.ex
def orders(%{item: item, args: args}, _, _) do
  batch({Ordering, :orders_by_item_name, args}, item.name, fn orders ->
    {:ok, Map.get(orders, item.name, [])}
  end)
end
```

To load the orders, we leverage the batch plugin that we covered in the last chapter. Although there aren't N+1 concerns when loading a single menu item, we'll be reusing these fields in the index at the end, and it's generally a wise approach to avoid N+1-style coding proactively. The batch plugin makes it particularly easy to handle the statistics, so we'll just use that for loading all the data here instead of setting up a Dataloader source for the Ordering context.

To recap how batch works, the orders/3 resolver sets up a batch key of {Ordering, :orders_by_item_name, args}, and it aggregates the item.name value, which means that it will call the Ordering.orders_by_item_name/2 function as Ordering.orders_by_item_name(args, aggregated_names). The output of that function will be a map containing orders for each menu item by name, so we can just pull out the orders for this specific item.

The batch function itself is where we use the order_items view we created earlier to do some pretty ordinary filtering:

```
10-chp.serverui/5-history/lib/plate_slate/ordering/ordering.ex
def orders_by_item_name(%{since: since}, names) do
  query = from [i, o] in name_query(since, names),
    order_by: [desc: o.ordered_at],
    select: %{name: i.name, order: o}
  query
  |> Repo.all
  |> Enum.group_by(& &1.name, & &1.order)
end
defp name_query(since, names) do
  from i in "order_items",
    join: o in Order, on: o.id == i.order_id,
    where: o.ordered_at >= type(^since, :date),
    where: i.name in ^names
end
```

The meat of the query happens in the name_query helper function, which we'll also use for the stats retrieval here in a moment. Together, these functions receive the :since argument and aggregated names, and create a mapping of menu item names to orders on that item. Aggregating the statistics on the orders works in a similar way:

```
10-chp.serverui/5-history/lib/plate_slate/ordering/ordering.ex
def orders_stats_by_name(%{since: since}, names) do
  Map.new Repo.all from i in name_query(since, names),
    group_by: i.name,
    select: {i.name, %{
      quantity: sum(i.quantity),
      gross: type(sum(fragment("? * ?", i.price, i.quantity)), :decimal)
    }}
end
```

The main thing to notice here is that we're computing both statistics at the same time, so the shape of the returned data structure will look like this:

```
%{
  "Chocolate Milkshake" => %{quantity: 4, gross: 12.0},
  "French Fries" => %{quantity: 2, gross: 1.0},
}
```

By returning both statistics, we can reduce the boilerplate in our resolver related to loading these statistics:

```
10-chp.serverui/5-history/lib/plate_slate_web/resolvers/ordering.ex
def stat(stat) do
  fn %{item: item, args: args}, _, _ ->
    batch({Ordering, :orders_stats_by_name, args}, item.name, fn results ->
      {:ok, results[item.name][stat] || 0}
    end)
  end
end
```

You can think of the stat/1 function as a resolver function builder. We pass in the statistic that we want from the schema like Resolvers.Ordering.stat(:quantity) or Resolvers.Ordering.stat(:gross), and then it returns a resolver function that sets up the generic batch. It then pulls out the specific statistic we care about via results[item.name][stat].

While the database design didn't make it trivial to connect menu items to orders, it provided us a good opportunity to experiment with some helpful batching techniques, and we learned about resolver building functions along the way. If you haven't reset your database since earlier in the book, you may still have some orders around. Otherwise, if you check out the book code for this chapter, you'll see that the seed data has been updated to include a user and a large number of orders over time. (Having a lot of orders will make the filtering by time a bit more interesting when we get to actually showing it in the UI.)

Displaying Order History

Our GraphQL schema is good to go at this point, so it's all UI work from here. What we want to do is put together a page that shows the details of a specific menu item, along with its order history and the statistics we compute. The controller action itself is nice and simple:

```
10-chp.serverui/5-history/lib/plate_slate_web/controllers/item_controller.ex
use Absinthe.Phoenix.Controller,
  schema: PlateSlateWeb.Schema,
  action: [mode: :internal]
# «Rest of controller»

@graphql """
query ($id: ID!, $since: Date) {
  menu_item(id: $id) @put {
    order_history(since: $since) {
      quantity
      gross
      orders
    }
  }
}
"""
def show(conn, %{data: %{menu_item: nil}}) do
  conn
  |> put_flash(:info, "Menu item not found")
  |> redirect(to: "/admin/items")
end
def show(conn, %{data: %{menu_item: item}}) do
  since = variables(conn)["since"] || "2018-01-01"
  render(conn, "show.html", item: item, since: since)
end
```

One thing that's different from before is that instead of including an @action directive on this particular GraphQL query, we're setting a configuration value on the use Absinthe.Phoenix.Controller invocation. When all of the GraphQL documents within a controller should all use the mode: :internal option, you can simply specify this on the use call, so that you don't have to add that boilerplate to every document.

The callback itself has two clauses: one if the ID we're given fails to turn up a menu item, and another if it doesn't fail. The query is exactly what we had envisioned earlier and will get us the info on a particular menu item along with its history. We're also passing in a since variable, which we'll drive from a date select in the template. In order to make sure the date input gets a value, we also need to pass since to our render function. The variables/1 function comes from Absinthe.Phoenix, and is a way for us to access the bare inputs to the GraphQL query, which is exactly what we need to fill the date input.

This template is the largest we've used in this chapter, so we'll look at it in two parts. Up at the top, we've got a header and the form to enter the date:

```
10-chp.serverui/5-history/lib/plate_slate_web/templates/item/show.html.eex
<h2>
  <%= @item.name %>
</h2>

<%= form_tag item_path(@conn, :show, @item), method: :get do %>
  <div class="form-group">
    <label for="since">Since</label>
    <input type="date" id="since" name="since" value="<%= @since %>"/>
  </div>
  <%= submit "Filter Orders", class: "btn btn-primary" %>
<% end %>
```

The form is pretty simple. The path we're using just routes back to where we are right now with whatever the new since value would be. If we have order information, we then use that to display some interesting history:

```
10-chp.serverui/5-history/lib/plate_slate_web/templates/item/show.html.eex
<%= if Enum.empty?(@item.order_history.orders) do %>
  <p>No units have been sold during this time period.</p>
<% else %>
  <h3>
    Sold
    <%= @item.order_history.quantity %>
    ($<%= Decimal.round(@item.order_history.gross, 2) %> gross)
  </h3>
```

```
<table class="table">
  <thead>
    <tr>
      <th>Date</th>
      <th>Count</th>
    </tr>
  </thead>
  <tbody>
    <%= for order <- @item.order_history.orders do %>
    <tr>
      <td><%= order.ordered_at |> DateTime.to_date %></td>
      <td><%= order.items |> Enum.map(&(&1.quantity)) |> Enum.sum %></td>
    </tr>
    <% end %>
  </tbody>
</table>
<% end %>

<p>
  <%= link "Back",
      to: item_path(@conn, :index),
      class: "btn btn-default btn-xs" %>
</p>
```

To see this template in action, we just need to get our server going again.
Start it with this:

```
$ iex -S mix phx.server
```

Now, let's browse to http://localhost:4000/admin/items and click the "show" button
on any of the menu item rows that have orders.

Reuben

Since 01/01/2018

`Filter Orders`

Sold 8 ($36.00 gross)

Date	Count
2018-01-21	4
2018-01-21	4

`Back`

There we have it! If you use the date select box, you can change the date and
see how this affects the list and order count.

If you don't see any orders, take a look at the seed data and make sure you actually have orders for the span of time you're searching! If not, either create some via GraphiQL or go to IEx and enter:

```
PlateSlate.Ordering.create_order(%{
  items: [%{menu_item_id: "1", quantity: 4}]
})
```

What's particularly cool is that we can add the same feature to the index page with almost no additional effort:

```
10-chp.serverui/5-history/lib/plate_slate_web/controllers/item_controller.ex
@graphql """
query {
  menu_items @put {
    category
    order_history {
      quantity
    }
  }
}
"""

def index(conn, result) do
  render(conn, "index.html", items: result.data.menu_items)
end
```

Here we're just getting the quantity value from the order_history, since it wouldn't make sense to try to add the orders themselves to the table. This value, however, fits in nicely in the template if we add another column:

```
10-chp.serverui/5-history/lib/plate_slate_web/templates/item/index.html.eex
<table class="table">
  <thead>
    <tr>
      <th>Menu Item</th>
      <th>Category</th>
➤     <th>Quantity</th>
      <th></th>
    </tr>
  </thead>
  <tbody>

<%= for item <- @items do %>
    <tr>
      <td><%= item.name %></td>
      <td><%= item.category.name %></td>
➤     <td><%= item.order_history.quantity %></td>
```

This additional column makes the index page a lot more useful as shown in the figure on page 219.

Listing Items

Menu Item	Category	Quantity			
Bánh mì	Sandwiches	0	Show	Edit	Delete
Chocolate Milkshake	Beverages	4	Show	Edit	Delete

So we've added a nice feature to both the menu item show and index page—by making what's effectively one change to our schema. The benefit of that one change, however, goes beyond the user interface. While we expanded the scope of our schema to support the UI, we've also kept our GraphQL API in sync—effortlessly. This symbiosis between UI and API is a compelling reason to use GraphQL to power both. By sharing the same data access pattern, it's easy to keep each apace with the other.

Moving On

Throughout this chapter, you've gotten a feel for a new way of building Phoenix controller actions, a declarative approach to defining their data requirements, and a way to reuse the GraphQL schema logic that we've already defined from within the same Elixir application. This approach is still new, and we've only scratched the surface on the possibilities.

Now that we've looked at server-side user interfaces, it's about time to move on to the dynamic world of client-side GraphQL frameworks. Let's take a moment and think about some interesting ways that you could expand the administrative interface using what you've learned.

1. You can add menu items—and list them—but what happens if you want to change or add a new one? Think about how you might add basic support for adding or editing menu items. They're just mutations!
2. Your menu could get pretty large. Think through how you might add a search box to the index to filter the list of menu items.
3. Build an administrative UI for categories. Follow the same pattern that we did throughout the chapter, but this time focus on categories by building PlateSlateWeb.CategoryController.

In the next (and final) chapter of the book, we'll take a look at the most popular GraphQL client-side frameworks, giving you a primer on how to integrate them with Absinthe, and what specialized support has already been prepackaged for you to use.

Integrating with the Frontend

Welcome to the client-side framework chapter, where you'll learn how to connect JavaScript-based web applications to a GraphQL API—including how to take advantage of Absinthe-specific features like Phoenix channel-based subscriptions using the plug-and-play packages that are already available.

Through this chapter, we're going to gradually step up the complexity of the front-end applications we're integrating. We'll start with a basic, single-file JavaScript application, then move on to the two most popular approaches to using GraphQL from JavaScript today: Relay (the original GraphQL framework) and Apollo Client.

The JavaScript ecosystem is full of choices, and we know that the choices that we've made in this chapter aren't going to appeal to every JavaScript developer's personal tastes. That's okay. If you're more comfortable with other frameworks and tools, you'll still find plenty of material here that you can repurpose to work with your day-to-day favorites.

Let's start by implementing the simplest of integrations, but one that still illustrates the most important feature: how to make a request to a GraphQL server from JavaScript. If you're planning on using Apollo or Relay, feel free to jump ahead, but this initial look at plain JavaScript will be especially useful to people building ultralight clients or working with another programming language.

Starting Simple

Using a GraphQL API from the client side doesn't necessitate a big framework or a lot of tooling. A plain old JavaScript *script* will do. We're going to start by building the simplest of JavaScript projects just to illustrate how to configure a basic client.

We'll set this up as a separate project from the PlateSlate Phoenix-based application. As noted in System Dependencies, on page xiv, you're going to need Node.js,[1] so if you don't already have a working installation, now's the time to get it set up and running. We recommend installation by using your favorite package manager, or a Node.js version manager if you see yourself using different versions in the future.

Once you have Node.js installed, you should be able to execute commands using the Node Package Manager (npm). Something like this should work:

```
$ npm --version
3.10.3
```

Now let's install yarn,[2] which will make management of our project dependencies easier:

```
$ npm install -g yarn
```

We'll make a new directory for our project (*alongside* rather than *inside* our Elixir PlateSlate application), change to that directory, and instruct yarn to bootstrap it with a basic package.json file to keep track of our project metadata and dependencies:

```
$ mkdir plate-slate-basic-ui
$ cd plate-slate-basic-ui
$ yarn init -y
```

The -y option here tells yarn just to assume we typed y (yes) to the various questions it would normally ask.

If you open up package.json in an editor, you'll see the basic boilerplate content that yarn added:

11-chp.frontend/plate-slate-basic-ui/1-start/package.json
```
{
  "name": "plate-slate-basic-ui",
  "version": "1.0.0",
  "main": "index.js",
  "license": "MIT"
}
```

There's not a lot here yet; we'll be adding a bit to this file shortly.

Now, let's create a subdirectory within our project that will hold the HTML and JavaScript files we'll be adding:

```
$ mkdir public
```

---

1. http://nodejs.org
2. https://yarnpkg.com

Dashes and Underscores

We use dashes instead of underscores when creating JavaScript projects because it's common JavaScript package naming style, and it makes it easy to identify Elixir vs. JavaScript projects from directory listings.

Inside that directory, we'll create a basic HTML document—something that we'll expand on later:

```
11-chp.frontend/plate-slate-basic-ui/2-server/public/index.html
<!doctype html>
<html lang="en">
  <head>
    <title>PlateSlate (Basic UI)</title>
  </head>
  <body>
    Hi.
  </body>
</html>
```

For the moment, we have it just greet the viewer; it doesn't hurt to be polite, and it would be nice to see something besides a blank page when we check to make sure we're serving the page. We could do that with a number of different tools, but since we're already using Node.js, let's configure a tiny static web server to make index.html available via a localhost port.

Adding a Static Web Server

The most common web server utility package for Node.js projects is Express,[3] and configuring it to serve a directory of static assets is pretty straightforward.

First, we need to add it as a development dependency using yarn:

```
$ yarn add express --dev
```

Now that we have Express available, let's write the configuration we need in our index.js file. We'll configure it to serve up our public/ directory on port 3000:

```
11-chp.frontend/plate-slate-basic-ui/2-server/index.js
const express = require('express');
const app = express();

app.use(express.static('public'));
app.listen(3000, () => console.log('Listening on port 3000!'))
```

---

3. http://expressjs.com

To make kicking off this little web server as easy as possible, let's add a script entry to our package.json file. It will just execute node ./ (which will run the script defined by the main setting—our index.js file):

```
11-chp.frontend/plate-slate-basic-ui/2-server/package.json
{
  "name": "plate-slate-basic-ui",
  "version": "1.0.0",
  "main": "index.js",
  "license": "MIT",
  "devDependencies": {
    "express": "^4.16.2"
  },
  "scripts": {
    "dev": "node ./"
  }
}
```

This lets us use yarn dev to kick off our web server:

```
$ yarn dev
Listening on port 3000!
```

If we check http://localhost:3000 in our browser, we'll see our Hi!.

So we have a (very) basic static web server set up, just using Node.js! Our web application is *just a bit* underwhelming at the moment. To test our ability to access data from our GraphQL API, we'd like to pull the list of menu items and display them.

Fetching a GraphQL Query

Let's shut down our fancy "Hi!" web server and work on our web application a bit more. We'll start by modifying our index.html document to do two things:

- Load a polyfill for the browser fetch[4] API
- Load our application code, which we'll put at public/js/app.js

---

Polyfill

A web polyfill is a piece of code that acts as a shim, adding a capability to older or less advanced browsers so that applications can transparently use modern browser APIs without needing to work around issues with browser-specific support.

This will involve two script tags—and we might as well remove our pithy greeting while we're at it:

---

4.   https://fetch.spec.whatwg.org/#fetch-api

11-chp.frontend/plate-slate-basic-ui/3-fetch/public/index.html

```html
<!doctype html>
<html lang="en">
  <head>
    <title>PlateSlate (Basic UI)</title>
    <script src="https://cdn.jsdelivr.net/npm/whatwg-fetch"></script>
    <script src="/js/app.js"></script>
  </head>
  <body>

  </body>
</html>
```

We'll define three named functions in our JavaScript application—first, the piece that uses fetch() to retrieve the menu items from our GraphQL API. Unsurprisingly, we'll call it fetchMenuItems():

11-chp.frontend/plate-slate-basic-ui/3-fetch/public/js/app.js

```javascript
function fetchMenuItems() {
  return window.fetch('http://localhost:4000/api', {
    method: 'POST',
    headers: {
      'Content-Type': 'application/json'
    },
    body: JSON.stringify({
      query: '{ menuItems { name } }'
    })
  }).then(function(response) {
    return response.json();
  });
}
```

Notice this looks like a completely normal HTTP POST—because it is. Since we're doing a query operation to get our menu items, we could be using GET, but it's easier and more consistent to encode our GraphQL document as part of an application/json POST body. We return the result of fetch(), which just happens to be a JavaScript Promise—an object that represents the completion or failure of an asynchronous action.

If fetchMenuItems() is unsuccessful, we want to display a simple message to users and log the details to the console. We'll do that with a function, displayFetchError():

11-chp.frontend/plate-slate-basic-ui/3-fetch/public/js/app.js

```javascript
function displayFetchError(response) {
  var element = document.createElement('p');
  element.innerHTML = 'Could not contact API.';
  console.error("Fetch Error", response);
  document.body.appendChild(element);
}
```

If fetchMenuItems() is successful, however, we'll take a look at the result from our GraphQL API and then show the appropriate information:

```
11-chp.frontend/plate-slate-basic-ui/3-fetch/public/js/app.js
function displayMenuItems(result) {
  var element;
  if (result.errors) {
    var element = document.createElement('p');
    element.innerHTML = 'Could not retrieve menu items.';
    console.error("GraphQL Errors", result.errors);
  } else if (result.data.menuItems) {
    var element = document.createElement('ul');
    result.data.menuItems.forEach(function(item) {
      var itemElement = document.createElement('li');
      itemElement.innerHTML = item.name;
      element.appendChild(itemElement);
    });
  }
  document.body.appendChild(element);
}
```

It's possible that the GraphQL API might return an error, so we deal with that similarly to how we handled a fetchMenuItems() failure: we'll display a simple error message and log the details. It's much more likely that we'll get a list of menu items back, however—and in that case, we'll build up a list of the menu items and display them for our users.

You'll notice that in both our failure and success cases, we're manipulating the HTML Document Object Model (DOM). To do this, our application script needs to make sure that our document is fully loaded—so we can safely muck around with the contents of its body.

We can do this by watching for the DOMContentLoaded event with an event listener:

```
11-chp.frontend/plate-slate-basic-ui/3-fetch/public/js/app.js
document.addEventListener('DOMContentLoaded', function() {
  // «Stuff to do once the page is loaded»
});
```

We'll go ahead and wire in our fetchMenuItems() there. We'll configure the resulting Promise object to trigger displayMenuItems() when it's successful, and displayFetchError() when it fails:

```
11-chp.frontend/plate-slate-basic-ui/3-fetch/public/js/app.js
document.addEventListener('DOMContentLoaded', function() {
➤   fetchMenuItems()
➤     .then(displayMenuItems)
➤     .catch(displayFetchError);
});
```

If we were to run both our PlateSlate GraphQL API (on port 4000) and our little web server (on port 3000) right now, we'd run full tilt into an issue with browser security, and we'd see something like this:

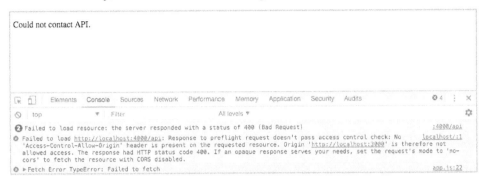

First off, congratulate yourself for a nicely inserted "Could not contact API" message, just as we planned for fetch errors.

The error messages you see in the console here are because we need to use cross-origin resource sharing (CORS)[5] to contact our server.

Configuring for CORS

CORS is a mechanism used by browsers and servers to allow resources with certain restrictions to be requested from another location on the web. It does this using a series of HTTP headers whose contents lay out a server's specific rules about what resources can be accessed and how.

The default rule for asynchronous JavaScript requests limits access to a same-origin policy, and because our web application isn't being served up by our PlateSlate itself, we need to configure our server to respond to the CORS-preflight requests appropriately, allowing cross-origin requests. Thankfully, there's a plug for that—cors_plug.[6] We'll use it directly in our Phoenix endpoint, with the default options.

Restrict Your CORS

You can restrict access to your server to a limited set of origin domains and HTTP methods by passing additional options to plug CORSPlug. Check the documentation for the cors_plug package for more information.

First, let's add the package to the list of declared dependencies in our PlateSlate mix.exs (the server, not our JavaScript UI, of course):

---

5.   https://fetch.spec.whatwg.org/#http-cors-protocol

6.   https://hex.pm/packages/cors_plug

11-chp.frontend/plate_slate/1-start/mix.exs
```
defp deps do
  [
    # «Other deps»
    {:cors_plug, "~> 1.5"},
  ]
end
```

We make sure we stop our PlateSlate Elixir application if it's still running, and install the package using mix:

```
$ mix deps.get
```

Once that is downloaded and ready to go, let's add the plug to our endpoint, which lives under lib/plate_slate_web. We will put it right after the socket configuration:

11-chp.frontend/plate_slate/1-start/lib/plate_slate_web/endpoint.ex
```
defmodule PlateSlateWeb.Endpoint do
  use Phoenix.Endpoint, otp_app: :plate_slate
  use Absinthe.Phoenix.Endpoint

  socket "/socket", PlateSlateWeb.UserSocket

  plug CORSPlug

  # «Rest of configuration»
end
```

We also need to tweak our web application to use CORS. We do this by setting the mode option for fetch():

11-chp.frontend/plate-slate-basic-ui/4-cors/public/js/app.js
```
function fetchMenuItems() {
  return window.fetch('http://localhost:4000/api', {
    method: 'POST',
    mode: 'cors',
    headers: {
      'Content-Type': 'application/json'
    },
    body: JSON.stringify({
      query: '{ menuItems { name } }'
    })
  }).then(function(response) {
    return response.json();
  });
}
```

If we start up our PlateSlate application (with mix phx.server) and our web application (with yarn dev), now we'll see a much more encouraging result in our web browser at http://localhost:3000 as shown in the figure on page 229.

- Bánh mì
- Chocolate Milkshake
- Croque Monsieur
- French Fries
- Lemonade
- Masala Chai
- Muffuletta
- Papadum
- Pasta Salad
- Reuben
- Soft Drink
- Thai Salad
- Vada Pav
- Vanilla Milkshake
- Water

Congratulations, you've rendered a list of menu items—in a tiny web application using basic, vanilla JavaScript from another server. Sure, the list is almost unforgivably ugly—Cascading Style Sheets (CSS) being an entirely different book, after all—but you're displaying live data, and the full capabilities of GraphQL queries are available to you, even from this toy-sized web application.

Want to show a menu item price? Displaying it—or any other data you could request via walking your data graph–is a simple matter of modifying your query and inserting the resulting data via the DOM elements of your choice. You're not limited to GraphQL query operations either. You can use mutation operations just as easily from an HTTP POST.

To use subscription operations, however, you're going to need to add some additional dependencies.

Choosing a Framework

Absinthe subscriptions, as you've read about in Chapter 6, Going Live with Subscriptions, on page 97, use Phoenix channels (by default, at least), and that takes some specialized handling. If you're going to support subscriptions, it's probably a good idea to go beyond the vanilla JavaScript that we've been using up to this point and look at more advanced GraphQL clients and framework projects that can make your life easier.

We'll cover two of them: Apollo Client and Relay.

At the current time, there are two major client-side JavaScript frameworks that developers use to build user interfaces on top of GraphQL: Relay and the Apollo GraphQL platform.

Beyond JavaScript

Just as on the server, your options for client-side GraphQL aren't strictly limited to JavaScript. We're limiting our examples to client-side JavaScript in the book only because it's got the widest, most active community of users and the most well-established use patterns.

If you are a proponent of Elm, ReasonML, ClojureScript, PureScript, or any other client-side language or framework on the web—as long as it can speak HTTP and WebSockets—you can make GraphQL work for you. The same goes for native mobile applications: Swift, Java, and other languages have already been integrated with GraphQL APIs.

It might take a little more footwork to find the right packages and tools that work for your language, but you can do it. Hopefully, learning about how JavaScript connects to a GraphQL server will help—either directly as something you can access externally from your language of choice, or as something that informs how you go about doing it directly.

Relay[7] is the original project that illustrated the use of GraphQL, released by Facebook at the same time in 2015, although it's progressed quite considerably since then. While the Apollo platform is, effectively, a collection of related tools and product offerings built around GraphQL, Relay is the more prescriptive, opinionated framework for building GraphQL-based web applications with React,[8] Facebook's library for building user interfaces. Relay sets certain additional expectations about the way you've built your GraphQL schema, and it supports some out-of-the-box patterns (like pagination) as a benefit of adhering to those constraints.

The Apollo GraphQL platform takes another approach. Originating from the Meteor Development Group,[9] Apollo is a large set of open source packages, projects, and tools that work in concert to provide a GraphQL client framework—a more a la carte approach than Relay. Apollo isn't tied to React and can be more readily layered on existing client applications. This flexibility has made Apollo a popular alternative to the more prepackaged Relay framework.

Both systems have Node.js-based server components that, since we're using Absinthe, we'll ignore for the purposes of this book. We'll focus on the client-side portions of Relay and the Apollo Platform (which is to say, Apollo Client).

---

7. https://facebook.github.io/relay
8. https://reactjs.org
9. https://www.meteor.io

We won't be able to give you a full workup of their relative pros and cons in the course of a single chapter, but hopefully you'll get a feel for their differences.

It's up to you which system you decide to use for your own projects. We recommend you dig into both more comprehensively after reading this chapter, perhaps by building on the simple example we'll create to use the PlateSlate API.

First up: Apollo Client, the more casual and flexible of the two options.

Using Apollo Client

For the sake of equal comparison, we're going to build our Apollo-based application on top of React. As we mentioned before, one of Apollo's benefits is that it isn't coupled to a specific UI framework (for example, we could also use Vue.js,[10] another popular option), but React is, by far, still the most popular choice for working with Apollo. Giving you the ability to build UI components with HTML, JavaScript, and even CSS in the same file, React has become one of the most widespread tools on the modern web.

We're going to build a fresh user interface for our PlateSlate application, displaying the same list of menu items that we did before. We'll also be adding support for live updating, showing you how you can use Apollo Client to work with Absinthe's implementation of GraphQL subscriptions.

We'll start by generating our application boilerplate. We're going to use a handy tool, create-react-app, that will build in all the development server and compilation toolchain configuration that we'll need to get down to work.

First, let's install create-react-app:

Rather than forcing you to structure your application in a specific way, Apollo Client gives you the ability to connect your web-based user interface—regardless of what you use to build it—to a GraphQL API.

```
$ npm install -g create-react-app
```

After it's installed, we'll generate our project, giving it the name of plate-slate-apollo-ui:

```
$ create-react-app plate-slate-apollo-ui
Creating a new React app in /path/to/plate-slate-apollo-ui.

Installing packages. This might take a couple of minutes.
Installing react, react-dom, and react-scripts...

«More output»
```

---

10. https://vuejs.org

```
Success! Created plate-slate-apollo-ui at /path/to/plate-slate-apollo-ui
Inside that directory, you can run several commands:

  yarn start
    Starts the development server.

  yarn build
    Bundles the app into static files for production.

  yarn test
    Starts the test runner.

  yarn eject
    Removes this tool and copies build dependencies, configuration files
    and scripts into the app directory. If you do this, you can't go back!

We suggest that you begin by typing:

  cd plate-slate-apollo-ui
  yarn start

Happy hacking!
```

That's a lot of output, but it's useful stuff. create-react-app generated our application with a development web server, a test harness, and a number of other tools we can use as we build our application.

Let's give the server a try, jumping into the project directory and running yarn start:

```
$ cd plate-slate-apollo-ui
$ yarn start
```

If the server starts up correctly, you should see a message showing how to connect to the application in your console—and your browser should automatically pull it up for you!

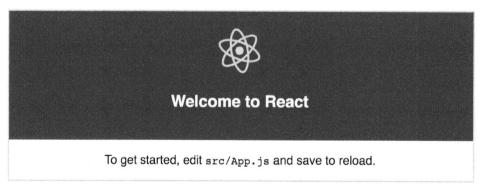

Welcome to React

To get started, edit `src/App.js` and save to reload.

Now that we're sure things work, let's edit our App.js and build out a basic menu list. If you're unfamiliar with React, don't worry. We're not going to get fancy and build out a complex set of components or styles.

At the moment, this is what the file looks like:

```
11-chp.frontend/plate-slate-apollo-ui/1-start/src/App.js
import React, { Component } from 'react';
import logo from './logo.svg';
import './App.css';

class App extends Component {
  render() {
    return (
      <div className="App">
        <header className="App-header">
          <img src={logo} className="App-logo" alt="logo" />
          <h1 className="App-title">Welcome to React</h1>
        </header>
        <p className="App-intro">
          To get started, edit <code>src/App.js</code> and save to reload.
        </p>
      </div>
    );
  }
}

export default App;
```

The most important thing for you to understand here is that it's defining a React component, and the return value of the component's render() function is what will be displayed to the user. This matches up with what we're seeing in our browser.

This Is JavaScript?

 If you're surprised by the appearance of import, class, the shorthand for function definitions, or the raw HTML just hanging out in a .js file, this might be the first time you've run into modern JavaScript (ES6) and JSX.[11] It's a brave new world!

Let's simplify things and render a simple listing of menu items. We'll start with some stub data, then switch it out for our real menu item data when we connect it to our API:

```
11-chp.frontend/plate-slate-apollo-ui/2-stub/src/App.js
Line 1  import React, { Component } from 'react';

        class App extends Component {

    5     // Retrieves current data for menu items
          get menuItems() {
            // TODO: Replace with real data!
```

---

11. https://facebook.github.io/jsx

```
        return [
          {id: "stub-1", name: "Stub Menu Item 1"},
10        {id: "stub-2", name: "Stub Menu Item 2"},
          {id: "stub-3", name: "Stub Menu Item 3"},
        ];
      }

15    renderMenuItem(menuItem) {
        return (
          <li key={menuItem.id}>{menuItem.name}</li>
        );
      }
20
      // Build the DOM
      render() {
        return (
          <ul>
25          {this.menuItems.map(menuItem => this.renderMenuItem(menuItem))}
          </ul>
        );
      }

30  }

    export default App;
```

We've changed the render() to build an unordered list, taking the data that menuItems() provides and passing it to renderMenuItem() to build each list item.

The key attribute you see on line 17 is required because it helps React keep track of list item identity across changes to our data, so it knows what's been added, removed, and changed. You need to make sure the values you pass to key are unique, and that's easy to do: our menu items will all have unique id values, and we've made our stub data items have the same property.

Now that we've rebuilt our menu list—this time on top of React—let's look at how we're going to integrate Apollo Client and the packages that support using it with Absinthe.

Wiring in GraphQL

We'll start by pulling in the @absinthe/socket-apollo-link package, an officially supported Absinthe JavaScript package that's custom-built to add support for Absinthe's use of Phoenix WebSockets and channels. The package will pull in a few dependencies it needs.

```
$ yarn add @absinthe/socket-apollo-link
```

We're going to create a directory, src/client, in our JavaScript application. It will contain all our GraphQL client-related configuration.

The first bit of configuration will be for the Absinthe WebSocket configuration. We'll put it in a new file, absinthe-socket-link.js:

```
11-chp.frontend/plate-slate-apollo-ui/3-config/src/client/absinthe-socket-link.js
import * as AbsintheSocket from "@absinthe/socket";
import { createAbsintheSocketLink } from "@absinthe/socket-apollo-link";
import { Socket as PhoenixSocket } from "phoenix";

export default createAbsintheSocketLink(AbsintheSocket.create(
  new PhoenixSocket("ws://localhost:4000/socket")
));
```

Most of this file is just importing the bits it needs: the base socket definition that @absinthe/socket provides, a utility function that knows how Apollo needs the socket to behave, and the underlying Phoenix socket code.

The most important thing to get right here is our socket URL. (If you remember, our PlateSlateWeb.UserSocket is available at /socket, based on the setup we did in PlateSlateWeb.Endpoint back on Setting Up Subscriptions, on page 98).

Mind Your URLs

You'll want to make sure that the URLs here are build-specific, supporting development, production, and any other targets you plan on using. The create-react-app boilerplate, like most React-based systems, leverages Webpack[12] to build our application, and you can use a Webpack plugin to support different build configurations.

Don't forget about the difference between ws:// and wss://. The latter indicates a secure WebSocket connection. You should probably only be using the insecure variant, ws://, in development.

Okay, so we have our WebSocket link configuration ready. Now let's add some basic setup for Apollo Client using it, and adding Apollo's standard in-memory caching facility. For the moment, we'll send all our GraphQL traffic over our WebSocket connection, but we'll build a hybrid configuration (sending query and mutation operations over HTTP) next.

First, let's pull in two new dependencies:

```
$ yarn add apollo-client
$ yarn add apollo-cache-inmemory
```

---

12. https://webpack.js.org

Here's the client configuration. It's even more simplistic than the socket's:

```
11-chp.frontend/plate-slate-apollo-ui/3-config/src/client/index.js
import ApolloClient from "apollo-client";
import { InMemoryCache } from "apollo-cache-inmemory";

import absintheSocketLink from "./absinthe-socket-link";

export default new ApolloClient({
  link: absintheSocketLink,
  cache: new InMemoryCache()
});
```

We start the file with imports. Our two new dependencies put in an appearance first, followed directly after by our WebSocket link. We then instantiate our client, providing the link and cache options. That's all the setup we need to do to have a working GraphQL client, sending requests and receiving responses over Phoenix's rock-solid WebSocket implementation.

Now all we need to do is make sure our user interface can get the data. It's time to throw away the menu item stub data.

Apollo Client doesn't know anything about React directly. A specialized package, react-apollo, provides the necessary integration features. We'll also pull in graphql-tag, used to define GraphQL documents in our application code.

```
$ yarn add react-apollo
$ yarn add graphql-tag
```

The application's main index.js needs to make use of our brand-new GraphQL client and provide it to our React component. We make the necessary changes to the file:

```
11-chp.frontend/plate-slate-apollo-ui/3-config/src/index.js
import React from 'react';
import ReactDOM from 'react-dom';
import './index.css';
import App from './App';
import registerServiceWorker from './registerServiceWorker';
➤ // GraphQL
➤ import { ApolloProvider } from 'react-apollo';
➤ import client from './client';

ReactDOM.render(
➤   <ApolloProvider client={client}>
➤     <App />
➤   </ApolloProvider>,
    document.getElementById('root')
);
registerServiceWorker();
```

The real work happens inside the component file, where we define the GraphQL query for the menu items and use the react-apollo graphql() function to build it into a higher-order component[13] that wraps the App component:

```
11-chp.frontend/plate-slate-apollo-ui/3-config/src/App.js
import React, { Component } from 'react';

// GraphQL
import { graphql } from 'react-apollo';
import gql from 'graphql-tag';

class App extends Component {

  // Retrieves current data for menu items
  get menuItems() {
    const { data } = this.props;
    if (data && data.menuItems) {
      return data.menuItems;
    } else {
      return [];
    }
  }

  renderMenuItem(menuItem) {
    return (
      <li key={menuItem.id}>{menuItem.name}</li>
    );
  }

  // Build the DOM
  render() {
    return (
      <ul>
        {this.menuItems.map(menuItem => this.renderMenuItem(menuItem))}
      </ul>
    );
  }

}

const query = gql`
  { menuItems { id name } }
`;

export default graphql(query)(App);
```

The nice thing about this approach is that you don't need to deal with the GraphQL request, and the result from your API is provided to the App component automatically as React properties. In the menuItems() getter, you can see where we check to see if the data property is available and whether it has menuItems, returning them if so.

---

13. https://reactjs.org/docs/higher-order-components.html

Let's see if it works! Start up your JavaScript application again with yarn:

```
$ yarn start
```

If you don't have the PlateSlate GraphQL API application still running some-where, when the browser pops up (if you open the Developer Tools), you'll see errors when the application attempts to connect via WebSocket:

```
⊗ ▸WebSocket connection to 'ws://localhost:4000/socket/websocket?vsn=2.0.0' failed: Error in connection    phoenix.js:817
    establishment: net::ERR_CONNECTION_REFUSED
  ◑ ▸WebSocket connection to 'ws://localhost:4000/socket/websocket?vsn=2.0.0' failed: Error in connection    phoenix.js:817
    establishment: net::ERR_CONNECTION_REFUSED
```

If everything is running as expected, the JavaScript application will connect and the Elixir application log will look something like this:

```
[debug] INCOMING "doc" on "__absinthe__:control" to Absinthe.Phoenix.Channel
  Transport:  Phoenix.Transports.WebSocket
  ≪Parameter details≫
[debug] ABSINTHE schema=PlateSlateWeb.Schema variables=%{}
---
{
  menuItems {
    id
    name
    __typename
  }
}
---
[debug] QUERY OK source="items" db=3.7ms decode=0.1ms
SELECT i0."id", i0."added_on", i0."description", i0."name", i0."price",
i0."allergy_info", i0."category_id", i0."inserted_at", i0."updated_at"
FROM "items" AS i0 ORDER BY i0."name" []
```

You can see the GraphQL query come across the Phoenix channel, and the Ecto query firing.

GraphQL Client-Side Caching

 You may notice the addition of _typename to our GraphQL query. This is done automatically by Apollo to help facilitate client-side caching, which is done by type.

Look at the browser! As shown in the top figure on page 239, our menu items look real again!

Let's dig in a little further on the browser side so we can check out exactly how we got the data.

If we open up our browser development tools, we can see the requests being sent across the WebSocket. We're using Chrome, so the information can be found under the Network tab, then by clicking on a WebSocket request's

- Bánh mì
- Chocolate Milkshake
- Croque Monsieur
- French Fries
- Lemonade
- Masala Chai
- Muffuletta
- Papadum
- Pasta Salad
- Reuben
- Soft Drink
- Thai Salad
- Vada Pav
- Vanilla Milkshake
- Water

Frames tab. Here you see the result of our GraphQL query (with the request and channel join right before it):

It's great to have GraphQL over WebSockets working, but we want to use normal HTTP requests for non–subscription-related operations. It's a straightforward process to modify our GraphQL client configuration to make that work.

Using a Hybrid Configuration

Giving our GraphQL client the ability to talk HTTP/S requires us to pull in another dependency, apollo-link-http:

```
$ yarn add apollo-link-http
```

Now we'll modify our client code and use a special function, ApolloLink.split(), to configure when each transport method should be used:

```
11-chp.frontend/plate-slate-apollo-ui/4-hybrid/src/client/index.js
import ApolloClient from "apollo-client";
import { InMemoryCache } from "apollo-cache-inmemory";
➤ import { ApolloLink } from "apollo-link";
➤ import { createHttpLink } from "apollo-link-http";
➤ import { hasSubscription } from "@jumpn/utils-graphql";

import absintheSocketLink from "./absinthe-socket-link";

➤ const link = new ApolloLink.split(
➤   operation => hasSubscription(operation.query),
➤   absintheSocketLink,
➤   createHttpLink({uri: "http://localhost:4000/api/graphql"})
➤ );
➤
➤ export default new ApolloClient({
➤   link,
➤   cache: new InMemoryCache()
➤ });
```

The hasSubscription() function, from one of @absinthe/socket's dependencies, is a handy utility that lets us check our GraphQL for a subscription. In the event one is found, we use our WebSocket link. Otherwise, we send the request over HTTP to the configured URL.

Let's see if this works.

After starting up our application again with yarn start (and making sure the API is still running in our other terminal), our page still displays our menu items, but this time the query happened over HTTP. In our Chrome Developer Tools panel, the request is accessible as a discrete item on the left-hand side (as graphql), and by clicking it we can preview the result as shown in the figure on page 241.

With all of this talk of subscriptions, it's probably time to make one work with our client-side application.

Using Subscriptions

We're going to add another subscription field to our GraphQL schema—this time so our user interface is notified when a new menu item is added. We're not going to connect it to any of our mutations, since for this example we're focused on just making sure the client integration works. (If you need a reminder of how Absinthe subscriptions are configured, see Chapter 6, Going Live with Subscriptions, on page 97.)

11-chp.frontend/plate_slate/2-subscription/lib/plate_slate_web/schema.ex

```elixir
subscription do

  # «Other fields»

  field :new_menu_item, :menu_item do
    config fn _args, _info ->
      {:ok, topic: "*"}
    end
  end
end
```

With our subscription in place, we just need to make some edits to our App component in the JavaScript application to support the client making the subscription and receiving its results.

At the bottom of App.js, we'll define the subscription and add some configuration to the graphql() higher-order component to handle sending the subscription document and inserting any new menu items that are received:

11-chp.frontend/plate-slate-apollo-ui/5-subscription/src/App.js

```javascript
Line 1  const query = gql`
          { menuItems { id name } }
        `;

     5  const subscription = gql`
          subscription {
            newMenuItem { id name }
          }
        `;
```

```
     export default graphql(query, {
       props: props => {
         return Object.assign(props, {
           subscribeToNewMenuItems: params => {
15           return props.data.subscribeToMore({
               document: subscription,
               updateQuery: (prev, { subscriptionData }) => {
                 if (!subscriptionData.data) {
                   return prev;
20               }
                 const newMenuItem = subscriptionData.data.newMenuItem;
                 return Object.assign({}, prev, {
                   menuItems: [newMenuItem, ...prev.menuItems]
                 });
25             }
             })
           }
         });
       }
30   })(App);
```

We're not going to go into depth about Apollo subscription configuration, but the most important pieces here are that we're defining a function, subscribeToNewMenu-Items(), on line 14, which uses subscribeToMore() to send our subscription—and update the components properties with updateQuery().

To create the subscription, we define a componentWillMount() function for our component. React will automatically call it for us, as it's a special life-cycle function. It calls the subscribeToNewMenuItems() function we defined, which kicks off our subscription:

```
11-chp.frontend/plate-slate-apollo-ui/5-subscription/src/App.js
componentWillMount() {
  this.props.subscribeToNewMenuItems();
}
```

If you have the PlateSlate GraphQL API application running, stop it and restart it using IEx so that you'll have a console you can use to execute functions in the application:

```
$ iex -S mix phx.server
```

Make sure the JavaScript application is running (refresh the browser window), and then in your Elixir console type the following. We're going to manually invoke our subscription publishing, passing it a new menu item:

```
iex> Absinthe.Subscription.publish(
       PlateSlateWeb.Endpoint,
       %{id: "stub-new-1", name: "New Menu Item"},
       new_menu_item: "*"
     )
```

With everything in place, here's what you'll see in your browser window. Notice that the new menu item is displayed right at the top of the menu item listing, and the WebSocket frames shows the subscription information we just sent:

Try it again if you like, substituting new menu item id and name values.

Over the last few pages, you've worked from a blank slate up to a working React application talking to Absinthe over HTTP and WebSockets using Apollo Client. Apollo Client is a great tool, but we're going to take a look at a more opinionated alternative: Relay.

Using Relay

If you're looking for a more opinionated, prepackaged GraphQL framework for your application, Relay is the gold standard. With an API that's been reimagined since its initial release in 2015, it's lighter, faster, and easier to use than before. "Relay Modern," as it's called, is worth a serious look when you evaluate a GraphQL framework for your application.

Let's reimplement our PlateSlate user interface using Relay Modern.

As with our Apollo example in the previous section, we'll use the create-react-app package to build the boilerplate for our new Relay application, just to save some time:

```
$ create-react-app plate-slate-relay-ui
```

Once our application is generated, we can verify that the development server is working correctly by going into the directory and running yarn start:

```
$ cd plate-slate-relay-ui
$ yarn start
```

This should open a browser window to http://localhost:3000 and show a basic starter page.

Up to this point, there's nothing Relay-related about the application at all. We'll pull in some basic Relay dependencies that we know will be needed.

```
$ yarn add react-relay
$ yarn add relay-compiler babel-plugin-relay --dev
```

The react-relay package provides the runtime features that Relay needs to interact with the React UI framework, while relay-compiler and babel-plugin-relay include development utilities that are used to prepare GraphQL queries, schemas, and related tooling for Relay's use.

Because we need to make some special modifications to our application's build process, we use create-react-app's ejection feature, which unpacks the configuration and scripts that create-react-app usually manages for us so that we can make changes:

```
$ yarn eject
```

Open up the package.json file. You'll see that a variety of project configuration options have been added.

We'll make one small change. Look for the "babel" section, and add the following "plugins" setting:

```
"babel": {
  "presets": [
    "react-app"
  ],
  "plugins": [
    "relay"
  ]
},
```

This will add the GraphQL transpiling support that Relay needs. Now, let's wire in our Absinthe socket so that the application can talk to the PlateSlate GraphQL API. We need the @absinthe/socket-relay package:

```
$ yarn add @absinthe/socket-relay
```

We'll use the package to build a Relay environment, which is how the framework bundles together the configuration that it needs to operate. Let's put it in relay-environment.js:

```
11-chp.frontend/plate-slate-relay-ui/1-start/src/relay-environment.js
import { createFetcher, createSubscriber } from "@absinthe/socket-relay";
import {
  Environment,
  Network,
  RecordSource,
  Store
} from "relay-runtime";

import absintheSocket from "./absinthe-socket";

export default new Environment({
  network: Network.create(
    createFetcher(absintheSocket),
    createSubscriber(absintheSocket)
  ),
  store: new Store(new RecordSource())
});
```

Similar to the way our Apollo Client application was configured, this lets us set up Relay cache storage and network-handling the way we want. Here we're using an in-memory cache and a WebSocket for our GraphQL requests. We configure the WebSocket itself in another file, absinthe-socket.js:

```
11-chp.frontend/plate-slate-relay-ui/1-start/src/absinthe-socket.js
import * as AbsintheSocket from "@absinthe/socket";
import { Socket as PhoenixSocket } from "phoenix";

export default AbsintheSocket.create(
  new PhoenixSocket("ws://localhost:4000/socket")
);
```

Our Relay application is configured, but it needs to have a static copy of the schema it will be using—the PlateSlate schema—in a format that the Relay compiler can understand. We can use a utility, get-graphql-schema, to grab it from our API using introspection and save it to a file. First we need to install it:

```
$ npm install -g get-graphql-schema
```

We run the utility, giving our API URL as the lone argument and piping the results to a new file, schema.graphql, at the root of the project:

```
$ get-graphql-schema http://localhost:4000/api/ > ./schema.graphql
```

Now let's build the App component. We'll make use of Relay's `QueryRenderer`, which takes the environment we've defined, our query (constructed using the graphql() function), and the logic to run based on the result of executing the query:

11-chp.frontend/plate-slate-relay-ui/1-start/src/App.js

```js
import React, { Component } from 'react';

import { QueryRenderer, graphql } from 'react-relay';

import environment from './relay-environment';

const query = graphql`
  query AppQuery { menuItems { id name } }
`;

class App extends Component {
  renderMenuItem(menuItem) {
    return (
      <li key={menuItem.id}>{menuItem.name}</li>
    );
  }

  render() {
    return (
      <QueryRenderer
        environment={environment}
        query={query}
        render={({ error, props }) => {
          if (error) {
            return (
              <div>{error.message}</div>
            );
          } else if (props) {
            return (
              <ul>
                {props.menuItems.map(this.renderMenuItem)}
              </ul>
            );
          } else {
            return (
              <div>Loading...</div>
            )
          }
        }}
      />
    );
  }
}

export default App;
```

It's important to note that the query we use here needs to have the operation name AppQuery, because that's what the Relay compiler will expect (the name of the component, which is App, followed by the type of operation, Query).

Now we just need to run the compiler to extract our query and prepare a generated copy. We'll add an entry to the "scripts" section of our package.json file so we can do that easily (now and in the future):

```
"scripts": {
  "start": "node scripts/start.js",
  "build": "node scripts/build.js",
  "test": "node scripts/test.js --env=jsdom",
  "compile": "relay-compiler --src ./src --schema ./schema.graphql"
},
```

Now let's use the new script entry:

```
$ yarn compile
relay-compiler --src ./src --schema ./schema.graphql
«Output»
Created:
 - AppQuery.graphql.js
```

Great! This built a new file, AppQuery.graphql.js, and put it in a new directory, src/_generated_. If you take a peek inside the file, you'll see something like this:

```
11-chp.frontend/plate-slate-relay-ui/2-compile/src/__generated__/AppQuery.graphql.js
    "text": "query AppQuery {\n  menuItems {\n    id\n    name\n  }\n}\n"
};

module.exports = batch;
```

Now we have everything that we need to try running the query. If you run your application again with yarn start (and make sure your PlateSlate GraphQL API is running in another terminal), here's what you should see:

- Bánh mì
- Chocolate Milkshake
- Croque Monsieur
- French Fries
- Lemonade
- Masala Chai
- Muffuletta
- Papadum
- Pasta Salad
- Reuben
- Soft Drink
- Thai Salad
- Vada Pav
- Vanilla Milkshake
- Water

Success!

Now let's see how we can take our Relay application to the next level: adding our newMenuItem subscription.

Adding a Subscription

Adding a subscription to a client-side Relay application involves packaging up the actual GraphQL subscription operation with a configuration that defines how it's requested and how data should be interpreted when it's received.

We'll add our subscription in a new directory, src/subscriptions, and call it NewMenu-ItemSubscription:

```
11-chp.frontend/plate-slate-relay-ui/3-subscription/src/subscriptions/NewMenuItemSubscription.js
import { graphql, requestSubscription } from 'react-relay';

import environment from '../relay-environment';

const newMenuItemSubscription = graphql`
  subscription NewMenuItemSubscription {
    newMenuItem { id name }
  }
`

export default () => {
  const subscriptionConfig = {
    subscription: newMenuItemSubscription,
    variables: {},
    updater: proxyStore => {
      // Get the new menu item
      const newMenuItem = proxyStore.getRootField('newMenuItem');
      // Get existing menu items
      const root = proxyStore.getRoot();
      const menuItems = root.getLinkedRecords('menuItems');
      // Prepend the new menu item
      root.setLinkedRecords([newMenuItem, ...menuItems], 'menuItems');
    },
    onError: error => console.log(`An error occured:`, error)
  }

  requestSubscription(
    environment,
    subscriptionConfig
  )

}
```

The file defines the subscription and couples it with an updater, which gets the reference to the new menu item in the cache and adds it to the menu item list. It provides a function that will request the subscription using requestSubscription.

Let's use that function from our App component. As with the Apollo example, we'll trigger the subscription from the componentWillMount React life-cycle function:

11-chp.frontend/plate-slate-relay-ui/3-subscription/src/App.js
```
import NewMenuItemSubscription from './subscriptions/NewMenuItemSubscription';

class App extends Component {

  componentDidMount() {
    NewMenuItemSubscription();
  }

  // «Rest of component»

}
```

We need to remember to compile our subscription. We use yarn compile again. It's smart enough to only compile the new pieces of GraphQL:

```
$ yarn compile
relay-compiler --src ./src --schema ./schema.graphql
«Output»
Created:
 - NewMenuItemSubscription.graphql.js
```

Great, now we'll give this a shot in our running Relay application. First, make sure that the PlateSlate GraphQL API application is running inside an IEx session, so that we can manually publish the result of a newMenuItem subscription for testing:

```
$ iex -S mix phx.server
```

Once both applications are up and running, execute the following in the IEx session, keeping an eye on the web browser:

```
iex> Absinthe.Subscription.publish(
       PlateSlateWeb.Endpoint,
       %{id: "stub-new-1", name: "New Menu Item"},
       new_menu_item: "*"
     )
```

If everything's working as it should, "New Menu Item" should suddenly appear at the top of the menu item list. The figure on page 250 shows what it should look like, complete with the details in Developer Tools.

Now that we have a working app with some impressive bells and whistles (even if it's missing a designer's touch, to say the least), let's look at some of the special patterns that Relay uses and that Absinthe supports: nodes and connections.

Supporting Relay Nodes

To support refetching records from a GraphQL server, Relay has certain expectations[14] about the way records are identified and can be retrieved.

Absinthe ships specialized support for the Node pattern as part of the absinthe_relay Elixir package. Let's configure our PlateSlate application to support refetching menu items using the macros that the package provides.

If you look at the source of mix.exs in our PlateSlate Elixir application, you can see that we've already included absinthe_relay as a dependency:

```
11-chp.frontend/plate_slate/3-node/mix.exs
defp deps do
  [
    # «Other deps»
    {:absinthe_relay, "~> 1.4.0"},
  ]
end
```

To add Node support in our schema, we need to do three things:

• Define a new interface, :node, that declares an :id field.

---

14. https://facebook.github.io/relay/graphql/objectidentification.htm

- Implement the :node interface in any object type we'd like to use it.
- Define a root-level query field, :node, that can fetch any implementing object type records by :id.

All of these can be done with a single macro: node.

First let's pull it into our application by modifying our schema:

11-chp.frontend/plate_slate/3-node/lib/plate_slate_web/schema.ex
```elixir
defmodule PlateSlateWeb.Schema do
  use Absinthe.Schema
  use Absinthe.Relay.Schema, :modern

  # «Rest of schema»

end
```

Note the special :modern argument that indicates we're targeting Relay v1 (Modern) client applications.

Setting a Relay Flavor

In future versions of absinthe_relay, the :modern argument to use Absinthe.Relay.Schema won't be necessary, as it will default without warnings. For the moment, be explicit and set :modern (or :classic, if you're supporting an older application).

We'll add the :node interface here in the main schema file using the node macro. It's almost identical to a normal use of interface; we don't have to provide a name or any of the field details, but we do need to tell Absinthe how to map records to the specific type of object by providing a resolve_type function. (If you're a bit rusty on how interfaces work, see Using Interfaces, on page 71.)

11-chp.frontend/plate_slate/3-node/lib/plate_slate_web/schema.ex
```elixir
node interface do
  resolve_type fn
    %PlateSlate.Menu.Item{}, _ ->
      :menu_item
    _, _ ->
      nil
  end
end
```

This will create an interface (:node) that expects one field (:id) to be defined—and the ID will be a global identifier. The fact the ID needs to be a global identifier makes sense, since the node *field* we'll be adding will need to look up any node object. Thankfully, absinthe_relay makes exposing object IDs using a globally unique scheme easy.

Let's configure our menu item object type as a node and see how it works. We use the node macro again, this time as node object. We'll edit our menu types file and make the change to our :menu_item type:

11-chp.frontend/plate_slate/3-node/lib/plate_slate_web/schema/menu_types.ex
```
defmodule PlateSlateWeb.Schema.MenuTypes do
  use Absinthe.Schema.Notation
  use Absinthe.Relay.Schema.Notation, :modern

  # «Other definitions»

  node object :menu_item do
    # «Rest of definition, with the :id field removed!»
  end

end
```

We've removed the :id field from the object definition, since the node macro will create one for us—with support for generating global IDs. If we start the application and use GraphiQL (at http://localhost:4000/graphiql) to list the menu items, we can see what the IDs look like:

By default, the IDs are base64-encoded versions of the object type name and the local (database) ID. We can verify this using IEx:

```
$ iex -S mix
iex> Base.decode64("TWVudUl0ZW06NA==")
{:ok, "MenuItem:4"}
```

In practice, Absinthe uses a special function, Absinthe.Relay.Node.from_global_id/2, which checks the ID against the schema:

```
$ iex -S mix
iex> Absinthe.Relay.Node.from_global_id("TWVudUl0ZW06NA==",
  PlateSlateWeb.Schema)

{:ok, %{id: "4", type: :menu_item}}
```

Now let's build our `node` field: the third and final piece that we need to add to support Relay's refetching. It will use `from_global_id/2` on the argument it's given and execute a resolver function we provide:

11-chp.frontend/plate_slate/3-node/lib/plate_slate_web/schema.ex

```
query do
  node field do
    resolve fn
      %{type: :menu_item, id: local_id}, _ ->
        {:ok, PlateSlate.Repo.get(PlateSlate.Menu.Item, local_id)}
      _, _ ->
        {:error, "Unknown node"}
    end
  end
  # «Other query fields»
end
```

Because the IDs are already parsed for us, we just need to match against the result. At the moment, we're handling menu items, but we could expand this to match other node types, too.

We can check the field works as expected using GraphiQL:

With these parts in place, our menu item object refetching is good to go. If we'd like to support any other node types, we just need to:

- Expand the :node interface resolve_type match

- Make sure the object definition uses the node macro and doesn't define its own :id field

- Expand the :node query field's argument match for parsed IDs

> ### Supporting Global IDs in Other Resolvers
>
> Passing opaque global IDs back to your client applications obviously means that they're going to be using those IDs in any subsequent queries, mutations, and subscriptions. To help handle these global IDs transparently, even when nested in arguments, Absinthe provides a piece of middleware, Absinthe.Relay.Node.ParseIDs.[a]
>
> ---
>
> a.   https://hexdocs.pm/absinthe_relay/Absinthe.Relay.Node.ParseIDs.html

Meeting Relay's expectation for globally identifiable records can feel like a high bar at first, but once you get used to using the node macro and the tools that ship with absinthe_relay to support it, it will feel like second nature.

Now let's look at a very useful pattern that Relay provides: connections.

Supporting Relay Connections

To support pagination, Relay has defined a set of conventions[15] used to model lists of records and the related metadata. As an example, let's review the :menu_items field in the PlateSlate schema. In its current, simplistic state, it looks something like this:

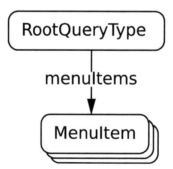

In short, the root query type has a field, menuItems (or :menu_items, in Absinthe's Elixir parlance), that returns a list of MenuItem (that is, :menu_item) records.

---

15. https://facebook.github.io/relay/graphql/connections.htm

If we model the field as a Relay connection, it will change to look something like this:

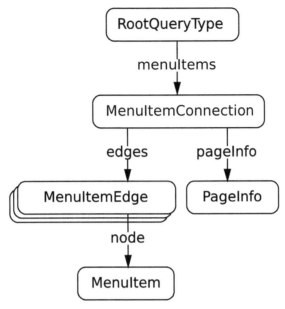

This necessitates the addition of two new object types:

- MenuItemConnection, an object type that contains the edges and the pageInfo fields

- MenuItemEdge, an object type modeling a single node result (the actual data) and its placement in the list

It also makes use of a statically defined type, PageInfo, with important paging information like hasNextPage and hasPreviousPage.

In addition, our field would need to accept some new arguments (first and since for forward pagination, last and before for backward pagination).

Cursor-Based Pagination

 Relay connection pagination is cursor-based, meaning that it's all about retrieving a number of records since or before a given (optional) cursor value. Every connection edge has a cursor.

This sure seems like a lot of things to do. Thankfully, as was the case with the global identification needs of Relay (and the node macro), the absinthe_relay Elixir package provides tools to make supporting connections a lot easier.

Let's go ahead and open up our PlateSlate schema and see what it would take to convert it to a full-blown Relay connection field. We're going to be using the connection macro, so if you didn't follow along with Supporting Relay Nodes, on page 250, make sure to include the use line you see here:

```
11-chp.frontend/plate_slate/4-connection/lib/plate_slate_web/schema.ex
defmodule PlateSlateWeb.Schema do
  use Absinthe.Schema
➤ use Absinthe.Relay.Schema, :modern

  # «Rest of schema»
  query do
    # «Other query fields»
➤   connection field :menu_items, node_type: :menu_item do
      arg :filter, :menu_item_filter
      arg :order, type: :sort_order, default_value: :asc
      resolve &Resolvers.Menu.menu_items/3
    end

  end

end
```

We have changed the :menu_items field by prefixing it with connection and, instead of declaring that it's of type list_of(:menu_item), we declare a :node_type. The connection macro uses this node type to infer the name of the associated connection type, which we'll add in our PlateSlateWeb.Schema.MenuTypes module here momentarily.

Note that the :filter and :order arguments were left untouched. While the connection macro automatically adds the pagination-related arguments for you, it doesn't get in the way of custom arguments that you might want (and we do) for your queries.

Here's the very minor changes that are necessary in our menu types file: pulling in the connection macro from Absinthe.Relay.Schema.Notation and using it to define our connection type, tied to the :menu_item node type:

```
11-chp.frontend/plate_slate/4-connection/lib/plate_slate_web/schema/menu_types.ex
defmodule PlateSlateWeb.Schema.MenuTypes do
  use Absinthe.Schema.Notation
➤ use Absinthe.Relay.Schema.Notation, :modern

  # «Other definitions»

➤ connection node_type: :menu_item

end
```

Not a lot here. You can customize the contents of the connection if you like (by providing a do block and the usual use of the field macro), but ours is just a vanilla connection with the usual node and pageInfo trappings, so we can leave it as a single line.

The most substantive changes that we need to do are in our field resolver, since we need to describe how the query will be executed:

```
11-chp.frontend/plate_slate/4-connection/lib/plate_slate_web/resolvers/menu.ex
def menu_items(_, args, _) do
  Absinthe.Relay.Connection.from_query(
    Menu.items_query(args),
    &PlateSlate.Repo.all/1,
    args
  )
end
```

Previously, this function just passed the arguments to Menu.list_items/1, but because we want to use Absinthe.Relay.Connection's useful from_query/4 function to handle the actual pagination of records and the construction of a valid :menu_item_connection result, instead we use Menu.items_query/2. Instead of returning the result of the database query, this returns the query itself (an Ecto.Queryable.t, to be precise), which from_query/4 uses (along with the repository function and the arguments) to take care of matters for us.

We just need to make a couple small changes to the behavior of Menu.items_ query/1, though. It needs to be made public (it's defined with defp at the moment), and it should gracefully handle additional arguments that it doesn't use (like the pagination arguments that the connection macro defined for us and that from_query/4 needs):

```
11-chp.frontend/plate_slate/4-connection/lib/plate_slate/menu/menu.ex
➤ def items_query(args) do
    Enum.reduce(args, Item, fn
      {:order, order}, query ->
        query |> order_by({^order, :name})
      {:filter, filter}, query ->
        query |> filter_with(filter)
➤     _, query ->
➤       query
    end)
  end
```

With the function made public so that our resolver can call it, and with the fall-through match keeping the function from exploding in the event of an argument it doesn't care about, we're ready to play with our connection.

Popping open a terminal, running the PlateSlate application (for one final, bittersweet time), and pointing our browser to GraphiQL running at http://localhost:4000/graphiql, we can query our menuItems using both our pagination and custom arguments.

Here we are paging in threes, and filtering for menu items that contain the letter "u."

```
GraphiQL    ▶    History ▾    Save                                              ‹ Docs

1 ▾ {                                              ▾ {
2 ▾   menuItems(first: 3, filter: {name: "u"}) {   ▾   "data": {
3       pageInfo {                                  ▾     "menuItems": {
4         hasPreviousPage                                 "pageInfo": {
5         hasNextPage                                       "hasPreviousPage": false,
6       }                                                   "hasNextPage": true
7 ▾     edges {                                           },
8         node {                               ▾         "edges": [
9           name                               ▾           {
10          id                                               "node": {
11        }                                                    "name": "Croque Monsieur",
12        cursor                                               "id": "TWVudU10ZW06Mg=="
13      }                                                    },
14    }                                                      "cursor": "YXJyYX1jb25uZWN0aW9uOjA="
15  }                                                      },
16 }                                            ▾           {
                                                             "node": {
                                                               "name": "Muffuletta",
                                                               "id": "TWVudU10ZW06Mw=="
                                                             },
                                                             "cursor": "YXJyYX1jb25uZWN0aW9uOjE="
                                                           },
                                               ▾           {
                                                             "node": {
                                                               "name": "Papadum",
                                                               "id": "TWVudU10ZW06Nw=="
                                                             },
                                                             "cursor": "YXJyYX1jb25uZWN0aW9uOjI="
                                                           }
                                                         }
                                                       }
                                                     }
          QUERY VARIABLES                            }
```

Another successful GraphQL query with Absinthe.

Relay Conventions Outside Relay

If you like Relay's take on global identification or record pagination, but don't want to use Relay itself, never fear. You can still make use of the absinthe_relay package on the server side with whatever client-side system that you want. While things might not work as transparently as they would with Relay, at the end of the day it's just GraphQL in and JSON out. If you build the necessary support into your client-side applications, there's nothing stopping you from using a Relay-supporting GraphQL API.

Wrapping Up

Through this chapter, you've discovered how to integrate a client-side application—vanilla, Apollo, or Relay—with an Absinthe-based GraphQL API, and you've learned about some of the framework-specific features that are available. The instructions here are mostly just illustrative; new client-side frameworks, tools, and even languages are constantly changing, and a lot of factors are involved in your choice of the right UI and GraphQL technologies for your team.

As a GraphQL server implementation, Absinthe can work with anything that talks GraphQL; just keep an eye on the project documentation[16] to see if there's been any specialized support added to make integrating with your technology of choice even easier.

Whether you were new to GraphQL, new to Elixir, or just wanted a refresher on how they can work together, we have covered a lot of material in this book—but this is just the beginning! GraphQL and Elixir are both relatively new technologies, after all. Where can we take them from here, working together?

---

16. https://hexdocs.pm/absinthe

GraphQL Types

Object

Description

GraphQL objects represent a list of named fields, each of which yields a value of a specific type.

Note that object types cannot be used for input (instead, see "InputObject" below).

Absinthe Macro

object

Examples

In an Absinthe schema:

```
@desc "A person"
object :person do
  field :name, non_null(:string)
  # «Other fields»
end
```

InputObject

Description

Defines a set of input fields; the input fields are either scalars, enums, or other input objects. This allows arguments to accept arbitrarily complex values.

Absinthe Macro

input_object

Examples

In an Absinthe schema:

```
@desc "Profile information to modify"
input_object :profile_input do
  field :name, non_null(:string)
  # «Other fields»
end
```

Enum

Description

Represents one of a finite set of possible values. GraphQL enums are not
references for a numeric value, but are unique values in their own right.
They serialize as a string: the name of the represented value.

Absinthe Macro

enum

Examples

In an Absinthe schema, defining the enum and the internal representation
it will map to:

```
@desc "The selected color channel"
enum :color_channel do

  @desc "Red Color Channel"
  value :red, as: :r

  @desc "Green Color Channel"
  value :green, as: :g

  @desc "Blue Color Channel"
  value :blue, as: :b

  # «Other values»
end
```

There is also a shorthand values option available, if default settings are
appropriate:

```
enum :color_channel, values: [:red, :green, :blue]
```

Interface

Description

    Represents a list of named fields and their arguments. GraphQL objects
    can then implement an interface, which guarantees that they will contain
    the specified fields.

Absinthe Macro

    interface

Examples

In an Absinthe schema, defining the interface and mapping results to the
associated GraphQL type:

```
@desc "A named object"
interface :named do
  field :name, :string
  # «Other fields to be implemented»
  resolve_type fn
    %Item{}, _ ->
      :item
    _, _ ->
      nil
  end
end
```

An object type implementing the interface:

```
@desc "An item"
object :item do
  interfaces [:named]
  field :name, :string
  # «Other fields»
end
```

Union

Description

    Represents an object that could be one of a list of GraphQL object types,
    but provides for no guaranteed fields between those types. They also differ
    from interfaces in that object types declare what interfaces they implement,
    but are not aware of what unions contain them.

Absinthe Macro

    union

Examples

In an Absinthe schema, defining the union and mapping results to the associated GraphQL type:

```
@desc "A search result"
union :search_result do
  types [:person, :business]
  resolve_type fn
    %Person{}, _ ->
      :person
    %Business{}, _ ->
      :business
    _, _ ->
      nil
  end
end
```

Scalar Types

Description

Represents a primitive value in GraphQL. GraphQL responses take the form of a hierarchical tree; the leaves on these trees are GraphQL scalars.

Absinthe Macro

scalar

Examples

In an Absinthe schema, defining a custom scalar type by providing functions to parse input and serialize results:

```
scalar :datetime, name: "DateTime" do
  serialize &DateTime.to_iso8601/1
  parse &parse_datetime/1
end
```

Built-in Scalars

A number of built-in scalar types are part of the specification and are predefined for you by Absinthe.

Boolean (Built-in)

Description

The Boolean scalar type represents true or false.

Absinthe Identifier

:boolean

Float (Built-in)

Description

The Float scalar type represents signed double-precision fractional values as specified by IEEE 754. Response formats that support an appropriate double-precision number type should use that type to represent this scalar.

Absinthe Identifier

:float

ID (Built-in)

Description

The ID scalar type represents a unique identifier, often used to refetch an object or as the key for a cache. The ID type is serialized in the same way as a String; however, it is not intended to be human-readable. While it is often numeric, it should always serialize as a String.

Absinthe Identifier

:id

Int (Built-in)

Description

The Int scalar type represents a signed 32-bit numeric non-fractional value. Response formats that support a 32-bit integer or a number type should use that type to represent this scalar.

Absinthe Identifier

:integer

String (Built-in)

Description

Represents textual data as UTF-8 character sequences. The String type is most often used by GraphQL to represent free-form human-readable text.

Absinthe Identifier

:string

Absinthe Scalars

Absinthe ships with a number of custom scalars predefined for convenience. They are found in Absinthe.Type.Custom and include:

- :datetime
- :naive_datetime
- :date
- :time
- :decimal (when the decimal package is a dependency)

To use these scalar types, add the following to your Absinthe schema:

```
import_types Absinthe.Type.Custom
```

Special Types

Lists (Collection Type)

Description

Lists are ordered sequences of values.

Examples

In an Absinthe schema, use the list_of/1 macro to declare the type as a list of a given type:

```
object :person do
  field :pets, list_of(:pets)
  # «Other fields»
end
```

Non-Null (Constraint)

Description

To declare a type that disallows null values, the GraphQL NonNull type can be used. This type wraps an underlying type, and this type acts identically to that wrapped type, with the exception that null values are not valid responses for the wrapping type.

Examples

In an Absinthe schema, use the non_null/1 macro to declare the type as non-nullable:

```
input_object :contact_input do
  field :name, non_null(:string)
  # «Other fields»
end
```

Null (Input Value)

GraphQL has two semantically different ways to represent the lack of a value:

- Explicitly providing the GraphQL literal value, null, or as a variable value. Absinthe will pass on that value as nil to resolvers.

- Implicitly not providing a value at all, in which case Absinthe will omit the value when invoking resolvers.

Bibliography

[Tho18]   Dave Thomas. *Programming Elixir 1.6*. The Pragmatic Bookshelf, Raleigh, NC, 2018.

[TV19]   Chris McCord, Bruce Tate and José Valim. *Programming Phoenix 1.4*. The Pragmatic Bookshelf, Raleigh, NC, 2019.

Index

Thank you!

How did you enjoy this book? Please let us know. Take a moment and email us at support@pragprog.com with your feedback. Tell us your story and you could win free ebooks. Please use the subject line "Book Feedback."

Ready for your next great Pragmatic Bookshelf book? Come on over to https://pragprog.com and use the coupon code BUYANOTHER2020 to save 30% on your next ebook.

Void where prohibited, restricted, or otherwise unwelcome. Do not use ebooks near water. If rash persists, see a doctor. Doesn't apply to *The Pragmatic Programmer* ebook because it's older than the Pragmatic Bookshelf itself. Side effects may include increased knowledge and skill, increased marketability, and deep satisfaction. Increase dosage regularly.

And thank you for your continued support,

Andy Hunt, Publisher

Learn Why, Then Learn How

Get started on your Elixir journey today.

Adopting Elixir

Adoption is more than programming. Elixir is an exciting new language, but to successfully get your application from start to finish, you're going to need to know more than just the language. You need the case studies and strategies in this book. Learn the best practices for the whole life of your application, from design and team-building, to managing stakeholders, to deployment and monitoring. Go beyond the syntax and the tools to learn the techniques you need to develop your Elixir application from concept to production.

Ben Marx, José Valim, Bruce Tate
(242 pages) ISBN: 9781680502527. $42.95
https://pragprog.com/book/tvmelixir

Functional Web Development with Elixir, OTP, and Phoenix

Elixir and Phoenix are generating tremendous excitement as an unbeatable platform for building modern web applications. For decades OTP has helped developers create incredibly robust, scalable applications with unparalleled uptime. Make the most of them as you build a stateful web app with Elixir, OTP, and Phoenix. Model domain entities without an ORM or a database. Manage server state and keep your code clean with OTP Behaviours. Layer on a Phoenix web interface without coupling it to the business logic. Open doors to powerful new techniques that will get you thinking about web development in fundamentally new ways.

Lance Halvorsen
(218 pages) ISBN: 9781680502435. $45.95
https://pragprog.com/book/lhelph

A Better Web with Phoenix and Elm

Elixir and Phoenix on the server side with Elm on the front end gets you the best of both worlds in both worlds!

Programming Phoenix

Don't accept the compromise between fast and beautiful: you can have it all. Phoenix creator Chris McCord, Elixir creator José Valim, and award-winning author Bruce Tate walk you through building an application that's fast and reliable. At every step, you'll learn from the Phoenix creators not just what to do, but why. Packed with insider insights, this definitive guide will be your constant companion in your journey from Phoenix novice to expert, as you build the next generation of web applications.

Chris McCord, Bruce Tate, and José Valim
(298 pages) ISBN: 9781680501452. $34
https://pragprog.com/book/phoenix

Programming Elm

Elm brings the safety and stability of functional programing to front-end development, making it one of the most popular new languages. Elm's functional nature and static typing means that run-time errors are nearly impossible, and it compiles to JavaScript for easy web deployment. This book helps you take advantage of this new language in your web site development. Learn how the Elm Architecture will help you create fast applications. Discover how to integrate Elm with JavaScript so you can update legacy applications. See how Elm tooling makes deployment quicker and easier.

Jeremy Fairbank
(250 pages) ISBN: 9781680502855. $40.95
https://pragprog.com/book/jfelm

Fix Your Hidden Problems

From technical debt to deployment in the very real, very messy world, we've got the tools you need to fix the hidden problems before they become disasters.

Software Design X-Rays

Are you working on a codebase where cost overruns, death marches, and heroic fights with legacy code monsters are the norm? Battle these adversaries with novel ways to identify and prioritize technical debt, based on behavioral data from how developers work with code. And that's just for starters. Because good code involves social design, as well as technical design, you can find surprising dependencies between people and code to resolve coordination bottlenecks among teams. Best of all, the techniques build on behavioral data that you already have: your version-control system. Join the fight for better code!

Adam Tornhill
(274 pages) ISBN: 9781680502725. $45.95
https://pragprog.com/book/atevol

Release It! Second Edition

A single dramatic software failure can cost a company millions of dollars—but can be avoided with simple changes to design and architecture. This new edition of the best-selling industry standard shows you how to create systems that run longer, with fewer failures, and recover better when bad things happen. New coverage includes DevOps, microservices, and cloud-native architecture. Stability antipatterns have grown to include systemic problems in large-scale systems. This is a must-have pragmatic guide to engineering for production systems.

Michael Nygard
(376 pages) ISBN: 9781680502398. $47.95
https://pragprog.com/book/mnee2

Long Live the Command Line!

Use tmux and Vim for incredible mouse-free productivity.

tmux 2

Your mouse is slowing you down. The time you spend context switching between your editor and your consoles eats away at your productivity. Take control of your environment with tmux, a terminal multiplexer that you can tailor to your workflow. With this updated second edition for tmux 2.3, you'll customize, script, and leverage tmux's unique abilities to craft a productive terminal environment that lets you keep your fingers on your keyboard's home row.

Brian P. Hogan
(102 pages) ISBN: 9781680502213. $21.95
https://pragprog.com/book/bhtmux2

Modern Vim

Turn Vim into a full-blown development environment using Vim 8's new features and this sequel to the beloved bestseller *Practical Vim*. Integrate your editor with tools for building, testing, linting, indexing, and searching your codebase. Discover the future of Vim with Neovim: a fork of Vim that includes a built-in terminal emulator that will transform your workflow. Whether you choose to switch to Neovim or stick with Vim 8, you'll be a better developer.

Drew Neil
(190 pages) ISBN: 9781680502626. $39.95
https://pragprog.com/book/modvim

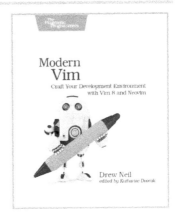

Exercises and Teams

From exercises to make you a better programmer to techniques for creating better teams, we've got you covered.

Exercises for Programmers

When you write software, you need to be at the top of your game. Great programmers practice to keep their skills sharp. Get sharp and stay sharp with more than fifty practice exercises rooted in real-world scenarios. If you're a new programmer, these challenges will help you learn what you need to break into the field, and if you're a seasoned pro, you can use these exercises to learn that hot new language for your next gig.

Brian P. Hogan
(118 pages) ISBN: 9781680501223. $24
https://pragprog.com/book/bhwb

Creating Great Teams

People are happiest and most productive if they can choose what they work on and who they work with. Self-selecting teams give people that choice. Build well-designed and efficient teams to get the most out of your organization, with step-by-step instructions on how to set up teams quickly and efficiently. You'll create a process that works for you, whether you need to form teams from scratch, improve the design of existing teams, or are on the verge of a big team re-shuffle.

Sandy Mamoli and David Mole
(102 pages) ISBN: 9781680501285. $17
https://pragprog.com/book/mmteams

Pragmatic Programming

We'll show you how to be more pragmatic and effective, for new code and old.

Your Code as a Crime Scene

Jack the Ripper and legacy codebases have more in common than you'd think. Inspired by forensic psychology methods, this book teaches you strategies to predict the future of your codebase, assess refactoring direction, and understand how your team influences the design. With its unique blend of forensic psychology and code analysis, this book arms you with the strategies you need, no matter what programming language you use.

Adam Tornhill
(218 pages) ISBN: 9781680500387. $36
https://pragprog.com/book/atcrime

The Nature of Software Development

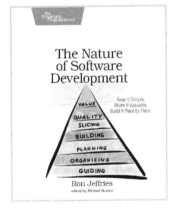

You need to get value from your software project. You need it "free, now, and perfect." We can't get you there, but we can help you get to "cheaper, sooner, and better." This book leads you from the desire for value down to the specific activities that help good Agile projects deliver better software sooner, and at a lower cost. Using simple sketches and a few words, the author invites you to follow his path of learning and understanding from a half century of software development and from his engagement with Agile methods from their very beginning.

Ron Jeffries
(176 pages) ISBN: 9781941222379. $24
https://pragprog.com/book/rjnsd

The Pragmatic Bookshelf

The Pragmatic Bookshelf features books written by professional developers for professional developers. The titles continue the well-known Pragmatic Programmer style and continue to garner awards and rave reviews. As development gets more and more difficult, the Pragmatic Programmers will be there with more titles and products to help you stay on top of your game.

Visit Us Online

This Book's Home Page
https://pragprog.com/book/wwgraphql
Source code from this book, errata, and other resources. Come give us feedback, too!

Keep Up to Date
https://pragprog.com
Join our announcement mailing list (low volume) or follow us on twitter @pragprog for new titles, sales, coupons, hot tips, and more.

New and Noteworthy
https://pragprog.com/news
Check out the latest pragmatic developments, new titles and other offerings.

Save on the ebook

Save on the ebook versions of this title. Owning the paper version of this book entitles you to purchase the electronic versions at a terrific discount.

PDFs are great for carrying around on your laptop—they are hyperlinked, have color, and are fully searchable. Most titles are also available for the iPhone and iPod touch, Amazon Kindle, and other popular e-book readers.

Buy now at *https://pragprog.com/coupon*

Contact Us

Online Orders:	*https://pragprog.com/catalog*
Customer Service:	*support@pragprog.com*
International Rights:	*translations@pragprog.com*
Academic Use:	*academic@pragprog.com*
Write for Us:	*http://write-for-us.pragprog.com*
Or Call:	+1 800-699-7764

Milton Keynes UK
Ingram Content Group UK Ltd.
UKHW010130080924
447992UK00007B/215